Bringing Religion into International Relations

Culture and Religion in International Relations

Series Editors
Yosef Lapid and Friedrich Kratochwil

Published by Palgrave Macmillan

Bringing Religion into International Relations

Jonathan Fox and Shmuel Sandler

BRINGING RELIGION INTO INTERNATIONAL RELATIONS
© Jonathan Fox and Shmuel Sandler, 2004

First published 2004 by
PALGRAVE MACMILLAN™
175 Fifth Avenue, New York, N.Y. 10010 and
Houndmills, Basingstoke, Hampshire, England RG21 6XS
Companies and representatives throughout the world

PALGRAVE MACMILLAN is the global academic imprint of the Palgrave Macmillan division of St. Martin's Press, LLC and of Palgrave Macmillan Ltd. Macmillan® is a registered trademark in the United States, United Kingdom and other countries. Palgrave is a registered trademark in the European Union and other countries.

ISBN 978-1-4039-7603-1

Library of Congress Cataloging-in-Publication Data
Fox, Jonathan, 1968–
    Bringing religion into international relations / Jonathan Fox and Shmuel Sandler.
        p. cm.—(Culture and religion in international relations)
    Includes bibliographical references and index.
    ISBN 1–4039–6551–X
        1. Religion and international affairs. I. Sandler, Shmuel. II. Title. III. Series.

BL65.I55+
201'.727—dc22   2003064012

A catalogue record for this book is available from the British Library.

Design by Newgen Imaging Systems (P) Ltd., Chennai, India.

First edition: June 2004
10 9 8 7 6 5 4 3 2 1

Printed in the United States of America.

Transferred to Digital Printing in 2007

*In memory of Daniel J. Elezar, a pioneer in
the study of religion in the public square*

CONTENTS

Chapter 1

Introduction

The attacks on the Twin Towers in New York City and the ensuing ones in Washington and Pennsylvania by Osama Bin Laden's religiously motivated Al-Qaeda organization seemingly caught the Western world by surprise. What was particularly surprising to the West is that religious phenomena could have such an impact in the heart of the Western world. That this surprise occurred is itself surprising given earlier indications of the growing phenomenon of religiously motivated conflicts in the international scene. These include previous terrorist attacks by Al-Qaeda, the tensions between India and Pakistan, the ongoing sectarian conflict in Northern Ireland, the successful religious revolutions in Iran and Afghanistan, the outbreak of the Al-Aqsa Intifada in Israel, stopping a peace process of almost a decade, and a score of other local conflicts of this type around the globe.

Even in the face of this evidence neither Americans nor other Western nations were ready for this new challenge to stability and harmony in their lives. The successful attack by a religious fanatic organization at the heart of the United States where no other state or group had ever done so denoted a new era of world politics. Should policy makers have turned to the relevant academic disciplines the situation was not much better. Despite Samuel Huntington's *Clash of Civilization* (1993; 1996) and Jurgensmeyer's *The New Cold War* (1993), the discipline of international relations was not ready for inclusion of the religious variable into the contending paradigms in the discipline as these new works insinuated. While very different in their approach and scope the common denominator between these two studies was the assertion that religious struggles will replace the ideological Cold War confrontation. They also represent some of the few exceptions to a more general rule of international relations scholarship ignoring religion. Thus, we must ask whether we are in need of a new paradigm that would include religion as a major explanation for international relations or is it politics as usual? Answering this question will be one of the challenges of this book.

Our approach to this challenge is implied in the title of the book. We need to bring religion into international relations. This does not mean rejecting previous theories of international relations. Nor do we suggest disregarding the methods of research that have been developed during the twentieth century. Rather, it means that we must include in our understanding and research of international relations the various manifestations of religion and their influence on the range of social and political phenomena that the discipline of international relations seeks to explain. In short, no understanding of international relations can be complete without bringing religion into the discipline.

Before we address these issues it is important to define what we mean by religion. Religion is one of those terms that is extremely difficult to define. Turner (1991: 243–245) demonstrates this in a discussion of the topic where he looks at several definitions of religion used by social scientists. He notes that most definitions are problematic for two reasons. First, they must make assumptions that all religions have a certain level of uniformity. For example, if a definition includes belief in a deity or some divine entity, religions like Buddhism that do not fit this definition would not be considered religions. Second, most definitions attempt to deal with existential issues that are not really relevant to social scientists trying to examine the impact of religion on society.

Our approach to the concept of religion does not rely on a specific definition of the concept. Rather we accept that it exists and influences human behavior and focus our efforts on discovering these influences. There are several such basic influences. First, it can influence people's worldviews, which in turn influences how they think and behave. Second, it is an aspect of identity. Third, it is a source of legitimacy, including political legitimacy. Fourth, it is associated with formal institutions that can influence the political process. This approach to religion is discussed in more detail in chapter 8 in light of the discussion in this book.

In order to answer the challenge of integrating religion into international relations theory we must contend with preliminary questions: Why was the discipline not prepared for religion? Why is it that a discipline that developed for almost a century and has intellectual roots extending hundreds of years has not included religion in its term of reference? We try to answer these questions comprehensively in chapter 2. Our overall argument is that the discipline of international relations is a microcosm of the Western social sciences, which for most of the twentieth century ignored religion. The founders of the social sciences and their heirs, including most major Western social thinkers, rejected religion as an explanation for the world. They believed that primordial factors such as ethnicity and religion had no part in modern society or in rational explanations for the way the world works. They also focused most of their studies on the West, where religion's influence was least apparent and argued that its influence in the non-West was a primordial remnant that would disappear as the non-West modernized. Ironically, rather than causing religion's demise, modernity has caused a resurgence of religion but this did not conform with the *Zeitgeist*. This resurgence, while visible in the West, was most visible outside of the West.

We propose that the combination of a Western-centric worldview and the influence of social sciences contributed to international relations scholars ignoring religion. We further argue that these phenomena, and thus the tendency to ignore religion, were stronger in international relations scholarship than in other social science disciplines. The ascendance of the international system from a religious war, the legitimizing principles, and political philosophy that accompanied its evolution contributed to the secular essence of the discipline of international relations. We identify other factors such as the reality of international relations being heavily influenced by behavioralism and the use of quantitative methodology as further causes for international relation's blind spot for religion. Those who use this approach to international relations are often accused of ignoring what they cannot measure and religion is among the most notoriously difficult things to measure.

Another explanation within the framework of international relations's Western-centrism is that the major theories of international relations are all based on assumptions that exclude religion as an important factor. The central role of factors like material power, economics, the state, and the nation in international relations theory left little room for the consideration of religion as a causal influence.

It is within this context that we must make this point about the relationship between state, nation, and religion. A common denominator between politicized religion and nationalism is that both were to have dissipated in the modern state system (Appleby, 1994). Social scientists in general and political scientists in particular envisioned that modernity would marginalize primordial loyalties. By creating the powerful territorial state, modern man would throw off his need to turn to God to supply his basic material and spiritual needs. In a like manner the state would replace his identity needs (Connolly, 1988: 7–8). Modernization would integrate ancient loyalties and mold them into a new identity or sacrosanct center. The new core encompassing institutions, identity, and service functions would replace the former diffused zone of authority (Shils, 1978: 4–10).

Despite common beliefs that see religion and nationalism as twin ideologies, that is, two phenomena that are always in concordance, this is not always the case. Religion sometimes is in contest with nationalism. The nation-state in advanced societies can serve the same societal roles as religion, and thus replace it. While the state segment provides institutions that convey authority and services, the nation and particularly the ethnic nation, provides identity via heritage or sociopsychological solidarity. The state via its control of territory provides security (Herz, 1957: 99–124) whereas the nation provides communal belonging, common origins, and eternity (Smith, 1981: 18–20) functions that man had previously conceded to God. These functions of the nation-state complement each other and can free man from the need to turn to God.

Surprisingly, primordial loyalties survived the onslaught of the modern state. Since this phenomenon was recognized, many explanations were given to the endurance of primordial forces (Fox, 2002a: 102). One answer lies in the double effect of modernity. Ernst Haas related the reappearance of nationalism in our era as a rational choice for societies that go through the strains of modernization (Haas, 1986). The same logic can be applied to the survival of religion. The process that destroys traditional society creates a vacuum that calls for transcendence. This statement echoes Huntington's statement from the 1960s that "the breakup of traditional societies may lead to psychological disintegration and anomie, lest these very conditions also create the need for new identities and loyalties" (Huntington, 1968: 37).

While our discussion in chapter 2 may provide an explanation for why religion was ignored by international relations theory, this is not enough. We, therefore, try in the ensuing chapters to identify religious influences on international phenomena that can serve as a starting point for international relations scholarship in its efforts to integrate religion into the discipline. It should be pointed out at the outset that we are not proposing a paradigmatic change. Our main purpose is to expand the boundaries of international relations theory by the inclusion of religion as a variable in the research of international politics. That is, we want to bring religion into international relations, not replace international relations theory with a new one positing that religion is the central causal factor of world politics. Our main aim is that eventually religion will find its rightful place in the discipline within existing paradigms. Moreover, our suggested areas of study are not an exhaustive list, rather a place to start.

We start with one of the major constituents of both domestic and international politics—legitimacy. We must recall that prior to the emergence of realism as the leading paradigm in international relations, the discipline consisted primarily of international law, a major source of what is and is not considered legitimate in the international arena. It is a fact that religious ideas were one of the bases for the doctrine of "just war", a major element of international law. Chapter 3 explores the linkage between political and religious legitimacy in international politics. This aspect of religious legitimacy plays a role in promoting both stability and conflict in regions like Latin America as well as the doctrine of Just War but is hardly considered in contemporary international relations theory.

It is only natural that we start our analysis with a basic feature like legitimacy. In politics legitimacy is the complementary device to physical power. Religion is a powerful source of legitimacy enabling the regime to survive and reduce the need for persuasion via the use of force. In foreign policy it can be similarly used to support war and peace. In international politics, religion can be a source of legitimacy for accommodation and collaboration between nations as well as for ferocious and extended wars like the Thirty Years War. In fact, religious legitimacy may bring about the avoidance of war because of a verdict by a religious authority or cause the opposite. In short, religious legitimacy can support the status quo or challenge it.

If, as we argue, religion was a source of legitimacy during the Cold War era, it is even more relevant in a world where normative factors are having an increasing influence on international relations. Furthermore, we can assume that the growth of nationalism and ethnicity as legitimizing ideas for the use of violence will be accompanied by religion as a legitimator of violence. As religion can be an aspect of identity, this trend will also be influenced by the attention given to identity in international politics. As part of our examination of this trend we also investigate whether political leaders are influenced in their international behavior by their personal religious views.

Another major influence of religion on the international arena is the linkage between domestic and international politics. This phenomenon of "linkage politics" identified as early as the 1960s by James Rosenau (1969) is especially relevant to religion. While the influence of religion on domestic politics has become increasingly clear to social scientists, this dimension also has yet to find its proper place in international relations theory. Hence, in chapter 4, we investigate whether domestic religious issues and conflicts cross state borders and, thus, penetrate into the international arena. It is clear that this internationalization of domestic conflicts is not unique to religious conflicts. Nevertheless, religious conflicts are among those that have been internationalized. Furthermore, we argue that sometimes it is religious conflicts in particular that have been internationalized. We introduce some empirical analysis of intervention in ethnic conflicts during the 1990s, which demonstrate that religious conflicts are more likely to attract intervention and that the interveners most often belong to the same religion as the groups on whose behalf they intervene. The chapter also examines, other ways in which religious conflicts cross borders, how local conflicts become internationalized, and how disputes over holy sites become international issues.

The natural spin-off of linkage politics has been transnational relations or the world politics paradigm proposed by Robert Keohane and Joseph Nye (Keohane and Nye, 1970, 1977). Religion as an actor or issue is most visible in areas that transcend state borders. It is this dimension of international relations that we try introduce in chapter 5. In the last decades religious fundamentalism has become an increasingly important factor in both international and domestic politics in most parts of the world and across religions. As we shall see, politicized religion by definition finds the international system its natural domain of activity. Religiously motivated terrorism, and the international struggle over the issue of human rights, including religious human rights, are the most noticeable global issues influenced by religion but not the only ones. Indeed transnational issues like women's rights and family planning have religious aspects or overtones. Unable to cover every aspect, in this chapter we provide in-depth analyses of the overlapping issues of terrorism, religious fundamentalism, and political Islam.

Even though our book is predominantly theory-oriented we try to introduce some empirical evidence in chapters 6 and 7. In doing so we chose to examine Samuel Huntington's controversial "clash of civilizations" theory in chapter 6. In chapter 7 we examine a salient international conflict with strong religious connotations—the Palestinian–Israeli conflict with a special emphasis on the Al-Aqsa Intifada. The two chapters also differ in their methodology. While Huntington's theory is examined via a comparative cross-sectional analysis the latter is examined as a case study.

Huntington himself, avoided the term religion in his well-celebrated clash of civilizations theory. Yet his definition of civilization is clearly religion oriented. Similarly, some of the participants in the debate, even when they address religion more explicitly, also try to avoid calling religion by its name. This phenomenon strengthens our argument that international relations as a Western-centric theory has an inherent difficulty in including religion in its terms of reference.

To be sure the attraction to Huntington's theory was to some extent motivated because it tried to define the nature of conflict in the post–Cold War era. According to Huntington civilizational conflicts will be the most common and intense forms of conflicts in the post–Cold War era. We point directly to more precise motifs—religion, ethnicity, and nationalism.

This chapter includes a discussion of Huntington's theory as well as the multiple arguments against it as well as a discussion of the overlapping concepts of culture, religion, and ethnicity and their importance to international relations. It also includes an empirical analysis of the comparative influence of religion, civilizations, and separatism on ethnic conflicts during the 1990s.

In chapter 7 we examine the role of religion in the Palestinian–Israeli conflict giving special attention to the themes discussed in previous chapters. Its main purpose is to complement our empirical research via a case study methodology. While the take-off point of our Palestinian–Israeli conflict analysis is the current Al-Aqsa Intifada, a name that provided the current stage of the conflict with a particular religious flavor, the analysis begins with the intercommunal conflict during Mandatory (pre–World War II) Palestine. We articulate the role of religion in influencing both Muslims and Jews involved in the conflict and try to evaluate its role in promoting violence. At the same time we do not ignore the secular rationale of both sides and reach the conclusion that while influenced by religious impulses and beliefs both sides are ultimately motivated by national and political interests and norms even more than by divine aspirations.

It is against this background that we must clarify some points regarding the scope of our work. The first regards the time period covered. Our deliberation is essentially limited to the modern era and within that period predisposed to the last decades of the twentieth century and the beginning of the new millennium. While we argue that religion has been applicable to all of the modern era, it undoubtedly became more pronounced since the 1980s. Another precaution that we must suggest at this point is that, as far as we could determine, only a few events within this time framework have been purely religious. Our purpose in this book is to examine religious aspects of international politics not to claim that all is religious.

Moreover, we are aware and caution our colleagues that religion is often used for nonreligious purposes. It could have been tempting for us to approach this enterprise by magnifying the religious dimension in international interactions, but than we would have been overstating our case.

More specifically we also learned, especially from our empirical research, that the motivations of religious actors are not always religious. In order for this conclusion to be challenged a broader study is needed. It is impossible to fully discuss all relevant cases within the context of one book. Accordingly, this one is intended to begin a dialogue that we hope will include many scholars doing their work in many contexts and continue for many years. We, thus, encourage broader comparative research that both challenges and expands upon the ideas we present here.

Finally, our work may be lacking in references to international relations scholarship. However, this is exactly our point. International relations theory has not developed much on religion, and hence we must draw on other disciplines. This is the best proof to our overall central argument that Western international relations scholarship has ignored religion. For this reason, our study is an interdisciplinary work and we feel no need to be apologetic about this fact. It also suits our main conclusion: while religion is not the main driving force behind international relations, international relations cannot be understood without taking religion into account. Religion's influence on international relations cannot be studied outside of the context of social sciences. Nor can international relations, if to a lesser degree than religion, find itself outside social sciences. Combining the two justifies our retrogression.

The following chapters are intended to begin this process of bringing religion into international relations. They draw upon the literature from the social sciences in general, as well as the international relations literature. In doing so they identify a number of ways religion influences international relations. The result, we believe, provides us with both a better understanding of international relations, an improved understanding of the role of religion in modern times, and hopefully will start fruitful debate on how to improve the theory of and research in international relations.

CHAPTER 2

THE OVERLOOKED DIMENSION

One of the questions we must ask when examining the role of religion in international relations is why has there been so little written on the topic? Religion is rarely included in most major theories of international relations and when it is addressed, it is usually through viewing it as a subcategory of some topic that is considered more important such as institutions, terrorism, society, or civilizations (Kabalkova, 2000: 682–683). In the few cases where it is addressed directly, "religion tends to be characterized as fundamentalist, extreme, radical, or militant" (Fawcett, 2000: 2) rather than as a normal element of the political process. That is, in the rare cases where the international relations literature deals with religion, it is presented as a secondary aspect of the topic at hand or an exception that has little impact.

Our basic argument is that this trend can only be fully understood when examining the discipline of international relations within the context of the social sciences in general. As discussed later in this chapter, it is clear that for much of the twentieth century most Western social scientists did not give religion much weight in their theories and, in fact, often predicted its demise as a significant social and political force. We further argue that this tendency is more strongly rooted within the field of international relations than in the rest of the social sciences. Also, as demonstrated later in this chapter, the other disciplines of the social sciences began to reevaluate the role of religion much earlier than did international relations scholarship. Thus, in addition to asking why religion was ignored by the social sciences in general, we also must ask why international relations scholarship in particular ignored religion.

The reasons for this disregard for religion are rooted in several interrelated trends that are discussed in more detail later in this chapter. First, the social sciences have their origins in the rejection of religion as an explanation for the world by major Western social thinkers. Thus, international relations evolved from the premise that primordial factors such as ethnicity and religion had no part in modern society or in rational explanations for the way the world works. Second, international relations is perhaps the most Western-centric of the social science disciplines. Because of this, the trend among Western social scientists to ignore religion is perhaps most prevalent among international relations scholars. Third, the study of international relations is heavily influenced by behavioralism and the use of quantitative methodology. Those who use this approach to international relations are often accused of ignoring what they cannot measure and religion is among the most notoriously difficult things to measure. Fourth, the major theories of international relations are all based on assumptions that exclude religion as an important factor. For instance, realism, perhaps the most influential of international relations paradigms, focuses on the pursuit of power as the driving force behind the relations between states. This pragmatic approach excludes less tangible factors such as religion in favor of more concrete factors such as territory, population, economic power, and military might. It also places states into a "black box" and ignores their domestic politics, the realm in which the influence of religion is most likely to become apparent. Each of these interrelated reasons why religion has been ignored in international relations is examined in more detail later.

The Modern Rejection of Religion

The majority of the most important eighteenth-, nineteenth-, and early-twentieth-century Western social thinkers who profoundly influenced the evolution the social sciences, such as Comte, Durkheim, Freud, Marx, Nietzsche, Toennies, Voltaire, and Weber, had one thing in common, they all believed that an age of enlightenment would replace religion as the basis for understanding and running the world (Appleby, 1994: 7–8; Shupe, 1990: 19; Turner, 1991). For instance, Nietzsche's "God is dead" thesis refers to the loss of credibility of Christian belief and the loss of commitment to absolute values (Turner, 1991: 40–42, 192). Similarly, Weber argued that secular ideologies were replacing religion as the basis of legitimacy and social control in nineteenth-century society (Turner, 1991: 190–193). In all, these social thinkers rejected religion as an explanation for the world and believed that in the modern industrial age more rational, scientific, and legalistic means were needed in order to explain the world we live in as well as to manage it. While clearly the understanding of religion and society by these scholars is considerably more complex than represented here, the theme that religion was to become a less important factor in the modern world was an essential element of this understanding.

Modern social scientists followed in the footsteps of these thinkers and developed paradigms that posited that religion had no meaningful role in modern politics and society. The political science version of this paradigm is modernization theory. Modernization theory posits that processes inherent in modernization would inevitably lead to the demise of primordial factors like ethnicity and religion in politics. These modern processes include economic development, urbanization, modern social institutions, pluralism, growing rates of literacy and education as well as advancements in science and technology.[1] While the modernization literature tended to focus on ethnicity, it was also clearly meant to apply to religion.[2] Modernization theory was the dominant paradigm among Western political scientists from the late 1950s through the mid-1970s.

The sociological analogue of modernization theory, known as secularization theory, focuses exclusively on religion and remained the dominant paradigm in sociology into the early 1990s. This paradigm posits that, society is becoming more secular for basically the same reasons political scientists subscribed to modernization theory. In fact, secularization theory has been described as a subset of modernization theory (Hadden, 1987b: 588). As societies become more modern and advanced, they become more secular. This process is facilitated by the modern state, which is based on rational and scientific principles and is guided by a legalistic and bureaucratic infrastructure. Religion is no longer needed to legitimize the state because the state is legitimized through the "will of the people" either through democratic institutions or through ideologies, such as Marxism or Fascism, which claim that the state represents the will of the people through other means. In addition, religion's traditional role of interpreting the natural order has been replaced by scientific rationalism, thus undermining another important role religion played in the past.

Thus according to secularization theory, in modern times, secular, rational, and scientific criteria and phenomena have replaced religion. Secular institutions have taken over many roles traditionally filled by religion. The resources and time devoted to religion, both by public institutions and individuals, has declined. Social norms that were once defined by religious precepts are now defined by technical, rational, and empirical criteria. That is, priests and ministers have been replaced by psychiatrists, psychologists, anthropologists, and sociologists. Larger society has replaced the small community as the basis for most social life. Accordingly, religion, which helps to maintain order within community, is no longer needed to maintain social order in a society that is no longer communally based.[3]

It is difficult to overemphasize the extent to which these paradigms were dominant in the social sciences during much of the twentieth century. Hadden (1987b: 587) points this out when he notes, "few forecasts have been uttered with more unshakable confidence than sociology's belief that religion is in the midst of its final death throes." He argues that this belief reached the level of a doctrine or ideology that resulted in the idea rarely being subjected to any real scrutiny. He concludes,

> With the benefit of hindsight, it is easy to understand how the presuppositions of the discipline have radically affected our thinking about religion. But only of late have scholars begun to explore how the discipline's theoretical presuppositions, emanating from the secularization model, have clouded clear-headed observation of data as well as theory construction. (Hadden, 1987b: 597)

As Hadden states, the social science assumption of a secular world has come under increasing scrutiny. By the early 1980s political scientists began to reexamine their assumptions regarding ethnicity and religion and by the late 1980s or early 1990s sociologists began to reassess secularization theory. For political scientists events including the rise of the religious right in the United States and the Iranian revolution had a profound influence in that these events that significantly influenced Western, and especially U.S. politics, could not be ignored. Many sociologists similarly found it difficult to ignore that people continued to be religious and religion continued to influence social institutions and behavior. Nevertheless until the events in Waco Texas, 1993, few academics considered religious violence in the West anything other than an epiphenomenon (Kaplan, 2002: 2).

Modernity as Causing the Resurgence of Religion

Ironically, this reassessment of the role of religion in society has resulted in an argument that is nearly exactly opposite to the argument made by modernization and secularization theory: modernization, rather than causing religion's demise, is responsible for its resurgence. The magnitude of the change in attitude toward religion caused by this reassessment cannot be underemphasized. In practice it represents a complete reversal in the role religion is believed to play in modern society in politics. While modernization and secularization theorists posited that modernity had made religion a primordial remnant that was fading away as an important social and political factor, the central argument of this reassessment is that modernity is increasing the role of religion in society and politics.

This reassessment is multifaceted and has identified multiple ways in which processes associated with modernization have contributed to the revitalization of religion. First, in many parts of the Third World, efforts at modernization have failed causing a religious backlash against the Western secular ideologies that were the basis for the governments which were in charge of these unsuccessful efforts at modernization. Furthermore, due to the processes of colonialism and cultural colonialism, Western secular ideas are considered foreign and, therefore, illegitimate, leaving only religion as a basis for legitimacy (Jusegensmeyer, 1993; Thomas, 2000: 817–819). Second, modernization has undermined traditional lifestyles, community values, and morals, which are based in part on religion, thus contributing to this religious backlash against modernity (Sahliyeh, 1990: 9; Haynes, 1994: 34; Thomas, 2000: 816). Third, modernization has allowed both the state and religious institutions to increase their spheres of influence, thus resulting in more clashes between the two (Shupe, 1990: 23–26). Fourth, modern political systems allow for mass participation in politics, which has allowed the religious sectors of society a means to impose their views on others (Rubin, 1994: 22–23). Fifth, modern communications has allowed religious groups to export their views more easily and the international media has made religious groups aware of the activities of other religious groups, often inspiring similar actions (Shupe, 1990: 22).

Sixth, a new trend in the sociology of religion, known as the rational choice or economic theory of religion, posits that the freedom of choice in many modern societies to select one's own religion has led to an increase in religiosity (the extent to which one is religious). This approach basically applies economic market behavior theory to religious behavior in a manner similar to the way Mancur Olson (1971) applied it to collective-action theory. The basic argument is that when religious monopolies are broken down, as they have been in much of the modern world, people engage in a cost–benefit analysis in selecting their religion. At the same time religious "producers" have an incentive to make their religions as attractive as possible to the body of "consumers" in the religious "market-place." The resulting "free market" has made religion more attractive to the "consumers" of religion, resulting in an increase in religiosity (Iannaccone, 1995a,b; Warner, 1993).[4]

Seventh, modern religious organizations contribute to political activity. On a general level, some form of organization is necessary for political mobilization and religious institutions provide ready-made organizations for this purpose that often have access to the media, considerable economic assets, and international communications networks. In fact, in many nondemocratic regimes the protected status of religious institutions makes them the only format in which people are allowed to organize. People who are active in religious organizations tend to develop organizational and leadership skills that are also useful for political activities. They are also often exposed to mobilization efforts by their religious organizations as well as political messages and morality messages which, themselves, are not so different from political messages. Religious organizations also help to develop interpersonal networks that are useful for political mobilization. However, it should be noted that under many circumstances religious organizations are conservative and prefer to support the status-quo (Fox, 1999a; Hadden, 1987a; Harris, 1994; Johnston and Figa, 1988; Verba et al., 1993).

Eighth, modernity does cause secularization in some parts of the religious economy in that many mainstream and dominant religions become more worldly. However this process results in a countervailing trend of other parts of the religious economy because there is a demand for less worldly religions. Thus secularization is one of two interrelated processes. First, mainstream organizations become more worldly as they and their elites become more intertwined with the establishment, which often desires to partake in religion without being overly restricted by religious precepts. Second, those who desire a more spiritual and otherworldly religious experience flee the mainstream religions to either sects that broke off from the mainstream religions or to different faiths altogether (Stark and Bainbridge, 1985: 1–2). These dual trends are reflected in the decline of mainstream faiths in Europe while at the same time Evangelical and postmodernist faiths are thriving there (Haynes, 1998: 66–67, 215–216).

The rise of religious fundamentalism in the late twentieth century is also attributed to modernization. Many explanations for fundamentalism focus on the dislocations caused by modernity's undermining of traditional society both on a personal and communal level. Thus, fundamentalism is concerned with defining, restoring, and reinforcing the basis of personal and communal identity that is being shaken or destroyed by modern dislocations and crises (Marty and Appleby, 1991: 602, 620; Esposito, 1998). In fact, in many ways religious fundamentalism is an organized criticism and rejection of modernity. Fundamentalists reject the replacement of religious morality and explanations for the world in which we live with scientific and rational explanations and moral systems (Mendelsohn: 1993; Tehranian, 1993). In addition, fundamentalist movements often make use of modern communications, propaganda, and organizational techniques, and engage in the distinctly modern behavior of using political action, including the mobilization of women, in order to further their agenda (Eisenstadt, 2000: 601–603). Thus, even though religious fundamentalism is often perceived as a return to the past, it is in fact a very modern phenomenon.

Today, while many political scientists do not overtly include religion in their theories and explanations, few actively deny that it influences the political process. Thus, the modernization theory's rejection of religion as a thing of the past is itself a thing of the past. Sociologists have been a bit slower and more reluctant to jump onto this bandwagon. Nevertheless, despite the long history of secularization theory in the social sciences and the fact that it played a central role in the development of the sociology of religion,

> recent theoretical and empirical papers on the sociology of religion appearing in top journals have generated interest and controversy. Indeed, for the first time since the 1960s, scholars who typically specialize in other substantive areas are doing research on, or theorizing about, the sociology of religion. This development is a tremendous surprise to many sociologists, who accepted the expectations of secularization theories that promised declining importance of religion in social life, diminished strength for religious organizations, and waning religious commitment among individuals. (Sherkat and Ellison, 1999: 364)

However, many sociologists continue to argue that secularization is occurring. This has resulted in a vigorous debate among sociologists that revolves around two issues. The first is whether secularization means people becoming less religious or whether it means a decline in religion's influence over public institutions. The second is whether either of these processes is, in fact, occurring. This debate is so central to the study of religion by sociologists that a recent volume of *Sociology of Religion* was devoted exclusively to this debate with extensive arguments on both sides of both of the aforementioned issues.[5]

The Profound Rejection of Religion in International Relations Theory and its Western Roots

Until now, our discussion of the rejection of religion in the Western social sciences has dealt with political science and sociology but not the study of international relations. This is because the rejection of religion by international relations scholars is perhaps more profound than its rejection by political scientists and sociologists. More specifically while sociologists and political scientists had a body of theory explaining why religion was believed to be of declining significance, there is no analogous body of theory in international relations. Rather, the study of international relations simply ignores religion and there is not even a debate over its role analogous to the debate among sociologists. That is, it is simply assumed that religion is not important to international relations and that no explanation or discussion of this assumption is necessary. In fact, the study of international relations was founded, at least in part, on the belief that the era of religion causing wars was over (Laustsen and Waever, 2000: 706). Furthermore, there has been no reassessment of this assumption analogous to the reassessments of modernization and secularization theory by political scientists and sociologists.

Whenever international relations scholars do deal with religion it is almost always as an element of some other overarching phenomenon or mediating variable. Perhaps one of the most prominent examples of this is Samuel Huntington's (1993a, 1996a) clash of civilizations theory. Huntington posits that in the post–Cold War era most conflicts will be between several civilizations that, by his own admission, are primarily defined by religion. This has resulted in a voluminous debate over whether Huntington is correct and, if he is not, what will be the basis for conflict now that the Cold War has ended. Despite the fact that religion is the primary basis of Huntington's civilizations, this debate has mostly avoided discussing religion. Most of Huntington's critics attack him along one of three avenues, none of which address the religious underpinnings of his arguments. First, many attack what they perceive as his methodological shortcomings and errors. That is, they argue that Huntington's research design was somehow flawed.[6] Second, many argue that, rather than civilizations, some other form of identity will be the most important basis for political groupings. These contending bases for political groupings include groupings smaller than civilizations such as the state, the nation, and ethnic groups as well as groupings larger than civilizations such as a unified world order. Finally, many argue that Huntington has ignored some important factor in world politics that makes his theory irrelevant. These factors include conflict management, population issues, environment issues, the power of modernity and secularism, military power, economic power, economic prosperity, information technology, and desires to emulate and align with the West (Fox, 2001a: 181–182).[7]

This debate provides an excellent example of the extent to which international relations scholars have been avoiding the issue of religion. Huntington proposed a theory that while to a great extent is based on religion, systematically avoided making it an overt element of his theory and preferred to couch his theory in the term "civilizations." This theory resulted in, perhaps, the largest debate in the study of international relations during the 1990s, at least in terms of volume. Yet almost all of the participants in the debate follow Huntington's lead and avoid the overt discussion of religion in international relations. Furthermore, even if one were to argue that Huntington's civilizations are synonymous with religion this would mean that he maintains that religion was not important in international relations until after the end of the Cold War, a contention that we dispute. Rather we argue that religion has always been an important factor in international relations but was overlooked.

Be that as it may, this treatment, or rather the nontreatment, of religion by international relations stands in stark contrast to the open reassessment of the role of religion in society by political scientists and sociologists over the past two decades. This implies that trends within the social sciences are not enough to explain why religion has been ignored by international relations theorists. If it were only this that was causing religion's role to be downplayed, all of the social sciences would likely have come to the conclusions that their previous assumptions regarding religion were wrong at the same time or at least within several years of each other. However, in fact, sociologists lagged about five or ten years behind political scientists and international relations scholars were still mostly indifferent to religion until the September 11, 2001 bombings of the World Trade Center and the Pentagon made religion difficult to ignore. It is argued here that this phenomenon of overlooking religion is a peculiarly Western phenomenon and the study of international relations is, in many ways, the most Western of the social sciences. In addition, the major paradigms of international relations for various reasons either focus on those aspects of human behavior that are least influenced by religion or are based on those political philosophies that are most entrenched in the arguments that religion is not relevant.

The West vs. the Rest

We borrow the term "the West vs. the rest" from Huntington's (1996b) article describing what he thinks will be the basis for conflict in the twenty-first century. However, we argue that inadvertently Huntington provided us with an explanation to the low status of religion in international relations theory. In other words this phrase better describes the twentieth-century divisions within the social sciences over whether religion is important. This is because the argument that religion is not important is a particularly Western argument. The eighteenth-, nineteenth-, and early-twentieth-century thinkers who originated this argument are Westerners who focused primarily on the West. Modernization theory, in essence, argued that the modern conditions that were believed to have caused the decline of religion in the West would have the same effect in the non-West. Those sociologists who supported, and continue to support, secularization theory base their arguments primarily on the United States and to a lesser extent other Western democracies. In fact, secularization theory has been described as "an ideological impulse strongly rooted in the Western Enlightenment, and one that resonates with the conventional wisdom of many Western elites" (Sherkat and Ellison, 1999: 364).

The influence of the Enlightenment on the belief that the modern world will be secularized is, perhaps, most obvious with regard to sociology. The founding generation of sociologists were mostly Europeans who were born in the context of the political and cultural upheaval caused by the Enlightenment. This upheaval included three sources of social tension that profoundly influenced the thinking of early sociologists. First, there was a new evolutionary worldview that included the belief that religion was standing in the way of progress. Second, advocates of new social arraignments were struggling against the status quo that included traditional religion. Third, reason and science were challenging religion's monopoly over people's minds and consciousness. As a result, the founding generations of sociologists were not disinterested analysts, they were advocates for the science and reason that was expected to crush the ignorance and superstition caused by religion. This heritage resulted in a deep-rooted assumption among Western sociologists that reached the proportions of a dogma or ideology that religion was not important. This was reinforced by a combination of selective recruitment of those with secular worldviews into the ranks of sociologists and the socialization of those who still believed religion important (Hadden, 1987b). Thus, many Western sociologists entangled their own values and group interests in their study of secularization (Lawrence, 1989: 62–63).

The assumption that religion is not important in politics is not limited to academic scholarship but is also an essential element of Western culture and socialization. Westerners, especially those from the United States are socialized from childhood to believe in classical liberalism which, among other things, advocates the separation of church and state. Future social scientists, as children studying the U.S. political system, learn that it is wrong for the government to endorse any religion and it is right for it to avoid all unnecessary interference with religion. While a full discussion of the influence of this socialization on the worldviews of social scientists is beyond the scope of this essay, it is unlikely that this socialization does not increase the likelihood that Western social scientists will overlook religion as an important factor in the study of international politics. Similarly, other modern ideologies that have been the basis for socialization in much of the world, such as Marxism, also contain biases against religion (Gopin, 2000: 37–40).

It is probably possible to argue that religion in the West is less important than it was in the past. As noted earlier, the concept of separation of church and state is an important element of liberal democracy. In fact, the secularism of the West is seen as a way to avoid the religious-based violence and fanaticism of the past (Keane, 2000: 10–11) and in the West the tensions between religion and secularism have been mitigated by institutionalizing these differences (Marquand and Nettler, 2000: 3). Also the modernization theory and secularization theory arguments were developed based on Western examples and if they are applicable anywhere, they are applicable to the West. Finally, there is considerable evidence that in Europe there is less Christian fundamentalism than elsewhere and participation in public worship as well as the influence of religious institutions on politics are lower than in the rest of the world and, furthermore, are declining (Crouch, 2000). However, as discussed earlier, these theories, to put it mildly, have come under serious debate even with regard to the West.

Interestingly one response to these criticisms of secularization theory is precisely that secularization is occurring in the West and only the West. Over the past 200 years, there is said to be a trend of privatization of religion and secularization of state in the West. This secularization has taken the form of less money donated to religious institutions, less new clergy, less attendance and membership, less political and social influence, and less people thinking religion is important. Church leaders are trying to take an interest in social issues probably because they fear the secular amoral direction Western society is heading and this tactic gives then a chance to influence an increasingly secular culture. Unfortunately, many think their success at this has been limited. However, this decline seems to be limited to traditional religious institutions. Evangelicals and postmodernist religious groups, in contrast, are thriving but remain a minority (Haynes, 1998). Even in the United States, which is perhaps the most religious country in the West, fundamentalists are a small minority that reached a peak of about 19 percent of the population in 1980 (Perkin, 2000: 80–82). Thus, despite arguments to the contrary, religion is still an important factor in Western culture.

This trend of downplaying religion's significance by scholars who study the West stands in stark contrast to those that study the non-Western world who have always considered religion important. If one were to try and convince an expert on the Middle East, for example, that religion in general and Islam in particular are not important political and social factors he would probably reject that argument out of hand. In fact, many argue that not only are Islamic groups important in the Middle East, a large part of their political agenda is to resist Western influence and to de-Westernize the international interpretations of modernity (Eisenstadt, 2000a: 608–609). Furthermore, political Islam is not seen as the revival of Islam but rather emphasizing that the religion, which was always there, is relevant to politics and is more legitimate than secular Western ideas and values (Halliday, 2000: 132).

Similarly an expert on Asia would be hard-pressed to explain many of the region's conflicts without including religion in the explanation, especially those conflicts in Sri Lanka and the Kashmir region of India to name a few. An expert on Africa could not ignore the civil war in Sudan and an expert on Latin America would need to take the role of the Catholic Church and liberation theology into account. Thus, for scholars who study these and other parts of the non-Western world, the fact that religion remains important both because people are religious and because religion has an influence on political and social institutions is a "no brainer" that needs little discussion or proof. It is simply taken for granted. Furthermore, Islam is not the only religion that is resisting Westernization. In most of the Third World Western political ideologies and values are considered by local religious traditions as foreign and immoral, causing a religious backlash against them (Juergensmeyer, 1993; Thomas, 2000).

However, even this evidence is dismissed by many of those who do compare the West and the non-West who

> construct a dichotomy between those "extreme" [non-western] brands of religion portrayed as being caught-up in, or even fermenting, bitter violence elsewhere, and the cozy mainstream denominational religions which form part of the cultural backdrop for those of us in the West who watch these "tribal" outbreaks on our TV screens from the safety of our living-rooms. (Fawcett, 2000: 2)

In other words, many of those in the West who deal with the non-West see religion's violent role as a primordial throwback that will disappear as the non-West modernizes.

Yet, there is a growing recognition, even among Westerners who focus on the West, that religion is not a thing of the past. It is arguable that the intrusion of information from the non-West into insular Western academic circles is one of the factors that has caused the reassessment of religion's role in politics and society. One of the watershed events that began to convince political scientists of religion's importance was the Iranian revolution. It was nearly impossible for U.S. political scientists to ignore the Iranian revolution due to the hostage crisis that was extensively covered by the U.S. media. Furthermore, the Iranian revolution was precisely a revolution against westernization (Moshiri, 1991). While it is unlikely that this was the only cause of the reassessment of modernization theory, it is also unlikely that it and other world events that contradicted the predictions of modernization theory did not play an important role in this reassessment.

These world events, which at least until the 1990s mostly took place outside of the Western world did not similarly influence sociologists who focused almost exclusively on the West. In this respect Western sociologists are even more insular than political scientists. Whereas political scientists must account for what goes on in other states and the influence of external factors in domestic politics, sociologists often look only at a single society or microcosm of that society. Thus, only evidence that comes from within the society they study is likely to influence their theories. Furthermore, evidence from the non-West would simply be interpreted by a secularization theorist as a result of the fact that the West was the first to modernize and other parts of the world lag behind it. In time, the non-West would also be expected to modernize and these religious revolutions, conflicts, and influences would then fade away for the same reason this is believed to have occurred in the West. However, if it becomes clear that religion continues to be important in the already modernized West, this would be harder to explain away.

The evidence within Western states that religion continues to be important is less blatant than it is in the non-West but by the 1990s it had become apparent enough that it was harder to ignore or explain away. There are several factors that likely influenced the thinking of sociologists. First, religious fundamentalism has become an increasingly important phenomenon throughout the world, including the West. In the early 1990s the first major interdisciplinary study on the topic, by Martin E. Marty and R. Scott Appleby was published and received considerable attention. Incidentally, neither Marty nor Appleby could be classified as social scientists as their areas of expertise are history and divinity but their project includes the work of many social scientists. Second, there was a growing recognition that people were at the very least not becoming less religious and may have been becoming more religious. In fact, one sociologist notes that the data never supported this aspect of the theory but since few sociologists collected data on this issue, this was a discrepancy that was easy to ignore (Hadden, 1987b: 599–603). Third, as the world becomes more interdependent it is harder for even sociologists to ignore what occurs outside of the societies that they study. This is both because the information is harder to avoid and because international influences on local societies and cultures are increasing. Fourth, the breakup of the Soviet bloc resulted in many high-profile ethnoreligious conflicts. While this occurred in Eastern Europe, which is not part of the West if you define the term narrowly, it certainly hit closer to home because these conflicts occurred mainly in European states where it was thought that religion had been nearly eradicated by decades of Communism. Despite this evidence, many sociologists still maintain that the process of secularization is continuing.[8]

The reasons that the study of international relations ignored religion until the events of September 11, 2001 are more complicated. One would assume that a field of study that is, by definition, international would include the abundant evidence from the non-West that religion continues to play a role in society and politics. However, despite this, the study of international relations is in many ways the most Western of the Western social sciences, not because of its subject matter, but because of the demographics of those who practice the discipline. That is, the study of international relations, at least in Western circles, is very Western because those who dominate the field are themselves Westerners and its origins are rooted in the experiences of the West.

The core of the discipline of international relations as we know it today evolved from the theories of national security developed after World War II by thinkers mostly from NATO states. Accordingly, the Cold War paradigm that dominated international relations theory focuses on East–West competition. This competition was between two secular ideologies: liberalism which combines capitalism and democracy and Communism, a notoriously secular ideology. Conflicts outside of the West were viewed as microcosms of this overarching secular conflict. Local causes, which often included religious ones, were downplayed at the expense of the larger geopolitical interests of the two major alliances and superpowers. Thus, even though the study of international relations deals with the entire world, it currently does so through a secular-minded Western lens.

Furthermore, as is discussed later in this chapter, there are structural aspects within most major and influential international relations theories that caused them to ignore religion.

The event that has, perhaps, caused international Western relations scholars to begin to reassess their tendency to overlook religion is the September 11, 2001 bombings of the World Trade Center in New York and the Pentagon in Washington DC. This watershed event made it difficult, if not impossible, to overlook the fact that at the very least there exist religiously motivated people who seek to influence the international status quo. This is because the attacks that killed thousands took place in what can be considered the heart of the West. This intrusion of the non-West into the West was more profound than any previous event. The Iranian revolution and other religious conflicts all took place far away from the United States. Most religiously motivated terrorist attacks on the United States took place outside of the United States and the few that took place in the United States, such as the 1993 bombing of the World Trade Center, killed only a few people.

Nevertheless, it is not clear that even these catastrophic bombings will cause the fact that religion does play an important role in international relations to be fully accepted by Western scholars. Much of the discussion of the events has been placed within the context of Huntington's civilizational argument, which as previously noted takes great pains to avoid dealing directly with religion. Also, many U.S. policy makers, including President Bush, have taken great pains to avoid painting the conflict as a religious one. It is portrayed as a war between civilized peoples and terrorism, not between the West and Islam. Osama Bin Laden's Qaeda organization is portrayed, perhaps correctly, as extremists who are not representative of Islam, and by inference also not representative of the true role religion plays in international relations. Thus, while it is too soon to say what impact these events will have on international relations scholarship, it is not clear that even this blatant intrusion of religion into the West will result in a general acknowledgment of the multiple ways in which religion influences international relations. It seems that the Western political tradition has produced a bias that explains the lacuna in integrating religion into IR theory. A closer look at the evolution of these theories is thus in order.

The Antireligious Origins of Major International Relations Theories

The nation-state is the core unit of world politics and has been ever since it made its first appearance on the world scene, especially since the end of World War I, when its legitimacy became virtually unimpeachable. Whether because of their legal status since the Peace of Westphalia (1648), or because of their control over the means of coercion, states constituted the essence of the international system. In order to avoid the debate whether the modern state is the product of the international system, or vice versa, the following analysis of the origins of the state will evolve from both micro and macro perspectives. The evolution of international relations theory will ensue the origins of the state. In both the evolution of the state system and the evolution of international relations theory our main concern here is to detect the subordinate role of religion in international politics.

The Origins of the Modern State

The birth of the modern state was rooted in the emergence and legitimation of an interstate system that replaced the earlier imperial and feudal orders. Prior to the emergence of the territorial state, legitimacy and effective power had been divided between two entities—the Holy Roman Empire or the Church of Rome, on the one hand, and a host of feudal lords, on the other. Whereas the emperor or the pope was the legitimate head of a united Christian Europe, actual power was decentralized among many feudal potentates. The monarchs of the territorial state to whom legitimacy was granted following the 1648 Peace of Westphalia had already been successful in their quest for a centralized control of power. As heirs to both the Holy Roman Empire and the feudal order, their survival depended on the ability of the territorial states they had created to fulfill the functions previously discharged by these two erstwhile systems of authority.

Religion had been the binding force of Europe following the disintegration of the Western Roman Empire in the fifth century. Having been the state religion of the Empire since the beginning of the fourth century Christianity ultimately survived the collapse of Rome. Throughout the Medieval years, Christianity provided identity to Europe a fact that was also carried over to the new era. During those years some of the major confrontations were either with the Pagan Barbarous tribes that penetrated Europe ultimately accepting monotheism and against the prophet in Arabia that also claimed revelation and ultimately generated the Muslim Empire. The Thirty Years War (1618–1648) and the ensuing Peace Treaty of Westphelia terminated this unity.

The new principle that replaced a united Christian Europe under the emperor and the pope was a pluralistic Europe of states, each legitimized by the monarch's divine right to rule. The basis of the feudal structure was the lord's ability to provide security to his subjects and his domain. By definition the monarch, his divine legitimacy apart, had an inherent interest in creating a strong state in which he provided security rather than the almighty. The doctrine of sovereignty rooted in divine norms, which developed as the central theoretical principle of the territorial state, was another step in the contraction of the role of God in foreign policy and international politics. The sovereign monarch became identified with the ability of the political authority to defend its subjects and territory against enemies from without and disorder from within. Sovereignty combined both external autonomy vis-a-vis other rulers and the capacity of the state to impose order on the territory under its control. The "prince" represented the highest secular authority within his territory. Moreover, his rule was contingent on his ability to provide security to the subjects within his territorial domain. Ideas articulated by Jean Bodin and Thomas Hobbes in their celebrated treatises provided the theoretical justification for dynastic sovereignty as well as the contractual logic that formed the basis of the state and of the international order (Herz, 1957; Puchala, 1971: 27–34). Within such a state system the role of the divine was in effect marginalized.

The American and the French Revolutions destroyed the "ancien regime," and the two political philosophers who had influenced these revolutions most—John Locke and Jean Jacques Rousseau—while not articulating the national idea expressly and deliberately, indirectly gave birth to a new legitimizing principle—self-determination. Principles like inalienable rights that are inhered in individuals and "the general will" underwrote the doctrine of popular sovereignty. The dramatic spectacle of a people rising up against their monarch and replacing him with organs of popular sovereignty provided not only a new legitimacy but destroyed even the small role that the divine played in the ancien regime. Following these revolutions even the divine right of kings to rule was gone. Moreover, in these two countries that later on turned into two different models of democracy, evolved a new relationship between church and state. One of the major losers in the French Revolution was the clergy, whereas in the United States the clergy was separated from government from the outset.

But the influence of the state evolved further. In polities like France and Britain, where the state had already been created, the advent of popular sovereignty did not imply a new form of state, only a new basis of legitimacy. These states grew in power both internally as well as in terms of international power. The emergence of strong states implied a smaller role for God in the lives of the individual and international society. The best expression for this climate in the international system was that Britain refused to join the Holy Alliance contrived by Tsar Alexander. Instead it preferred the Quadruple Alliance that provided security against French repeated aggression (Albrecht-Carrie, 1972: 7). Another demonstration of the secular nature of the international system was the alliance between Christian Britain and France with the Muslim Ottoman Sultan against

Russia in the Crimean War (1853–1856). Ironically, the trigger to the war was a quarrel between the Orthodox monks with the Western Christian missions over the holy places in Palestine. Britain saw in the Tsar's support of the Orthodox Church the continuation of Russia's Southward encroachment and hence supported Muslim Turkey against Christian Russia.

The nineteenth century was also the era of national revolutions during which the ethnic nation gave birth to the state. The decline of monarchical legitimacy and the rise of the doctrine of popular sovereignty gave birth to demands for self-rule within a political structure identical to and emerging from the ethnic composition of society. By contrast to the preceding 150 years when territorial states were established around princedoms, most of the new states represented a common ethnonational heritage. Europe was replete with stateless ethnic groups, many of whom were carrying collective memories of glorious ancient pasts. These ethnic groups were either crowded in with other disparate ethnic groups under the administrative rule of empires or internally fragmented into many separate entities, as in the German and Italian cases. Their heritage was to a large extent loaded with religious expressions. The Balkan nations for whom Christianity was a major agent in their identity revolted against Turkish rule trying to a limited extent to revive also the ethnic identities that had been dormant for hundreds of years (Albrecht-Carrie, 1972: 12). Significantly, because of international norms the states they established on the ruins of the Muslim Ottoman Empire however had a national basis not a religious one.

Italy and Germany, whose fractured political lives had failed to reflect the common traditions that bound them, each merged into a large sovereign state, thereby altering the balance of power in Europe and eventually resulting in two world wars. The state of Belgium was created in the wake of a common uprising by two different nations and religious sects because of the geopolitical security interests of the great powers. The revolutions of 1848, the "spring of nations," amply demonstrated that the national movement was an all-European phenomenon—even if its final legitimacy would have to await the post–World War I period.

Yet, despite the interest-based alliance and the great powers' realpolitics we must notice that the holy alliance was infused by a religious sense. Nineteenth-century Europe was still primarily Christian and the Ottoman Empire was in withdrawal. These remnants of religion seemed to totally fade out in the twentieth century.

A century after the Congress of Vienna, at the Versailles Peace Conference the right to self-determination was formally accepted as a sufficient ground for claims to sovereignty and this on a global scale. The effects of this recognition influenced not only the domestic structure of states but also their foreign dealings and, consequently, the global international order. In this new international order there was no room for divine intervention.

The Nation-State

The new principle of legitimacy that formally dominated international relations after Versailles was self-determination. The polity that emerged in the wake of World War I—the nation-state—was a merger of two distinguishable authority systems bound together by a common denominator—the national interest. But if the essence of the state is its functional performance the constituting factor of the ethnic nation is its historical origin. Based on this distinction, the *national interest*, the most celebrated concept employed by realism, received a new dimension in the new international system that emerged following World War I.

The mandate of the state is to provide security. The concern of the nation, rooted as it is in its ethnic character, is its historic mission. Thus, whereas the state component of the polity is prone to define its core objectives in terms of physical survival, the national component requires that short-term goals take into account the fulfillment of historical aspirations. Not every nation-state, by definition, will be motivated equally by both attributes; different categories of nation-states could be constructed according to a priority scale. States would usually rate their security as a core goal and their historical aspirations in long-range terms. Others would integrate their historical aspirations or ideological worldview into their core objectives. When polities define their interest in survival terms rather than missionary terms such as "manifest destiny" or "chosen nation" their national interest is secular. An elect nation would see its core values to spread its civilizing light or new mission among the infidels. Christianity and Islam in the Middle Ages, and in the modern era some revolutionaries of the French, the Bolshevik, and the Nazis ideologues defined the foreign policies of their states in missionary terms (Smith, 2000: 804–805). By doing so they went beyond the concrete definition of foreign-policy ends of the nation-state as the realist school saw it (Holsti, 1983: 129–140). For the school of realism there was hardly any difference between religious or ideological missionaries.

A common denominator of the nation and the state is territory. Nations can exist without unifying ethnic bonds on any territory—as do many modern nations like the United States or Australia. It is the state that enables the nation to control its territory and allows it to participate in international politics. In different terms: both the nation and the state are needed for functioning on the modern international scene but both need space.

Territory would usually be a statist concept, whereas land has more of a primordial implication. For the state, territory is the critical condition for functioning as a political entity; for the nation, land represents historical continuity. Territory allows the state to participate in international politics and provides security for its citizens. From a purely statist perspective, factors like natural boundaries and strategic depth determine desirable borders. A national approach, on the other hand, will determine its requirements by historical memories and loyalties, even by ancient records of national settlement. A religious approach would attach sacred attributes to its goals.

The nation and the state are two frameworks of authority that constitute the modern polity and do not always precisely overlap each other. While the nation has its roots in the ethnic community that preceded the appearance of the state, the state is a political–territorial construct. "The modern state," as A.D. Smith defined it, "refers to a set of autonomous and abstract institutions within a given territory; the modern nation refers to a sense of historic community associated with a unique 'homeland'." The nation, which is a modern development of the ethnic community, added the territorial element to the sense of common origin, history, and culture.

Besides territory the nation like the ethnic group "are founded on the sense of common origin and descent from a founding ancestor, even if he is mythical, and both also refer back to a common place of origin, the group's original habitat . . . Even where the ethnic community has lost touch with 'its' original habitat, the reborn and revived nation requires 'its own' territory—as the Turks did Anatolia and the Jews Israel—in which it may flourish" (Smith, 1981: 187–188).

Significantly, despite their secular systems of authority, each component of the modern state—the nation and the state—developed religious features in their system of legitimation and mobilization process. Thus while A.D. Smith wrote recently about "The Sacred Dimension of Nationalism," Robert Bellah had suggested three decades earlier the concept of "civil religion" (Smith, 2000: 791–814; Bellah, 1970). This division is not a coincident. Bellah wrote about the United States and hence spoke about a state religion while Smith is more influenced by the European experience and hence refers to the religious-ethnonational linkage. Still as far as international legitimacy is concerned the legitimizing principle continued to be self-determination, thus implying the sovereignty of the people not God.

It is against this background of the evolution of the international system and its main actors that we turn now to an analysis of international relations theories. We start with realism, a theory that with time fulfilled the function of a paradigm. This approach provided not only a framework for the secular state but also introduced a comprehensive field of study. The core of this field of study consisted of materialistic elements that at least from first sight seemed very distant from transcendence (Molov, 2002: 31).

The Evolution of International Relations Theory

The realist school was established following World War II, and despite many challenges it is the only approach that reached the status of a paradigm in international relations (Vasquez, 1998). It stressed the centrality of the pursuit of power in international politics and the importance of investigating actual rather than morally desirable behavior. This school took for granted the notion that the state was the central actor in international politics. The nation, in contrast, was seen as an attribute of power, so were elements like national morale and national character (Morgenthau, 1956: 97–105, 122–132). The attitudes of realists to providence is influenced by their approach to ideology that, as we indicated earlier, they see as disturbing the normal flow of international politics and disturbing the stability of a balance of power. For instance the tendency of the United States to pursue its foreign policy as a crusade is a weakness (Spanier, 1967: 1–17; Morgenthau, 1969: 15–18). Morgenthau criticized international morality because each nation saw its own morality as binding all of humanity. "In this, the ethics of international politics reverts to the politics and morality of tribalism, of the Crusaders, and of the religious wars." And he continues and attacks nationalistic universalism on the same basis:

> Thus, carrying their idols before them, the nationalistic masses of our time meet in the international arena, each group convinced that it executes the mandate of history, . . . and that it fulfills, a sacred mission ordained by providence, however defined. Little do they know that they meet under an empty sky from which the gods have departed. (Morgenthau, 1956: 234)

From a theoretical perspective, the emergence of a realist school in international relations positioned the state and power in the center of academic research. The behavioral revolution of the 1950s and 1960s expanded the agenda of political analysis in favor of other conceptual categories such as the role of the personality and perceptions in decision making processes or the political system. The emphasis on the individual enabled some role for religion. The study of socialization process, personality and perceptions (images), takes into account the impact of religious upbringing, or religiosity in foreign-policy making. Yet, the problem they encountered was first to verify the role of the religious variable on the personality of the decision maker and second the effect of all the psychological makeup on foreign-policy behavior (Sullivan, 1976: 23–65). Similarly, the application of systems and decision-making theories to foreign-policy analysis allowed for inclusion of religious factors in foreign policy. Within this approach religion could play a role in the political process, via religious parties or pressure groups, or the political culture. But, from our perspective, again the religious factor gets lost in the overall framework.

Both power and the state as well as foreign-policy behavior analysis seemed to suffer decline with the emergence of the world politics school. The "world politics" approach lumped its theoretical predecessors whether traditionalists or behavioralists, within one category: the state-centric view of international relations. By pointing to their central common denominator and concomitant shortcoming they aspired ultimately to become a new paradigm of international relations. In contrast to the realist school, the world politics position argued that the agenda of interstate relations has not always been dominated by security and power aspirations. Moreover, military force has not always been the sole or even the main means of achieving state goals. The web of global interactions is managed by power considerations as well as by rules and standards that have evolved to accommodate the growing interdependence between states and international organizations (Keohane and Nye, 1977).

Inadvertently, in its search for a paradigmatic shift, this school of thought by pointing to transnational relations drew our attention to religious forces, actors, issues, and interactions on the world scene that the state-centric view ignored or undervalued (Keohane and Nye, 1970: 371–398; Vallier, 1970, 129–152). Still, the religion factor is comparable to that of terrorist or multinational organizations.

Nevertheless and not surprisingly, because of its overwhelming centrality in world politics, a slow but incomplete return to the nation-state occurred while world politics was celebrating its new standing. An inquiry into the components of the nation-state came from two quarters, both outside of international relations and each concentrated on a different element. One was the so-called school of statism in comparative politics. Another source for investigation was the modern use of the concept of ethnonationalism elaborated earlier. Walker Connor and especially Anthony Smith, the two most celebrated fathers of this school, raised questions relevant to international relations. The end of the Cold War and the rebirth of the old-new nations in Eastern Europe made inquiry into the nation-state even more pertinent.

What began as an isolated conceptual observation late in the 1960s (Nettl, 1968: 559–592) became a quite significant issue a decade later: a number of studies appeared that reintroduced the state as the central variable in politics (Tilly, 1975; Krasner, 1978, 1984; Evans et al. 1985).[9] Stephen Krasner noted that the literature on the state was concerned with two central issues: "the extent of state autonomy and the degree of congruity between the state and its environment" (Krasner, 1984: 224). Indeed, most statists seemed to be preoccupied with the relations between state and society. Nevertheless, they have not proceeded to apply this interest to the relationship between the state and religion, and then to the foreign-policy dimension. Despite this renewal of interest of state–society relationship, no inquiry was made into the role of religion as containing state autonomy and its impact on foreign policy.

Also international relations theory found it difficult to part with the centrality of the state. The reaction to world politics in international relations was neorealism. The neorealists provide an explanation of international behavior primarily at the international or world politics level. As Kenneth Waltz put it when responding to John Vasquez's attack on the realist paradigm, "Old realists see causes as running directly from states to the outcomes, . . . New realists see states forming a structure by their interactions and then being strongly affected by the structure their interactions have formed" (Waltz, 1997: 913). Despite the emphasis on anarchy and the security dilemma neorealists perceived the state as the core unit of international relations (Waltz, 1979: 88–99). Neorealists see the *structure* of the international system, as defined to a large extent by the distribution of power, as solely responsible for international order. By putting the center of gravity on power and the state as the basic unit in world politics there was no room for spiritualism in international politics. In their eyes international regimes and international institutions play no role in promoting order at the international level.

Some change in the role of religion in international relations should have theoretically occurred with the emergence of two new approaches — neoliberalism and constructivism. In contrast to neorealists who see international order as solely connected to the balance of power neoliberals allowed an independent role for norms in promoting international order; or as they defined it international institutions.[10]

As expected the demotion of the state and power, and promotion of norms, the idea of world civilization and world citizenship, and free trade that promotes peace, did not bring back religion into the discourse of international politics. We may identify some historical connection of the neoliberal tradition to early Christian philosophers who perceived the economic division of the world as God's intention to promote interdependence (Baldwin, 1993: 11). However, Grotius and Kant, considered as the forefathers of the vision of a world community or international society, did not perceive any role for the divine in managing this world civilization. K.J. Holsti tried to trace the origins of the global society vision to Stoic philosophers and Christendom but also admitted the limits of this linkage (Holsti, 1987: 42–44). The law of nations (ius gentium — Grotius) or the idea of a community of democratic nations (Kant), rather than religious unity, according to the neoliberal approach, function as the basis for an international society and world peace.

Constructivism, the most critical theory of realism, went even further and totally rejected any role for structure of power in international order and viewed cooperation as growing out of a reformed process of international relations. Constructivist theory, which grew out from critical theory and postmodernism, focuses on the process of identity and interest formation, which it argues has been the most crucial factor in determining anarchy and international order. Alexander Wendt for instance, states clearly that structure has no role in international politics "and that if today we find ourselves in a self-help world, this is due to process, not structure. . . . Structure has no existence or casual powers apart from process. . . . Anarchy is what states make of it" (Wendt, 1992: 394–395).[11]

Bringing Europe as an example Alexander Wendt suggests, "four decades of cooperation may have transformed a positive interdependence of outcomes into a collective 'European identity' in terms of which states increasingly define their 'self' interest."

For an approach that sees the Westphelian international system as the creation of man, the divine is in trouble. Hence constructivists were less inclined even than the realists of bringing God back into international affairs. Since according to postmodernism "Reality is not God-given or

Nature-given, but human imposed" (Vasquez, 1998: 218), there is no single way of understanding or explaining the evolution of international relations. Though the new approach challenged the testing of empirical reality and hence the scientific approach to world politics, nevertheless it did not encourage transcendence. Instead of a scientific approach postmodernism and constructivism insinuated relativism, a trend that also does not cultivates religion. Ultimately, God's role is further degraded when all is in man's mind and under his control even more than when the state is replacing Him in supervising international politics.

The afore-mentioned debate between realists and nonrealists was also reflected in the very well-celebrated debate between Fukayuma and Huntington. While the first clearly belonged to the liberal tradition and spoke about the possibility of eternal peace the latter maintained that conflict is not over even in the post-Soviet era but would rather change faces. But the novelty of Huntington from our perspective, as noted earlier, is that he managed to bury the role of religion in international conflict in a more neutral language of culture and civilization.

It goes without saying that Marxism and neo-Marxism, a family of paradigms that competed with the others discussed here, also assumed religion to be irrelevant.

Religion and the Quantification of International Relations

Our tour de horizon of international relations theory and the role of the divine in it cannot be full without a short glance at methodology, a debate that in the 1960s as mentioned above, preoccupied the center stage of the discipline. A major branch of international relations scholarship focuses on quantitative methodology. That is, many of those who study international relations distill the various factors involved in various research questions into standardized measures and use statistical techniques in order to assess the dynamics of the phenomena that they are examining. This methodology has been extremely useful in the study of international conflict and has allowed scholars to examine the complex interactions between many potential causes of international and domestic conflict while comparing hundreds of cases. This is a task that, arguably, could not have been accomplished using the comparative method that relies primarily on human insight and introspection.

However, this methodology, which constitutes a significant proportion of the scholarship in international relations, has been criticized on grounds that are particularly relevant to the study of religion's role in international relations. Specifically, those who use this methodology are often accused of ignoring variables that are hard to measure. That is, since quantitative methodology cannot deal with factors that cannot be distilled into numerical variables, any phenomenon that defies easy measurement tends to be ignored.

Religion is, perhaps, one of the hardest variables to measure. This is true for two reasons. First, the lack of attention given by scholars to the topic provides a poor basis on which to develop variables. Most of the theories and variables that have been quantified are based on an extensive qualitative literature on the relevant topic. Thus, the scarcity of international relations literature on the topic of religion has probably hampered efforts to conceptualize how it may be measured. In fact, it is arguable that this lack of literature on the topic has resulted in an attitude that religion is not important enough to quantify. Second, it is clear that the only truly accurate measure would involve reading the minds of political actors in order to discover their true motivations. Since this is not currently possible, many researchers using quantitative methods probably choose not to measure religion at all.

In the rare instances when religion is included in quantitative studies, the measures are generally relatively crude. Some studies simply measure the number of religions involved in a conflict or whether the groups involved in a dyadic conflict are of different religions. For example, Henderson (1997) measures whether the two states involved in an international conflict have populations that adhere to different religions and Rummel (1997), while examining domestic conflict, similarly measures the number of different religions present in a state. Some studies measure specific aspects of the influence of religion that are informative, but limited in scope. For example, in a series of studies on ethnic conflict Fox (1997, 1999a,b, 2000a,b,d, 2001c) developed several such variables including measures for religious discrimination, grievances expressed over that discrimination, religious legitimacy, and religious institutions. Perhaps, the most sophisticated general measure of religion's influence on conflict was also developed by this series of studies and measures whether religious issues are more important compared to political economic, cultural, and autonomy issues, based on the extent of these types of discrimination and grievances expressed over that discrimination. However, this measure is still of the "more than" or "less than" variety as opposed to a more accurate scale. Also, the measure developed for religious legitimacy turned out to be less accurate than a simple measure of whether or not a state has an official religion.

Thus, while all of these measures of religion succeed at measuring some aspects of the influence of religion on political behavior, they are all relatively crude variables, especially when compared to the multiple and sophisticated ways in which other variables are measured. For example, there are multiple ways to measure economic inequality. First, some measure land usage and distribution. Second, some measure income inequality. This type of measurement itself is done in diverse ways. It can be measured for sectors, households, or individuals. It can include either pre- or post-tax income. It can also relate to economically active males or the whole population. Third, some measure other economic differentials between groups. These differentials can include any combination of factors including education, home ownership, unemployment rates, occupational status, and numbers living below the poverty line. Fourth, some measure economic treatment by the government, which can include discrimination, representation in government, comparative shares in political power, or public expenditures (Lichbach, 1989: 442).

However, to be fair, it is easier to measure a more concrete phenomenon such as economic inequality than it is to measure something as intangible as religion. Nevertheless, just because a perfect measurement of the influence of religion on political behavior is probably not an achievable goal does not mean that improved measures are not possible and desirable.[12] Also, it can be said that in the case of economic inequality there is too much information. That is, the "statistical measurement of economic inequality involves so many competing requirements that the hope for a single universally agreed upon index . . . is doomed" (Lichbach, 1989: 441).

Furthermore, it is interesting to note that, other than Henderson's (1997) study, all of the studies that include religion as a variable focus on domestic and not international conflict. Although, as discussed in detail in chapter 4, domestic conflicts are becoming international issues and studies on domestic conflict are often published in international relations journals, the core of international relations remains the study of international conflict. The lack of quantitative studies of international conflict and war that so much as include religion as one of many intervening variables is indicative of the failure of international relations to account for religion.

Conclusions

The role of religion in the social sciences in general, and in the study of international relations in particular, is an interesting paradox. On one hand, religion is an essential element of their origins but, on the other hand, until very recently they have ignored religion. More specifically, the social sciences, including the study of international relations, were founded upon the rejection of religion as a basis for understanding society. Social scientists hoped that secular ideologies, science, and rationalism would provide a basis for a better life in modern times than did the religious basis for society and government of the past. This resulted in an ideological rejection of religion as an explanatory factor. In some disciplines such as sociology, this ideology was overt but in others, such as international relations, it was less overt and buried within the origins and evolutions of the discipline. To a great extent, this tendency to ignore religion is rooted in the Western centrism of the social sciences. That international relations theory is the discipline that most profoundly ignores religion can be explained by the fact that in many ways it is the most Western of the social sciences.

If one looks closely at some major elements of international relations theory, one can still find these religious roots. For example, Smith (1999, 2000) has shown that many forms of nationalism have their roots in religious identities and that nationalism has many similarities to religion. The neoliberal tradition is linked to the thoughts of Christian philosophers (Baldwin, 1993: 11). Secular states develop civil norms of behavior with characteristics similar to religion (Bellah, 1970). The origin of the modern Westphalian state system is linked to the Protestant reformation (Philpott, 2000). Totalitarianism and ethnic cleansing have both been linked to ideas inherent in European Christianity (Osiander, 2000). Finally, the elements of modernity that were expected to bring about religion's demise, have ironically, been linked to its resurgence.

Thus, although the ideological themes and motifs of the paradigms that have driven international relations and the other social sciences have blinded the practitioners of these disciplines to the importance of religion as a social and political force, religion can still be found within them. Given this, while religion may be the missing dimension of international relations, it is not lost for good. That is, the building blocks for a theory of religion and international relations exist and can be found both within the roots of international relations theory and elsewhere within the body of knowledge of the social sciences. The rest of this book is intended to unearth some of these elements in order to create a better understanding of the role of religion in international relations.

CHAPTER 3

RELIGION AND LEGITIMACY

Legitimacy is an important aspect of international relations and few would deny that religion is an excellent source of legitimacy. Legitimacy can be described as "the normative belief by an actor that a rule or institution ought to be obeyed" (Hurd, 1999: 381). In other words, to convince another that your cause is legitimate, is to convince him that you are morally correct and he should support your cause or at least not oppose it. Thus, legitimacy can be a powerful asset to foreign-policy makers that can be directed at several audiences. It can be used to convince policy makers from other states. It can be used to undermine policy makers from other states who oppose you by convincing the populations of their states that you are correct. It can also help to mobilize support for policies within your own state, both among the population and other policy makers. It is also an important element of the stability of the international system. Other important elements of international stability include a balance of power and acceptance of the norms and structure of the international system (Kissinger, 1957).

To a certain extent there are distinct boundaries that define what is legitimate and what is not legitimate. For example, self-defense is generally considered legitimate and genocide is not. However, there is a considerable middle ground in which it is unclear whether an action should be considered legitimate. In these cases, it is up to policy makers to convince others that their action is legitimate. Thus, legitimacy, including religious legitimacy, has a dual role in foreign policy. It defines what is and is not beyond the pale as well as provides a means for policy makers to justify their actions to others. Accordingly, this chapter examines both how religious legitimacy influences foreign policy and how policy makers use it as a tool to further their own goals with an emphasis on the latter. This includes an examination of the impact of religion on the norms of the international system. It also includes an examination of how religion is used by policy makers to achieve their goals. Both of these roles of religious legitimacy in international relations have rarely been examined thoroughly. Thus, further scrutiny is necessary of the extent and limits of its influence on international norms as well as its potential uses and limitations as a tool as well as the costs of its use.

Foreign-policy tools can be divided into two categories. The first category is composed of tangible or material assets. This includes the traditional sources of power described in the international relations literature such as military and economic assets. The uses of this type of tool to further foreign policy are well known and are not discussed here.[1] The second category is persuasion. One way to persuade others, whether this persuasion involves foreign policy or any other topic, is to convince others that your cause is legitimate.

However, as is discussed later in this chapter, religious legitimacy is a complicated tool. The state rarely has a monopoly over religious legitimacy and others, both from within and outside of the state, can use it to oppose policies. It is both a common justification for war and the basis for those who advocate peace as well as one of the bases for what is considered appropriate behavior during a war. It is both a tool for mobilizing identity groups for causes that are not particularly religious and an essential element of many of those identities. It can support activities that would otherwise not be popular as well as mold itself to support activities and policies that are so popular that to oppose them would be ill-advised. Furthermore, religion can act as a motivating force, either through the worldviews of policy makers or through the constraints placed on policy makers by the religious worldviews of their constituents.

Religion as a Basis for Political Legitimacy

The argument that religion is a potential source of legitimacy is not a new one nor is it particularly in dispute. Even those who believe that the world is becoming secular and religion is becoming irrelevant in modern times concede that in those times and places where religion is relevant, it can legitimate a wide range of institutions and activities. For example, Marx's classic argument that religion is the opiate of the masses makes the dual argument that it should be recognized that religion is a false consciousness, but it is nevertheless a powerful force that can legitimate an economic system that is against the interests of the majority of society.

Despite the power of religion to legitimate policies and governments there is very little in the international relations literature that directly addresses the role of religious legitimacy in international relations. However, the literature on domestic politics and society does address the role of religious legitimacy. Thus, an examination of the complex ways religious legitimacy influences the domestic arena should shed some light on how it may influence international affairs.

Until a few centuries ago, it was taken for granted that religion was a source of legitimacy for the state. In fact, until the Enlightenment it was the sole basis for legitimacy in Europe. The right to rule came from God and was granted to the rulers through the Church. Thus, the common man had no right to question who ruled and how they ruled (Turner, 1991: 178–198). However, in the modern era this has changed and religion is no longer the sole basis for the legitimacy of most states. Currently, most states claim legitimacy through representing the will of the people. In governments based on the ideology of liberalism, as well as in many governments that are not, this is achieved through democratic representation or the appearance of democratic representation. Most other modern ideologies also draw their legitimacy from the will of the people. The various forms of Communist ideologies claim to represent the true economic interests of the workers who comprise the vast majority of society. Fascist ideologies are based on the argument that the leader is somehow more enlightened and closer to the truth than everyone else and is the embodiment of the state itself. Therefore it is in everyone's best interests to follow him. Nationalism, which is not incompatible with any of the aforementioned ideologies, legitimizes the state as the political embodiment of a nation.

The development of the role of religion in the international system paralleled its role in supporting the state. The international system that emerged following the Peace of Westphalia despite the advancement of sovereignty nevertheless kept the "divine right of Kings to rule" as its legitimizing principle. Prince Meternich and Lord Castlreagh the two main figures at the Vienna Congress tried to keep this principle thus avoiding the new international order that the French Revolution and the conquests of Napoleon Bonaparte implied for Europe. The Holly Alliance that emerged following Vienna also radiated an endeavor to maintain a Christian Europe. However, following the treaty of Versailles self-determination replaced the divine right of kings to become the legitimizing principle of the international system. Significantly, as the conveners of the Vienna Congress had expected this new normative value system opened a Pandora Box resulting in two world wars, a Cold War, and plenitude of interstate and intrastate wars throughout the twentieth century.

Yet, even in modern times, religion is still a source of legitimacy for the state, if only one among many. That is, even though justification of state power rests on ideologies like nationalism, the pursuit of democracy, and humanitarian values, among others, a "strong residual element of religion, which clearly exists even in western societies [and] can still perform basic legitimizing or oppositional functions within such ideologies" (Kokoslakis, 1985: 371). Geertz (1977: 267–278) makes a similar argument when he notes, "thrones may be out of fashion and pageantry too; but political authority still requires a cultural framework in which to define itself and advance its claims, and so does opposition to it."

For example, in Indonesia, it is very important for a leader to have religious legitimacy. Among the Javanese, the dominant ethnic group in Indonesia, power is believed to have a spiritual essence known as *wayhu* that is given to chosen people. As a result, all five of Indonesia's presidents since independence have sought to create the impression that they possessed *wayhu*. They all made frequent visits to holy places both during and before their terms of office. President Wahid, who ruled briefly for 21 months in 2000–2001 was the most overtly religious being a Muslim cleric. Indonesia's first president is "said to have surrounded himself with magic charms and with dwarfs, albinos, and others believed to have spiritual qualities." President Suharto, one of Indonesia's longest-serving presidents, is said to have gained his *wayhu* through his wife. When she died people began to believe that he had lost his *wayhu* and was removed from power two years later.[2] Clearly his removal from power was also due to Indonesia's economic problems and corruption as well as the desire for a less autocratic style of government, but the removal of President Suharto's aura of legitimacy likely facilitated his downfall.

In fact, many would have it that religious legitimacy is, in recent times, becoming a more important basis for legitimating governments. This is because, especially in the Third World, the Western secular ideologies that guide most states are falling into disrepute for a variety of reasons. First, they have always been perceived as foreign ideologies imposed from outside by elites who are overly influenced by the West, in contrast to local religious traditions that are indigenous and, therefore, more legitimate (Juergensmeyer, 1993). Second, the governments based on these ideologies and promising freedom, economic prosperity, and social justice have fallen far short of these promises, thus undermining their legitimacy (Juergensmeyer, 1993). Third, the modernization policies of these governments have led to many unsettling consequences including the alienation of those left out of the process and the breakdown in community values both of which have led to a religious backlash (Sahliyeh, 1990: 9; Thomas, 2000: 816; Haynes, 1994: 34). Fourth, modern communications technology has allowed religious institutions to extend their influence (Shupe, 1990: 22). Fifth, greater political participation has led to increased participation by those with religious agendas (Rubin, 1994: 22–23). Sixth, greater religious freedom and more individual choice in selecting a religion has led to greater individual interest in religion (Iannaccone, 1995a,b).

Religion can legitimate not only governments but also policies followed by governments, including policies that might otherwise be considered objectionable in an era where human rights are one of the major considerations. This can include severe discrimination and even violence against religious minority groups. Little (1996a) calls this type of behavior violent intolerance. The oppression of religious minorities can be justified as necessary because the religious minority is considered an enemy or threat to the well-being or religious values of the majority. This "necessity defense" allows extreme actions against an enemy whose very existence constitutes a danger. It is also one of the common justifications for genocide (Fein, 1990) and terrorism (Rapoport, 1984; Hoffman, 1995).

One example of this is the treatment of the Bahai minority in Iran. The Bahai are considered by the country's Shi'i Islamic regime to be apostates and counterrevolutionaries. This belief is based solely on religious ideology and, in fact, the Bahai pose little danger to the Iranian state. Nevertheless, in order to protect the state from what it believes to be an imminent threat, the Iranian government has instituted a set of policies designed to destroy Iran's Bahai community. The Bahai are denied recognition as a religion that has serious repercussions in that personal status in Iran is derived from one's religion. This means that a Bahai who wishes to marry must officially convert to Islam, thus separating himself from his religious community, or marry under the auspices of his faith and risk criminal charges of cohabiting with someone to whom he is not married. Similarly, the Bahai are also forbidden to bury their dead according to Bahai tradition, and many have been arrested for attempting to do so. Furthermore, in August 1983, the Iranian government officially declared membership in a Bahai institution to be a criminal offense. Other elements of this persecution include: the seizure of communal property including places of worship, schools, hospitals, and privately owned businesses; arrests and executions for allegedly criminal offenses; looting and arson by the Iranian populace; and vilification in the state-run media.[3] Thus, the Iranian government uses religion to legitimate its assault on the Bahai people that, in all probability violates the UN Convention against Genocide, which prohibits "acts intended to destroy in whole or in part, a national, ethnical, racial, or religious group as such" including "deliberately inflicting on the group conditions of life calculated to bring about its destruction in whole or in part."

Often religion can legitimate what politicians cannot achieve by other means. For instance, Glynn (1998) documents that one of the few efforts at racial reconciliation in the United States that has had any success are local efforts by black and white Evangelical churches. There are many political difficulties and controversies surrounding efforts at reconciliation including apologizing for slavery when the perpetrators and victims are long dead and most U.S. whites are not descended from slave owners. However, what is politically difficult can be much easier in a religious context. Glynn argues that these efforts have succeeded where political efforts have failed for three reasons. First, religious concepts of proper human relations are more exacting than secular concepts of reasonableness, fairness, or justice. Thus, this higher religious standard that is internalized by those who attempt the reconciliation may succeed where the secular solution of legislating attitudes has failed. Second, the Christian concept of sin combined with the idea of divine forgiveness is a good way to overlook grievances and avoid the issue of blame. One of the most difficult elements of resolving a conflict is over the issue of whom to blame. The concept of divinely inspired forgiveness gives both sides a chance to feel that their grievances have been addressed without having to antagonize the other side with issues of blame and reparation, which may otherwise have been unresolvable. Finally, when the two sides share a religion or come from similar traditions, the reconciliation can be reenforced with common rituals such as praying together.

This example illustrates that religion's power to legitimate policies and actions also has a positive side. It can potentially be used to legitimate and support resolving conflicts. For instance, there are several elements within the Judeo-Christian tradition that can be used to support nonviolence and reconciliation. These include, empathy, pacifism, the sanctity of life, focusing inward on improving oneself rather than outward on potential enemies, and the idea of a perfect and just society (Gopin, 2000: 20–23).

This dual potential of religion to support hatred and violence on one hand and peace and reconciliation on the other is due to the fact that most religions are internally pluralist in that they have multiple traditions and religious leaders must choose between them and often reinterpret them to deal with new situations (Appleby, 2000: 30–33). Thus, both religious and political leaders have wide discretion in how they use religious legitimacy to further their goals. They can draw upon the concept of love thy neighbor as well as upon the concept of holy war. In fact, the divergent interpretations of religious doctrine often have their roots in social and political interests (Lewy, 1974: 555–556).

Just as religion can support both peace and violence, it is a two-edged sword that can support both the government and those who oppose it. The dynamics through which religions support governments are well known. It is in the interest of a religion to increase number of adherents and enforce its belief. The best way to do this is through early socialization, which is best achieved through privileged access to education system and other government support for the religion, including legislating religious law as state law and eliminating rivals through government intervention. Political actors are willing to do this because they are primarily interested in survival and want to eliminate credible political rivals. Religious leaders can help achieve this by delivering the support of their constituents by giving the government an aura of religious legitimacy. Thus there is essentially a social contract of mutual support between political and religious elites (Gill and Keshavarzian, 1999; Kowalewski and Greil, 1990).

However, religious elites do not always support the state. Often religious elites decide to oppose the state. This can occur for a variety of interrelated reasons. First, if a state has an official religion that supports it, political opposition may be considered religious opposition. This may require those opposing the state to seek out alternative religions or religious institutions to justify their opposition. Second, when a religious minority rebels against a state, there is a strong likelihood that the minority's religion will be used to support that rebellion (Lincoln, 1985). Third, religion is an effective compensator for the powerless (Stark and Bainbridge, 1985). Fourth, when religious elites feel that the state's policies are against their interests or the opposition movement is likely to further their interests (Fox, 1999b). Fifth, when failing to support the opposition movement or continuing to support the state will cause the religion to lose members (Gill, 1998). Sixth, a religion may support an opposition movement against a state it considers to be morally deficient.

The Dual Role of Religious Legitimacy in Latin America

One example of this dual tendency of religion to both support and oppose governments is the Catholic Church in Latin America. Traditionally the

Catholic Church enjoyed a mutually supportive relationship with most Latin American governments and benefitted from the advantages of this mutual support. With a few exceptions, the Church defended its institutional interests through collaboration with political and economic elites and, in return, supported the rule of these elites. However, since World War II, elements of the Church, especially those at the grass-roots level, have supported the rights of the political and economic have-nots against the hierarchy. This often resulted in the upper and lower echelons of the Catholic hierarchy working at cross-purposes with the upper echelons supporting the state and the lower echelons opposing it, or at least many of its policies (Haynes, 1998: 42–48).

One form this opposition has taken is liberation theology, which is essentially a combination of Catholic and Marxist ideology that had its heyday from the 1960s to the 1980s. It is intended to help to understand as well as improve the desperate conditions of Latin America's poor. Liberation theologians claim that scriptures do not provide tools to analyze contemporary society and therefore must be joined with a secular social science, usually Marxist class analysis. It combines these two sources to develop a sense of social justice and to determine a course of political action to achieve this goal. For example, Jesus is considered a revolutionary who opposed oppression by the establishment in his own time. The political program of Liberation Theology has been pursued through base Christian communities (CEBs), which are usually lay-led due to the scarcity of priests among the region's poor. The goal of these CEBs is to empower people by increasing literacy and political awareness as well as to give the poor a more organized political voice. These CEBs produced many of the labor union and political leaders that have since championed the cause of the poor (Berryman, 1987; Haynes, 1998: 48–49; Pottenger, 1989; Roelofs, 1988).

Since the 1990s, Protestant denominations have been making major inroads in many Latin American states. Their success is due, at least in part, to the fact that the Catholic Church is perceived as distant from the common people and the Catholic Church has been associated with the establishment that has failed to bring the benefits of modernity to the region's poor. It is clearly the poor and marginalized who are most attracted to Protestantism (Haynes, 1998: 51–56). This has resulted in an interesting dynamic within the Catholic Church. In states where Protestantism has been making serious inroads into Catholicism, the Catholic Church has begun to champion anti-regime causes, presumably in order to maintain its support among the people (Gill, 1998). Thus, it can be argued that the Catholic Church in Latin America follows a policy of doing whatever will increase its hegemony in Latin America and will use its control over religious legitimacy to either support or oppose the state based on which policy will best further this goal. As a result, at different times and places it has both supported and opposed Latin American governments, proving that religion can be a double-edged sword.

The Limits of Religious Legitimacy

Religion is a versatile tool that can legitimate both war and peace and can support governments and policies as well as oppose them. However, this tool also has limitations. One major limitation is the tensions between religion and secularism. Whether or not the role of religion is decreasing in modern times, it is clear that there are many people who are not religious and are unlikely to be swayed by religious arguments. In fact, in some cases, invoking religious legitimacy may have the opposite effect. For example, many decades of tensions between religious and secular elements of Israeli society has resulted in a significant political polarization of the two populations. These tensions are over a variety of issues. Religious political parties wish to legislate religious laws as state law, including laws regarding dietary issues and what businesses and public services should be open on the Sabbath. Few from the ultraorthodox community are required to do the military service that is compulsory for the rest of the population. Also, there has been a continuing battle between secular and religious parties over political control of the country's educational system as well as for financial resources for the parallel secular and religious school systems. As a result of these tensions, and others, an appeal to religion in support of a policy can easily provoke a negative reaction from many elements of Israel's secular community. They resent what they see as religion being forced upon them and those who are religious being given special privileges and, therefore, if they are influenced by appeals to religious legitimacy, this influence has the opposite of the desired effect.

Similarly, not all people come from the same religious tradition and appeals to people from other traditions are less likely to be successful than appeals to members of the same tradition.

Another aspect of Israeli politics highlights a second limit on religious legitimacy. Many of Israel's ultraorthodox sects believe that there should not be a Jewish state until the messiah comes to establish it. In short, they feel that the state is illegitimate on religious grounds (Sandler, 1996: 133–135). In contrast, the Religious Zionists, another branch of Jewish orthodoxy adopted an ethnonational approach to Israel's foreign policy and became the most ardent supporters of The Land of Israel movement and the hard core of the settlers movement in Judea, Smaria, and the Gaza Strip (Sandler, 1993: 150–157). Thus, when using religion to legitimize a policy, or as in Israel's case the state itself, it is important to remember that not everyone will share your interpretation of religious doctrine and, as a result, may oppose you on religious grounds. These disagreements and the failure to legitimize the Oslo Peace Process ultimately resulted in the political assassination of Prime Minister Rabin in 1995 (Sandler, 1996: 147–148).

Another limitation of religious legitimacy is that some policies are so popular that religious legitimacy is simply not enough to change people's minds. In fact, it is possible that opposing a policy can do damage to the credibility of religion. Fawcett (2000) documents how this occurred in South Africa. She argues that churches rely on the collective cultural power of their population base. When the political order changes, they need to reposition themselves in order to benefit from the cultural power. That is, religious legitimacy is dependent upon the support of the population and religious institutions that position themselves too far outside of the political and cultural mainstream lose much of their influence.

The Dutch Reformed Church of South Africa supported Apartheid when it was popular but changed its stance in parallel with political institutions, both reacting to and supporting political changes. When Apartheid was at its height, opposing it would not only have been unsuccessful, it would have harmed the Church. Sermons against Apartheid would have only driven white South Africans to other churches or caused them to replace those in charge of the Dutch Reformed Church. However, as it became more apparent that the system of segregation was ending, the Church repositioned itself on the issue and actually participated in the process of legitimating and facilitating reconciliation. Thus, in South Africa, as well as elsewhere, religious legitimacy is not a unidirectional tool that can be used at will. Rather it is a multifaceted process that is both influenced by political and social factors as well as a strong influence on them. In short, religion can be a strong source of moral persuasion as long as the morality it supports is not too far out of line with the moral base of the population it is used to persuade.

The Uses of Religious Legitimacy in International Relations

All of this has a variety of implications for the role of religious legitimacy as an instrument of foreign policy. First, religion is a powerful source of legitimacy and, therefore, a powerful tool of persuasion. It can be used on a variety of populations that those who make foreign policy may want to convince. These include other policy makers in their own state, policy makers of other states, their own state's population, and the populations of other states. Second, religious legitimacy is a versatile tool. Religious traditions tend to be complex and have multiple traditions within them upon which foreign-policy makers can draw. Thus, they can be used to support both violent warlike policies as well as peaceful benevolent policies. In fact, religious legitimacy can support policies that otherwise may be unsupportable.

Third, religion is a double-edged sword. While policy makers can invoke it to support their policies, others can invoke it against them. In fact, the very same people policy makers wish to convince using religion are those who can use it against them. Those who oppose them within their own state, be they other policy makers, the political opposition, religious elites, or simply members of the population can denounce policies or proposed policies as against religious precepts. Policy makers from other states can undermine policies by branding them as against religious precepts as well as use religion to mobilize their own populations against the policy. This can also be done by opposition parties, religious elites, and others in other states. Given all of this, playing the religion card can backfire on a policy maker. In addition, policy makers must be aware that others may play the religion card against them.

Fourth, religious legitimacy may be versatile but it also has its limitations. Some people and elements of the population will not be convinced by religious arguments. Thus, in most cases, policy makers need something more than religious legitimacy to support a policy. In other words, religious legitimacy can be useful in furthering foreign policy goals but it is very difficult to achieve these goals using only religious legitimacy. Also, it is difficult, if not impossible, to successfully use religion to support policies that are considered beyond the pale. That is, some policies are so unpopular that not only will religion fail to convince people, trying to do so may damage future uses of religion to legitimate other policies or brand those trying to use religious legitimacy as fanatics.

Fifth, religion is a cultural-specific tool. For example invoking Jesus is unlikely to sway Jews and Muslims, much less Hindus. Thus, appeals to religious legitimacy are limited by the homogeneity of the audience. This means that the more religiously specific an appeal, the less people it is likely to convince, though, presumably, those who fall within the range of this appeal are more likely to be convinced. The other side of this coin is that the broader appeals will influence a more diverse audience but may be less convincing. Although it is possible to make appeals across religious traditions, a Christian, for example, invoking precepts common to Christianity and Islam or a Christian invoking Islam to convince a Muslim will be less persuasive than a Muslim invoking the same precepts.

Sixth, not all actors who use religious legitimacy are traditional policy makers or would-be policy makers. Religious elites and other nongovernment actors can effectively involve religious legitimacy toward a policy goal. One example of this is the role of the World Council of Churches (WCC) in the fall of South Africa's Apartheid government. The WCC, from its inception, represented hundreds of Christian denominations encompassing millions and eventually hundreds of millions of Christians. In 1970 it established a program to combat racism and decided to devote at least half of the funds from this program to oppose Apartheid. While these funds never exceeded a few hundred thousand dollars a year, the symbolic value of these donations contributed to the downfall of the Apartheid system of government in several ways. First, the impact of these donations was considerably greater than a simple appeal against racism because the WCC showed that its commitment was a serious one to the extent that it was willing to financially support a liberation movement. The symbolic and legitimacy value of these donations far exceeded the importance of the money itself, given that these funds were nowhere near what is generally needed to finance a successful liberation movement.

Second, the support of the WCC gave many blacks in South Africa the courage to "make their voices heard" within their own churches, which in turn influenced the thinking of those churches (Warr, 1999: 499–504). This is particularly important because the eventual support of South Africa's Dutch Reformed Church for the end of Apartheid both hastened and smoothed the transition to a more inclusive system (Fawcett, 2000). Third, the open opposition of a body that represented hundreds of millions of Christians posed a severe legitimacy problem to South Africa's government, which thought of itself as ruling a Christian nation. The WCC also endorsed international sanctions against South Africa and was instrumental in causing hundreds of businesses and numerous individuals to stop supporting companies that did business with South Africa. This divestment campaign cost South Africa almost $10 billion from 1984 to 1989 (Warr, 1999: 504–506).

Why is Religious Legitimacy Influential in IR?

While the aforementioned discussion makes it clear that religion is a potential tool of persuasion available to foreign-policy actors, it does not address the extent of the influence of this tool. That is, there remains the question of why are religious arguments convincing at all in an international arena where power and pragmatism still dominates? It is clear religion is a useful tool in mobilizing domestic support for a policy, but it is less clear that it is a match for the realist tools for international politics. That is, when pragmatic concerns and religious legitimacy collide, will religious concerns be trumped?

It is argued here that there are three reasons to believe that religious legitimacy should be influential in international relations. First, normative factors are having an increasing influence on international relations. Second, the growing literature on instrumentalism demonstrates that other cultural factors such as nationalism and ethnicity have provided legitimacy for political activities. Third, identity is clearly an influence on international politics and religion is an influence on identity.

Normative Power in International Relations

While it is clear that power politics have not gone away, there are many indications that normative concerns, of which religion is one, do influence foreign-policy behavior. International norms influence the international system by "providing solutions to coordination problems, reducing transaction costs, providing a language and grammar of international politics, and constituting the state actors themselves" (Cortell and Davis, 2000: 65–66). International norms also influence domestic politics and even make domestic issues international ones. The international norm of human rights is one example of this. Violations of human rights that were committed within Peru by the government of former dictator Pinochet resulted in the attempt to extradite him to Spain for trial many years after the fact. War crimes and crimes against humanity committed in Rwanda and the former Yugoslavia have resulted in international tribunals bringing the perpetrators of these crimes, including Yugoslavian President Milsovek. States engaging in international war almost always invoke the international norm of self-defense that is one of the few acceptable justifications for war according to the UN Charter. Since the end of the Cold War humanitarian intervention in domestic crises has increased as have the placement of international troops and observers to implement and maintain peace settlements.

Normative arguments can acquire power utility when norms become institutionalized as conventions. That is, when norms become socially embedded in a system, be it national, subnational, or international, to the extent that they are tied up with the social identities of the actors in that system, these actors are impelled to heed these norms. Thus, norms can be used to influence the behavior of others to the extent that they accept these norms. Some would even argue that the military and economic power are ultimately based on universally accepted norms. It is arguable that the power of economics is based on the social conventions of a medium of exchange and that military power is based on the social convention of an anarchic system (Hall, 1997).

Be that as it may, it is clear that international norms are slowly becoming incorporated into domestic politics through several processes and, thus, increasing their influence. First, international norms often coincide with local cultural values. In these cases the international norms can be incorporated into domestic culture as an expression of local values. However, in many cases these international norms contrast with local norms creating a friction between them. For example, the international norm of women's rights often clashes with religious and cultural perceptions of the proper and traditional role of women. Second, political leaders often invoke international norms in support of their causes, even if they do not believe in these norms. Despite this, repeatedly invoking an international norm can facilitate its incorporation into the domestic value system. For instance, when Palestinian leaders invoke the concept of human rights in their criticisms of the treatment of Palestinians by Israel, they open themselves up to criticism based on the way they treat their own people. Third, international norms often coincide with domestic material and political interests. Fourth, international laws are often legislated as domestic law. One way this occurs is when states sign international treaties and conventions, international norms become domestic laws. This is one reason why southern U.S. senators opposed ratifying the UN Convention on Genocide for many years. The convention would have made it against the federal law to commit "acts intended to destroy in whole or in part, a national, ethnical, racial, or religious group as such." The "in part" segment of the convention could have been interpreted as a racially motivated killing of a single black. This would have allowed the murder trial to take place in federal court where the perpetrators would have had a significantly lower chance of acquittal. Probably for this reason, when the United States finally ratified the convention, it included a reservation that it does not accept the "in part" component of the convention. Fifth, there is a continuing process of socialization at the international level toward the acceptance of many international norms. For instance, the international norms of nuclear anti-proliferation were probably a major reason why Ukraine decided to renounce nuclear weapons (Cortell and Davis, 2000: 72–84).

An example of the power of international norms is the success of indigenous peoples throughout the world in achieving increased autonomy and control over natural resources. Indigenous peoples are perhaps among the most powerless in the world as measured by traditional realist concerns. In fact they have been referred to as the fourth world. Yet in recent years many indigenous groups have achieved major political victories. For instance, natives in Canada and Australia have received considerable control over their own land and resources. Indigenous peoples in many states have mobilized politically and have a considerably increased say in their own affairs. Though these movements have not always been fully successful as was the case with the Zapotista rebellion against Mexico, which resulted in a continuing military standoff.

Why have peoples who are so powerless in terms of traditional political and economic measures had so much success in attaining their goals? The only answer is that there has been a shift in international norms. Originally the Westphalian state system accepted the law of conquest as an international norm. Based on this norm colonies were established by European powers and states like the United States conquered indigenous peoples. However this norm began to shift by the early twentieth century with the United States and the USSR emerging as world powers and both denouncing colonialism. The League of Nations and later the United Nations embraced the value of self-determination, which was used to end colonialism (Wilmer, 1993). While many Third World states, due to their multiethnic populations, felt that the right to self-determination was fulfilled by independence, many ethnic and national groups, including indigenous groups, sought to expand the concept of self-determination to include themselves. In fact the desire for self-determination is the most accurate predictor of which ethnic minorities will violently rebel (Gurr, 1993a,b). The success of many indigenous and other ethnic groups at gaining various forms of autonomy and independence in recent times and the international support for these movements indicates that this expanded concept of self-determination is becoming an important international norm.

While this example of the influence of norms on international relations may not be particularly religious, it does establish that norms play a role in international relations. Since religion is a major source of norms, this implies that religion can influence international relations in this manner.

Instrumentalism

While the concept of religion as a tool for politicians is rarely discussed in international relations theory, there is a body of theory that examines how politicians can use other aspects of culture to further political causes. This body of theory, known as instrumentalism, generally focuses on ethnicity and nationalism. It posits that the reason factors like ethnicity and nationalism are important is not because the true goals of politicians are ethnic or national, but rather because politicians have other goals in mind and play on national and ethnic sentiments in order to achieve these goals. These goals can include finding a way to divide a political or economic pie that is not big enough for all and the desire for power for its own sake as well as many others. Thus, in essence instrumentalist theory posits that factors like nationalism and ethnicity are politically relevant precisely because they are useful tools to further political and material ends.[4]

An extreme extension of instrumentalist theory found within ethnic conflict theory, known as constructionism, takes this argument a step further. While instrumentalist theory posits that ethnicity and nationalism are used by political entrepreneurs to further political and material goals, constructionist theory posits that they are created in order to further political and material goals. This view holds that group identity is situational and based on practical considerations and is closely related to the realist school of international relations. It stresses the argument that nationalism and ethnicity are based on the utility of pursuing interests and power and ignores where culture came from and how that affects interests (Comoroff and Stern, 1995: 5–7). While instrumentalism and especially constructionism are not universally accepted as the sole explanation for ethnic and nationalist behavior by those who study these topics, they are generally accepted as descriptions of one of the forms ethnic and national politics can take (Gurr, 1993a: 4–5).

This concept that one explanation for the political aspects of ethnicity and nationalism is that they are used to further goals that are not necessarily national or ethnic can be applied to religion. In fact, Hasencleaver and Rittberger (2000) do precisely this. They argue that the instrumentalist and constructionist perspectives can be used to understand the role of religion in politics. The instrumentalist view of religion posits that religion is a manifestation of other more basic social forces. Domestically elites use religion as a tool in seeking their own power and for mobilization efforts. Internationally it can also be used as a tool of power and interest. The constructionalist view of religion is applicable to politics and religion when leaders use new interpretations of their religions in order to justify their actions.

Religion is clearly a useful tool to mobilize people for political causes. Church attendance in the United States is correlated with voter turnout. Participation in religious activities also increases political participation. Those who play leadership roles in religious organizations develop skills that are useful for political organization. Also, religious motivations, organizations, and social interaction are resources that can be used for political purposes (Harris, 1994: 46–48). In fact, religious organizations are particularly suited for facilitating mobilization. They often have a protected status in society, shielding them from outside interference. They often have privileged access to the media and other international communications networks. They usually have high levels of legitimacy. They can often bring together diverse groups of people that could not be organized under another format (Johnston and Figa, 1988: 35–38).

These instrumentalist and constructionist views of religion are reflected in a literature within sociology known as functionalism. This literature posits that religion is not a basic force in society and is, rather, a reflection of more basic social interests. That is, it is social forces other than religion that determine the basic direction of society and use religion as a tool to enforce and facilitate that direction. A classic example of this is Marx's argument that religion is the opiate of the masses, which means that those who control the economy use religion to keep those at the bottom of the economic ladder in line. This particular argument is indirectly found in the international relations literature known as dependency literature, which posits that capitalism has been internationalized with the core states exploiting the periphery states. While most of this literature does not directly address religion it is consistent with dependency theory to argue that religion is one of the ways that the exploited workers in the periphery are kept in line.

The functions religion is said to have in society, according to functionalist theory, include unifying society, preventing social conflict, control of society by elites, helping people deal with difficult situations, explaining the physical universe, and answering unanswerable questions like what occurs after death (Wilson, 1982; Turner, 1991). Many of these functions are potentially useful to policy makers, including international policy makers. If policy elites are able to use religion to unify and control society this would minimize domestic opposition and maximize domestic support for their policies. If policy elites can take this a step further and use their concept of religion to define the political universe for their population, this makes it nearly impossible to oppose them. That is, if a policy, such as defining the states' enemies, is cast in religious terms, opposing this policy is not merely disagreeing with a political strategy, it is opposing a religious precept. It is to defy what is moral and right. Thus, a policy maker who can successfully portray a political cause as a religious one has a powerful tool for mobilizing support and silencing opposition. This is true whether or not the policy maker believes his religious characterization of the policy is true. However, it is necessary that he convinces his audience of the truth of his religious claims.

A clear example of a policy elite that has successfully achieved this is the Iranian government. Through a combination of political power and control over the media and the religious education of their population, they have created a theological regime where all policy, domestic and international, must be in accordance with religious precepts. Even the "moderate" forces within the Iranian government agree with this and merely disagree with the conservatives on how Islamic law should be interpreted and applied. The foreign policy of the Iranian government, which was originally established by Khomeini, is antagonistic to the West, which is seen as a threat to Islamic values. Recent attempts at moderating this stance by the moderate elements of the Iranian government have been strongly opposed by the government's conservative elements.

Religious states such as Iran are not the only ones that use religious images to define and portray enemies. For instance, U.S. President Ronald Reagan characterized the Soviet Union as "the evil empire" and President George W. Bush called North Korea, Iraq, and Iran the "axis of evil." While these characterizations clearly did not have the same level of influence in the United States that Iran's characterization of the West as the "great Satan" had in Iran, that these U.S. presidents chose to use them at all demonstrates that they felt it would have some influence on some elements of the U.S. population.

Primordialism, Identity, and the Civilizations Debate

Primordialism, the theory that competes with instrumentalism and constructionism as an explanation for ethnicity's political relevance, also provides a reason to believe that international relations is influenced by religious legitimacy. Primordialist theory posits that ethnicity and nationalism are important because they are intimately linked to identity. That is, they represent primordial kin-like ties between people and this makes them politically relevant.

These identities are usually reinforced by one or more of several types of myth. Myths of origin tell the group where it came from both temporally and spatially and usually include the purpose or goal of the group. Myths of migration and/or liberation tell of the group's wanderings and road to freedom. Myths concerning the nature of the group's ancestor or founder provide the group with a model for correct behavior. Myths of a heroic age, idealized past, or golden age tell of when the group was great and glorious and provide a model for group political aspirations. Myths of the group's decline or even exile explain why the group is in its current situation and often who is to blame. Finally, myths of rebirth and reawakening provide the community both with hope and a means to summon it to political action (Douglass, 1988: 201–202).

This explanation for ethnicity and nationalism is easily applied to religion. Most modern religions are at least as old as the average ethnic or national identity and are often, but by no means always, linked to ethnic and national identities. They also contain the same type of myths as do ethnic identities. For example, Judaism, as portrayed in the Old Testament, involved all of these types of myths described above. It tells of the creation of the world and the trials and tribulations of Abraham and his immediate decedants who founded the religion as well as the prophets who continued to reenforce it over the centuries. These stories provide archetypes whose behavior provides a picture of proper morality as well as a sense of the Jewish mission in the world. It tells of the Jewish society run by religious precepts and of the military victories by the Jews when they followed this code and of their defeats when it was ignored. It tells of the years of slavery in Egypt and God's miraculous efforts to free the Jews followed by the giving of the law and wandering in the Sinai desert, which helped to forge the Jews into a nation. It also tells of the destruction of the ancient Jewish state due to the sins of the people and promises a future return to Israel during a messianic age.

Images such as these can easily provide the basis for religious mobilization. Religious Zionism in Israel, for example, makes use of biblical images to reenforce political ideologies. The historical process of the return of the Jews to Israel is portrayed in messianic terms. Much of religious Zionism is based on reinterpretation of sacred texts. Historical events are believed to reflect God's plan and when properly interpreted can provide instructions for behavior, including political behavior (Don-Yehyia, 1994: 268–270). The redeeming of the land is seen as part of a prelude to the coming of the messiah. Thus, keeping every piece of land is seen as a religious precept and perhaps even an endeavor that justifies a holy war.

The Palestinians are also guided, in part, by religious models. They hold that the state of Israel is part of historical Islamic lands and should remain in Islamic hands. This is especially true of Jerusalem, which is the third most holy city for Muslims. The presence of a non-Islamic state in the region both now and in the past when it was held by Christian crusaders calls for *jihad*, a holy war, against the intruders.[5] Thus, religious ideologies and religious identities are among the many sources of considerable tensions between Israel and the Palestinians, a dispute with considerable international implications. This dispute, during the Cold War, attracted the involvement of both superpowers. Mediation between the two groups has involved heads of state including the president of the United States. Arab anger over Israeli actions played a role in OPEC oil policies, which caused major international economic crises during the 1970s. Also, the Israeli–Palestinian conflict came close to disrupting the allied effort against Iraq during the First Gulf War.[6]

Yet, international relations theory tends to ignore the importance of primordial ethnic and, especially, religious ties (Carment and James, 1997a: 207, 1997b: 16–18). However this trend is changing in the form of the debate over Samuel Huntington's (1993a, 1996a,b) clash of civilizations theory. Huntington posits that in the post–Cold War era most conflicts will be between several cultural-groupings that he calls civilizations which, by his own admission, are primarily defined by religion. Thus Huntington argues that primordial ties, though at a more general level than ethnic or national ties, will be the basis for future conflict, both international and

domestic. This aspect of his theory, among others, has sparked a voluminous and vigorous debate over what will be the future basis of conflict. It
is beyond the scope of this work to describe the entire debate and, therefore, this discussion focuses only on those aspects of the debate relevant to
whether primordial religious ties influence international politics.

Many argue that civilizations, be they religiously defined or not, will not
be the basis of post–Cold War conflict. Some argue that conflicts will more
often be within civilization than between them and the major basis for
conflict will continue to be ethnic and national groupings and sometimes
sub-ethnic and subnational groupings (Kirkpatrick et al., 1993; Halliday,
1997; Rosecrance, 1998; Walt, 1997). Others make the opposite argument
that for various reasons, the world is uniting and will rise above conflicts
(Ahari, 1997; Anwar, 1998; Ikenberry, 1997; Tipson, 1997). Also, most quantitative studies of the clash of civilizations theory tend to refute
Huntington's arguments.[7] However, many agree with Huntington's theory
and use it to make policy proscriptions.[8]

Interestingly, most of Huntington's critics who argue that conflict will not
be between civilizations, such as those described earlier, do not dispute that
conflict will be fought between identity groups. They simply argue that
those identity groups will not be civilizational and will, rather, be national or
ethnic. It is undisputed that religion can be a source of these types of identity. For instance, Seul (1999: 558) argues, "no other repositories of cultural
meaning have historically offered so much in response to the human need to
develop a secure identity. Consequently, religion often is at the core of individual and group identity." Falconer (1990: 274–275) documents how religious
institutions often provide theological framework for identities and historical memories. Others make similar arguments with regard to identity in general (Voye, 1999: 280–284), ethnic identities (Carment and James, 1998: 68;
Little, 1991: xx; Gurr, 1993a: 3), and national identities (Smith, 1999, 2000).

There are also many who make arguments consistent with the supposi-
tion that some aspect of religious belief can contribute to religious identity.
The argument that religion is an important source of people's worldviews,
which clearly influence people's identity, is a common one (Geertz, 1973;
Greely, 1982; Kabalkova, 2000; Stark and Bainbridge, 1979; Wentz, 1987).
The literatures on many specific types of conflict include religious ideologies and identities as one of the motivations. For instance, many argue that
not only is religion a motivation for terrorism, religious terrorism is qualitatively different from other forms of terrorism (Drake, 1998; Rapoport,
1984, 1988, 1990; Hoffman, 1995). In fact, one's religious perspective can
influence what one considers terrorism (Kennedy, 1999). Religion is a
source of discrimination, a major cause of conflict (Little, 1991; 1996a,b). It
can be a justification for genocide and ethnic cleansing (Fein, 1990: 49;
Osiander, 2000: 785). Religion in its milleniarian form is associated with
violence (Lewy, 1974; Rapoport, 1990: 120, 1991a: 131; Taylor, 1991: 121–155;
Zitrin, 1998). Some even argue that violence is an inseparable element of
religion (Juergensmeyer, 1991; Rapoport, 1991a; Girard, 1977; Zitrin, 1998).

The cross-sectional quantitative literature supports the argument that religious identities can contribute to conflict. Rummel (1997) connects religious diversity within a state to ethnic conflict. Henderson (1997) similarly shows states that have populations of different religions are more likely to go to war. Also, in a series of studies on ethnic conflict, Fox (1997, 1999a,b, 2000a,b,d, 2001e, 2002a,c, 2003a) connects various religious factors to conflict. These findings include: that the dynamic of ethnoreligious conflicts are different from those of other ethnic conflicts; when religious issues are important in a conflict, the extent of both discrimination and rebellion increases; religious legitimacy influences both the extent and type of grievances expressed by ethnic minorities; religious institutions facilitate conflict when religion is an important issue in that conflict but inhibit it when the conflict is not over religious issues; while Islamic groups are not more conflict-prone than other religious groups, religion tends to be more important in conflicts involving them; religion influences the extent of discrimination against ethnic minorities; religion can exacerbate separatist conflicts; religious conflicts attract more international intervention; and interveners in ethnic conflicts are mostly religiously similar to those minorities on whose behalf they intervene.

Given all of this, it is fair to say that the proposition that religion contributes to identity which, in turn, contributes to conflict is considerably less in dispute than Huntington's proposition that this will specifically manifest itself through his concept of civilizations. This brief review of the literature on religion and identity shows that religious identities are often linked to both domestic and international conflicts. Thus, religious identities are arguably a useful tool for policy makers who wish to justify their decisions.

This argument that religious identity is something primordial is not incompatible with the instrumentalist and constructionist theories described earlier. That religion can become politically relevant when political entrepreneurs "play the religion card" to further their policies, the instrumentalist argument, does not mean that religion cannot become politically important through other avenues such as identity. The constructionist argument that some religions are created or recreated to serve political interests does not deny that others are not. Furthermore, even those religions that are successfully constructed, so to speak, create feelings of identity and belonging similar to those religions that have been around for millennia. Thus, it is hard to believe that religious identities, be they primordial or new, do not have an influence on politics in general and international politics in particular, both as a basic motivating force and as a tool for policy makers.

Religion and the Legitimacy of War

Thus far, we have argued that religious legitimacy can influence international relations. However, it is possible to make an even stronger argument. This is because, the international laws of war, a major normative element of international relations, at least in part, are founded upon religious theology. The Western tradition of international law dates back to St. Augustine's *City Of God*, which is both a theological justification for a Christian ruler to engage in war and a set of guidelines for when war is permissible.[9] The Western conception of *just war*, which is the major basis of current international law, evolved over the centuries from this starting point. It coalesced into a form more recognizable as the direct antecedent of today's conception of just war between the twelfth and fifteenth centuries and, in addition to the Christian moral influences, was also based on the tradition of chivalry and Roman law (Johnson, 2000: 427). Since the Treaty of Westphalia the overt religious element of the international law of war has receded (Bryan, 1995) probably due to the antireligious bias of thinking since the Enlightenment, described in chapter 2.

Nevertheless the current international law of war is the direct descendant of a religious conception of what is moral and cannot be fully removed from its religious origins and is an overtly normative aspect of international relations. In fact the just war tradition has been described as a "theory of statecraft that is religiously and morally supportive of nonviolent legal and political approaches to conflict resolution. Just war theory points, in other words, toward a concept of peace while determining the ways and means in which discriminate and proportionate armed force can contribute to the pursuit of that peace" (Weigel, 1992: 178).

The international law of war is divided into two categories *jus ad bellum*, when a war itself is just, and *jus in bello*, the rules guiding behavior during a war. Wars of aggression are not allowed. It is only wars of self-defense, defense of others, and humanitarian intervention that are allowed. *Jus in bello* is even more overtly influenced by normative concerns. Noncombatants must be protected and the concepts of necessity, utility, and proportionality are given considerable weight. To elaborate, the means used in warfare, especially those that may also harm noncombatants, must be both means that can be expected to contribute to victory and necessary to achieve that victory. In addition, the harm done must be proportional to the contribution toward victory. In addition, many weapons have been prohibited due to their cruel nature.[10]

Interestingly, the moral injunctions of the Western just war tradition are reflected by an independent Islamic conception of the morality of war. However, it is important to remember that despite these similarities there are also significant differences between the Western and Islamic traditions. The differences are most pronounced with regard to *jus ad bellum*, when it is considered moral to go to war. This is especially apparent with regard to the concept of holy war. The tradition of holy war no longer characterizes mainstream Christianity but it is still considered legitimate in the Islamic community as a response to grave danger to the community (Skreslet, 1999). In fact, the concept of holy war did not catch on in Christianity until the papacy supported it in the late eleventh century and has since been disowned my most modern Christian states and has not been truly embraced by any Western state since the Thirty Years War (Partner, 1998).

Thus, while the concept of holy war is currently marginal in Christianity, the concept of *jihad*, Islamic holy war, remains legitimate in the Islamic world and is still available as a tool of statecraft (Partner, 1998). In fact, the whole concept of when it is legitimate to go to war is tied to religion. For instance, Islamic law differentiates between wars against other Muslims and wars against non-Muslims. Wars against other Muslims are discouraged and tend to be limited to self-defense, preserving Islamic values, or if those starting the war have a just cause as well as enough support that they are not easily defeated. In any case such wars may not be fought for reasons of greed or gain (El Fadal, 1999: 145–148; Hashimi, 1999: 164–167).

In contrast, Islamic rulers are given considerable discretion in starting wars against non-Muslims in order to protect Muslim lands and interests. This can include spreading Islam by conquering new territories. However, before force may be used the potential victims of conquest must be given a chance to convert to Islam or, if they refuse to do this, accept the superiority of Islam and pay tribute to the Islamic state. In the final accounting, the main considerations in engaging in such a war are the rights of Muslims and interests of Islam, as defined by the ruler, and very limited consideration is given to rights of non-Muslims (El Fadal, 1999: 151–154; Hashimi, 1999: 162–167; Kennedy, 1999: 9–11).

Thus, any Muslim ruler making war against a non-Islamic state can find justification to legitimize a war of aggression as a *jihad* as opposed to a Western ruler who is more limited by the Western just war prohibitions against such wars. It is possible to reconcile this tension between the Western and Islamic concepts of *jus ad bellum* by arguing that since there is no unified Islamic religious political authority there is no ruler qualified to declare *jihad*. However, in practice *jihad* is often invoked to spread Islamic political control, especially to recover territories that were once under Islamic control such as Israel and Chechnia (Johnson, 1997). Some radical Islamic thinkers argue that *jihad* in defense of Islam can also be invoked to fight political and social injustice and to counter political enemies that pose no physical threat to Muslims (Juergensmeyer, 2000: 81–83). Thus, in all, the Islamic conception of *jus ad bellum* is, at least in practice, much less restrictive than the more narrowly defined concepts of self-defense that guide Western concepts of just war.

The Islamic laws regarding *jus in bello*, the tactics and means of war, are more in line with the Western conception of just war, but by no means identical. In fact, most Muslims accept the international law on behavior in war as compatible with Islamic rules, and even influenced by them, and those aspects of Islamic law that are incompatible with Western rules are considered by many to be obsolete (Hashimi, 1999: 158). While noncombatants are to be protected, the burden of protecting them is not on the perpetrator of the act but the commander who is supposed to be defending them. It is the defending commander's job to make sure that noncombatants are out of the way of the fighting. However, in any case, noncombatants may not be targeted (Hashimi, 1999: 171; Kennedy, 1999: 12–13). Who is a noncombatant is subject to debate, but the Islamic definition of combatants is very broad. Nearly all agree that women and children are not combatants. Various other interpretations include as combatants political and military leaders, military medical personnel, anyone else who directly helps the war effort, and anyone who has the capacity to join in the fighting, whether they intend to or not. A minority even allow any nonbeliever to be killed. Thus, anyone who does not lack the physical or mental capacity to fight as well as anyone who voluntarily aids the enemy can be killed (Hashimi, 1999: 168–170). Western concepts of who is a combatant is more limited, encompassing mainly soldiers and perhaps those otherwise directly engaged in the war effort.

Islamic laws regarding permissible tactics more closely mirror the Western concepts of necessity, utility, and proportionality. Medieval scholars are divided over what tactics may be used. One school says any tactic, except burning, is permissible but a more severe method should not be used when a more lenient one will accomplish the task. The other school also restricts poisoning. There is general agreement on the concept of necessity in order to limit noncombatant fatalities. Because of this weapons of mass destruction (a classic medieval example is the use of flooding) is discouraged and should be used mainly in the form of a threat for deterrence and should only be used if deterrence fails and it is absolutely necessary (Hashimi, 1999: 171–173).

The similarities and differences between the Western and Islamic traditions of just war notwithstanding, it is clear that this is an aspect of international relations that is directly influenced by religious conceptions of morality. That is, it is at least in part religious ideas that determine whether the decision to go to war, as well as behavior during a war is legitimate. This goes beyond religion being a tool available to foreign-policy makers. It constitutes a normative restriction on their behavior with which they must deal, if only to construct a rationale for their policies.

Many may counter this assertion with the argument that the international law of war is merely the language policy makers use to discuss their actions and the true motivations for war are based on realist concerns. Even if this were the case, that leaders must at least pay lip service to the international law of war indicates that it must at least have some relevance. Furthermore, the norm against aggression is a strong one that has visible impact on the international scene, especially since the end of the Cold War. The reaction to Iraqi aggression against Kuwait that resulted in the First Gulf War is but one example of this. That Saddam Hussein resorted to Islamic rhetoric to justify his resistance against the NATO-led coalition only reenforces the argument that the resort to war is, perhaps, the area of international relations that is most overtly influenced by religion.[11]

Beyond Legitimacy—Religion as a Motivating Force

The argument that religion can influence one's views is not new or particularly in dispute. Religion is often part of people's worldviews and influences their perception of events and their actions. While it is clear that some, or even many, individuals in this modern day and age do not give much weight to religion, it is indisputable that there are many who do and that at least some policy makers fall into this category.

Most who discuss the influence of religion on human beings, argue that it in some way influences how we think. For example, Stark and Bainbridge (1985: 366) note that sociologists of religion assume that "people almost universally possess a coherent, overarching, and articulated 'Weltanschauung,' 'world view,' 'perspective,' 'frame of reference,' 'value orientation,' or 'meaning system' that is often based on religion." Spiro (1966: 94) argues, "every religious system consists . . . of a cognitive system." Williams (1994: 790–791) in his discussion of fundamentalist social movements describes their belief systems as "frames" that are the "schemata of interpretation" that people use to "give meaning to events, organize experiences, and provide guides for actions." Geertz (1973) argues that not only do religions include a belief system, most people find religion necessary to interpret the world around them, especially when bad things happen. Even some of those social scientists who inspired the trend of replacing religion with rationalism acknowledge that religion influences beliefs. Durkheim (1964: 47) defines religion as "a unified system of beliefs and practices relative to sacred things, that is to say, things set apart and forbidden—beliefs and practices which unite into one single moral community called a Church, all those who adhere to them."[12] Weber also strongly connected religion with beliefs (Hickey, 1984: 62; Kalberg, 1990: 61; Scheepers and Van Der Silk, 1998: 679). Finally, Marx's famous description of religion as the "opiate of the masses" acknowledges its influence on beliefs and behavior.[13]

Several survey-based studies also find that religious affiliation influences political attitudes and behavior. These findings include: that those who are religiously affiliated tend to be more politically conservative than those who are not (Hayes, 1995); that Christians and Jews group political issues into categories differently (Miller, 1996); that, in general, religiosity is inversely related to domestic violence but men who have more conservative religious views than their partners are more likely to engage in domestic violence (Ellison et al., 1999); that the nature of one's religiosity is linked to one's propensity toward conflict (Nielson and Fultz, 1995); that religiosity and authoritarianism are linked (Leak and Randall, 1995); that religious fundamentalism is linked with prejudice against blacks, women, homosexuals, and Communists (Kirkpatrick, 1993); that attitudes of Americans toward religious fundamentalists influence their decision to vote Democratic or Republican (Bolce and De Maio, 1999); and that religious denomination, when controlling for factors like education and income, is a strong predictor of moral attitudes (Ebaugh and Haney, 1978; Jelen, 1984; Harris and Mills, 1985; Scheepers and Van Der Silk, 1988).

There are two potential ways in which religious belief systems can influence international politics. The first is that these belief systems can influence the outlook and behavior of policy makers. Weber describes the process by which this happens through a concept called psychological premiums. He argues that religions place psychological premiums on actions that serve as filters for evaluating how one should behave (Kalberg, 1990: 63–66).[14] Wentz (1987) argues that these belief systems are so essential to our thought process that we will not only ignore any information that challenges them, we will even defend our belief systems from outside challenges at all costs. Laustsen and Waever (2000: 719) similarly argue that they result in particularly extreme and intractable responses because "religion deals with the constitution of being as such. Hence, one can not be pragmatic on concerns challenging this being." Carment and James (1998: 68) note that such threats to basic values are among the causes of ethnic conflicts.

Thus religiously inspired views held by policy makers and the policies based upon them could result in nearly intractable policies which, in turn, can lead to international incidents including war. In an empirical example of this phenomenon, Khosla (1999: 1152) and Fox (2001e) demonstrate that religious sects are more likely to draw international intervention on their behalf than any other type of ethnic group. Similarly Henderson (1997, 1998) finds that religious differences are among the causes of international war.

The September 11, 2001 attacks drew attention to the role of religion especially the Wahhabi theology on terror originating from Saudi Arabia, where this religious creed is dominant. It is significant that the Saudi elites, which to a large extent depend on the West's and especially U.S. support are now being blamed for the rise of Bin Laden and Al-Qaeda (Gaus, 2001: 109–122; Gold, 2003).

Another excellent example of the influence of religious worldviews on policy is the Arab–Israeli conflict in its many manifestations over the past century. Both sides of the conflict have made exclusive claims to the same territory that are at least in part based on religion. This dispute has led to several major wars that involved superpowers and a series of terrorist attacks and violent uprisings. The conflict has also resulted in a "peace process" that has involved the United States and other major powers, the United Nations, and many states in the region. Even if the "peace process" is eventually successful and results in a settlement, it is more than likely that there will be religious-based opposition on both sides to that settlement. While some may argue that both sides of the conflict have often relied on secular ideologies to guide them, the religious claims of both sides to Israel cannot be denied. The recent troubles that resulted after Israeli politician Ariel Sharon's visit to the Temple Mount in Jerusalem, a site considered holy by both Jews and Muslims, is case in point.

Furthermore many like Anthony Smith (1999, 2000) trace the origins of secular ideologies like nationalism to religion. It is also telling that many, if not most, of those on both sides who object to the Palestinian–Israeli peace process are members of the religious nationalist camps.

This example also brings to light the second way religion can directly influence the decisions of policy makers, the constraints placed on policy makers by widely held beliefs within the population they represent. That is, even in autocratic governments, policy makers would be unwise to make a decision that runs directly counter to some belief, moral, or value that is widely and deeply held by their constituents. Thus both Israeli and Arab leaders have had to very carefully weigh what their populations would accept when making agreements. In another example of this phenomenon, while pure realist concerns dictated that Arab states like Saudi Arabia, and Egypt to side with the United States in its military opposition to Iraq during the Gulf War, religious concerns made the decision more complicated. There was considerable opposition in the Arab world to an Islamic state siding with a non-Islamic state against another Islamic state. There was also considerable opposition to allowing a non-Muslim army on to what they consider to be holy Islamic territory.

Also, not only do religious-based attitudes among constituents on specific issues constrain policy makers, religion also influences the political and cultural mediums in which they act. For example, several studies have found that states with Islamic populations are disproportionally autocratic.[15] While, other than the studies on this specific topic, few quantitative studies of the influence of religion on political structures exist, it is fair to argue that the connection between Islam and autocracy is only the tip of the iceberg. Samuel Huntington (1993a, 1996a) makes this assumption when he argues that international conflict in the post–Cold War era will be between civilizations which are, for the most part, based on religion.[16] In part, he is making the argument that religion is linked with issues of identity, another strong influence on both belief systems and international politics.

Many disagree with many of Huntington's arguments, however they generally do not oppose his argument that identity is an important influence on politics. They, rather, argue whether post–Cold War identities will be civilizational. Some argue that the relevant level of identity will be national or even subnational.[17] Others argue that the world is unifying into a single identity.[18] Be that as it may, the vigorous nature of this debate underscores the influence many scholars believe identity, including religious identity, has on political behavior.[19] This is particularly important given that many believe religion to be one of the most important influences on identity (Laustsen and Waever, 2000: 709; Fox, 2001e).

Given all of this, the debates among sociologists described in chapter 2 on whether people are becoming less religious and whether the influence of religion over social and political institutions is declining is very pertinent to the study of international politics. If people are, in fact, becoming less religious this would mean that religion would be less of an influence on policy makers, both because policy makers themselves would be, on average, less religious and because a less religious population would mean less or weakened religious constraints on policy options. These constraints would also weaken if religion is, in fact, moving from the public to the private sphere.

However, many would argue that even if religion is moving to the private sphere, it would still continue to influence policy because many modern ideologies that influence policy making have religious origin. As noted earlier, this is especially true of nationalism. Even if this is the case, this influence would be an indirect influence where religion influences a mediating variable which, in turn, influences policy. This is clearly an influence of a lower order than a direct influence of religion on policy decisions.

Conclusions

The purpose of this chapter has been to demonstrate that religious legitimacy influences international politics, both as a tool that policy makers can and do use for foreign policy and as an independent influence. None would dispute that this was the case before the Enlightenment. Furthermore we have demonstrated that religion continues to be a potent and useful tool of foreign policy that can be used to justify and build support for policies. Occasionally, religion can even justify what nothing else can justify. Also, religious conceptions of morality are inextricably intertwined with the moral justifications and guidelines of war.

However religion is one aspect of international relations among many and has many limitations and complications. It is a double-edged sword that can be used by non-policy makers or other policy makers to oppose policies or to unwelcomely influence the decisions of policy makers. It can only be used to influence those that hold compatible beliefs and may antagonize those that do not. Finally, religious legitimacy is a powerful tool of persuasion but it is limited to persuasion and rarely has any material power that would be recognized by a realist.

Nevertheless, there are numerous theoretical and concrete reasons to believe that religious legitimacy influences the practice of international politics. There is a strong tradition that normative concerns, such as religion, influence political decisions, including those regarding foreign policy. There is also a considerable literature which posits that other cultural factors like ethnicity and nationalism are useful tools for policy makers and other political actors, as well as being sources of identity that influence political behavior. Finally, we cite numerous concrete examples in this chapter of religious legitimacy influencing political behavior. These diverse examples include the basis for political legitimacy in Indonesia, the treatment of the Bahai minority in Iran, the religious foreign policy of Iran's theocratic government, efforts at racial accommodation in the United States, the link between participation in church activity and political participation in the United States, U.S. President Ronald Regan's religious characterization of the former USSR as an "evil empire," the "axis of evil" used by President George W. Bush to describe terrorist states to justify his attack on Iraq, the dual role of religious legitimacy in both legitimizing and opposing Latin America's governments, the negative influence of religious legitimacy on many secular Israelis, the messianic justifications for religious Zionism in Israel, the religious justifications for the Palestinian struggle against Israel, the role of South Africa's Dutch Reformed Church in first supporting then opposing Apartheid, the role of the WCC in the fall of Apartheid, the role of normative power in the success of many indigenous peoples' movements, and Saddam Hussein's appeals to Islam to justify his behavior during the Gulf War. Furthermore, these examples are only a few among many.

Given all of this, it is hard to deny that religious legitimacy plays a role in foreign policy. However it is important to emphasize that we do not argue that it is the dominant factor in international relations. Rather we argue that it is one factor among many and is, perhaps, the least recognized of the important influences on international relations. Thus, we do not downgrade realist arguments that concrete power is a major driving force of international relations; we merely argue that they are not the only factor to be considered and that religious legitimacy is a potentially powerful force that should not be ignored.

CHAPTER 4

LOCAL RELIGIOUS CONFLICTS ARE INTERNATIONAL ISSUES

Domestic conflicts, including religious conflicts, are becoming increasingly international issues. Since the end of the Cold War, a greater proportion of world conflicts are domestic ones (David, 1997; Huntington, 2000). Many of these domestic conflicts, in turn, become internationalized (Sarkees et al., 2003: 49–70; Fearon and Laitin, 2003: 75–90). This can occur for several reasons. First, they often cross borders and can destabilize an entire region as did the various ethnic and national conflicts in the former Yugoslavia. Second, the successes of groups on one side of the world can often inspire similar groups on the other to rebel. Third, the growing presence of the international media publicizes these conflicts throughout the world. Fourth, since the end of the Cold War superpower rivalry international intervention has become more feasible and, thereby, more common. Fifth, those involved in domestic conflicts often seek to use international forums and pressure in order to further their aims. Sixth, conflicts often result in international refugee flows. Seventh, the groups involved in the conflict often have national, religious, or ethnic ties with groups living in other states. Eighth, international organizations and forums are increasingly used by the parties in conflicts and their allies in order to further their goals.

It is clear that this internationalization of domestic conflicts is not unique to religious conflicts. Nevertheless, religious conflicts are among those that have been internationalized. Furthermore, we argue that sometimes it is religious conflicts in particular that have been internationalized.

Religion and International Intervention

International intervention in domestic conflicts has been increasing since the end of the Cold War. Most of this intervention is, at least in theory, due to the increased acceptance of humanitarian intervention. That is, the interveners generally intervene for humanitarian reasons or at least use humanitarianism as a pretext. While this clearly has implications on the changing nature of sovereignty and the role of international organizations in world politics, little attention has been paid to the role religion plays in these interventions. In addition to the more publicized interventions such as those in East Timor and Kosovo, many smaller-scale military interventions occurred in the form of providing military combat training, cross-border sanctuaries, or in-country combat units. For example, during the 1990s, Iran, a Shi'i Islamic country, provided military support for Shi'i minorities in Iraq and Afghanistan. Saudi Arabia and Pakistan, both Sunni Islamic states, militarily intervened on behalf of Afghanistan's Sunni Islamic Pashtun majority. Pakistan also continually involves itself in the conflict in India's Islamic Kashmir region. Russia's Islamic Chechen region has received support from many Islamic states including Turkey, Saudi Arabia, and Abkhazia. The Hindu Tamils of Sri Lanka have received support from India, a Hindu state. Also, Russia has intervened on behalf of fellow Russians in the Islamic former Soviet republics of Tajikistan, Turkmenistan, and Uzbekistan.[1]

These examples, while illustrative, are by no means conclusive proof that religion influences international intervention. This is because, as is the case with so many issues in international politics, for every example cited earlier, one can cite a counterexample where states intervened on behalf of groups that belong to different religions than the intervener. The intervention by the mostly Christian NATO states in Kosovo, an Islamic region of Yugoslavia, would be one such counterexample.

Therefore, rather than selectively citing examples, we have chosen to take a more systematic approach to supporting our argument that religion influences the decision to intervene in a conflict. We do so by using the Minorities at Risk (MAR) dataset. The MAR dataset contains information on 337 ethnic minorities worldwide. That is, MAR dataset includes all instances of where ethnic minorities throughout the world were in conflict or had the potential to be in conflict with the majority groups in their state during the 1945–2000 period and, thus, had the potential to attract intervention.[2] However, the dataset includes information on intervention only for the 1990–1995 period and the 275 ethnic minorities that were active in that period.

Using this method allows us to include all cases of serious ethnic conflict between 1990 and 1995, the period in which the intervention data is available in the MAR dataset, in our analysis. Thus, our analysis includes all examples of intervention in major ethnic conflicts during this time period leaving no counterexamples to be cited. While, clearly it would be preferable to include all interventions during this period, including interventions in nonethnic conflict, this is not currently possible because the relevant data exists only for ethnic conflict.

The MAR data distinguishes between political and military intervention. Political intervention includes ideological encouragement, nonmilitary financial support, access to external markets and communications, the use of peacekeeping units, and instituting a blockade. Military intervention includes funds for military supplies, direct military equipment donations or sales, military training, the provision of military advisors, rescue missions, cross-border raids, cross-border sanctuaries, and in-country combat units.

The variables used here measure simply whether an intervention by a foreign government occurred or not. This is done separately for political and military intervention.[3] Also, additional information, collected separately, is available on the religions of the majority and minority groups involved in the 275 conflicts contained in the study. This variable divides the conflicts into three categories: the religions of the two groups are the same; the groups are of different denominations of the same religion; and the groups are of different religions.[4] A variable using the same three categories is used to identify religious affinities between foreign governments who intervene in an ethnic conflict and the ethnic minority on whose behalf they intervene.[5] This analysis also includes variables that measure the specific religions of both the minority groups[6] and the interveners using three categories: Christian, Islamic, and other. While there are clearly major divisions within both Christianity and Islam, not to mention many of the different religions within the "other" category, these more general categories have been selected so that each category has a sufficient number of cases for meaningful statistical analysis. All other variables are taken directly from the MAR dataset.

It is important to note one major flaw in this method of analysis. It is able to assess whether conflicts between groups that differ religiously or minorities of particular religions attract more intervention and whether interveners are more likely to be religiously similar to those groups on whose behalf they intervene. However, this study has no means of directly measuring the motivations of interveners. Thus, any conclusions presented here of the motivations of the interveners can only be inferred from their actions. In other words, while this study can show whether religious conflicts attract more intervention and that those with religious affinities are more likely to intervene, this study cannot provide any direct evidence that this is due to religious motivations.

The first question asked here is whether religious conflicts more often attract intervention? The answer, shown in table 4.1, is yes for political intervention but no for military intervention. Ethnic minorities that differ either in religion or denomination from the majority group in their state attract political intervention by foreign states nearly twice as often as do minorities that are of the same religion as the majority group in their state. In contrast, there is little difference between the extent of military intervention in religious, denominational, and same-religion conflicts.

Table 4.1   Percentage of Ethic Conflicts in Which Intervention Occurred, Controlling for Religious Differences Between the Groups

Difference in religion between conflicting groups	*No. of cases*	*Military (%)*	*Political* (%)*	*All* (%)*
Same religion	142	19.1	33.8	40.8
Different denominations	32	15.6	59.4	62.5
Different religions	101	18.8	61.4	64.4

Note
* = Significance (Chi-Squared) of table including this column and column for "no intervention" <.001.

Table 4.2　Percentage of Ethic Conflicts in Which Intervention Occurred, Controlling for Religion of Minority Group

Religion of minority group	No. of cases	Military** (%)	Political (%)	All* (%)
Christian	139	15.2	41.7	44.6
Islam	74	33.8	56.8	64.9
Other	62	8.1	46.8	53.2

Notes

* = Significance (Chi-Squared) of table including this column and column for "no intervention" <.05;

** = Significance (Chi-Squared) of table including this column and column for "no intervention" <.001.

The second question asked here is whether minorities of certain religions attract conflicts more often? The answer, shown in table 4.2, is yes. Islamic minorities attract both political and military intervention more often than Christian and other minorities. Islamic minorities attract military intervention almost two-and-a-quarter times as often as do Christian minorities and over four times as often as "other" groups. They also attract political intervention about 136 percent as often as Christian minorities and about 121 percent as often as "other" minorities.

The third question asked here is whether governments intervene more often on behalf of minorities religiously similar to them? In order to answer this question, as well as the following one, we look not at the number of ethnic minorities that experience intervention but, rather, at the universe of interveners. This is because some ethnic conflicts drew no intervention while others drew intervention by multiple states. Since we are interested in the behavior of the interveners, they are the unit of analysis we use to answer this question.

The answer to this question, shown in tables 4.3 and 4.4, is yes, in general, the greatest proportion of foreign intervention, both military and political, is by states that are religiously similar to those minorities on whose behalf they intervene. In addition, this tendency increases in strength when the conflicts are religious ones. Furthermore, foreign political intervention by religiously similar groups is even more likely in denominational conflicts. Thus, there is ample evidence that religious affinities is one of the factors that makes foreign intervention more likely in religious conflicts. Given this, it is fair to conclude that results imply that not only do ethnic conflicts between groups of different religions attract more political intervention, this increase may be due to the religious affinities of the interveners.

The fourth question asked here is whether interveners of specific religions are more likely to intervene on behalf of groups religiously similar to them. The answer, shown in tables 4.5 and 4.6, is yes. Islamic states are the most likely to intervene on behalf of other Islamic groups. Only

Table 4.3   The Influence of Religious Affinities on Political
Intervention by Foreign Governments in Religious Conflicts

Difference in religion between conflicting groups	*No. of cases*	*Religious affinities between intervener and minority group (%)*		
		Same religion	*Different denominations*	*Different religion*
Same religion	72	44.4	30.6	25.0
Different denominations	22	81.8	4.5	13.6
Different religions	93	55.9	18.3	25.8

Note: Chi-Square for table = .020.

Table 4.4   The Influence of Religious Affinities on Military
Intervention by Foreign Governments in Religious Conflicts

Difference in religion between conflicting groups	*No. of cases*	*Religious affinities between intervener and minority group (%)*		
		Same religion	*Different denominations*	*Different religion*
Same religion	43	46.5	27.9	25.6
Different denominations	9	66.7	0.0	33.3
Different religions	30	63.3	23.3	13.3

Note: Chi-Square for table = .242.

Table 4.5   The Influence of Religious Affinities on Political
Intervention by Foreign Governments in Conflicts
Involving Christian, Islamic, and Other Minorities

Religion of intervener	*No. of cases*	*Religious affinities between intervener and minority group (%)*		
		Same religion	*Different denominations*	*Different religion*
Christian	94	42.6	27.7	29.8
Islam	63	69.8	22.2	7.9
Other	30	60.0	0.0	40.0

Note: Chi-Square for table = .000.

7.9 percent of political interventions by Islamic states are on behalf of non-Islamic groups as are only 10.3 percent of their military interventions. Christian states intervene politically on behalf of non-Christian states nearly four times as often and militarily over twice as often. That these results are less pronounced for Christian interveners is probably due to the

Table 4.6   The Influence of Religious Affinities on Military
Intervention by Foreign Governments in Conflicts Involving
Christian, Islamic, and Other Minorities

Religion of intervener	No. of cases	Religious affinities between intervener and minority group (%)		
		Same religion	Different denominations	Different religion
Christian	37	48.6	29.7	21.6
Islam	39	69.2	20.5	10.3
Other	6	0.0	0.0	100.0

Note: Chi-Square for table = .000.

fact that the United States and most other world powers that are among the most common interveners (Khosla, 1999) are Christian states. In fact, when removing intervention by the United States from the analysis, the percentage of Christian interveners who are of the same religion as the minority group on whose behalf they intervene rises to 62.5 percent for political intervention and 61.5 percent for military intervention, numbers much more similar to those of Muslim states.[7]

Because intervention does not occur in a vacuum we must ask a final question: Do these results indicate that whether a conflict is religious, religious affinities between interveners and intervenees, and the specific religions of interveners and intervenees all influence the extent of international intervention hold-up when controlling for other factors? There are many factors other than religion that can influence the extent of intervention for which we can control. First, ethnic[8] and cultural[9] differences between the two groups involved in the conflict can arguably increase the extent of intervention for the same reasons as religious differences. Second, the more intense a conflict, the more likely is intervention. Accordingly, we include measures for the extent of protest and rebellion between 1990 and 1995.[10] Intervention is becoming increasingly more common for humanitarian reasons. Accordingly we include a variable measuring the extent of discrimination against minority group.[11] Democratic governments are less likely to experience intervention because they tend to have built-in conflict resolution procedures, which make intervention less necessary and conversely autocratic governments are more likely to create the discriminatory atmosphere that makes intervention seem necessary.[12] When conflicts often spread across borders and destabilize entire regions intervention is more likely in order to contain the spreading conflict. Accordingly, we include variables for the extent of conflict in the region during the 1980s and 1990s.[13]

The analysis also includes the variable measuring religious differences between the conflicting parties and variables measuring whether the minority is Christian or Muslim.[14] Unfortunately it is not possible to include the religious affinities between the interveners and the beneficiaries of the intervention in the analysis because this information was coded only for those cases where foreign intervention occurred. Thus, including this variable would eliminate all cases where foreign intervention did not occur from the analysis, which would in turn, make doing such an analysis impossible by creating a dependent variable with only one possible value. Also, there is no readily apparent way to create a variable measuring this phenomenon that would not have unacceptable levels of covariance with the dependent variables.

The multivariate analysis, shown in table 4.7, confirms the findings of the bivariate analysis. That is, even when controlling for many other factors the extent of religious differences between the groups involved in the conflict significantly influence political intervention and Muslim minorities experience military intervention more often.

In all, the results presented here clearly show that the extent of intervention in ethnic conflicts is influenced by religious factors. Religious conflicts attract more political intervention by foreign governments. Religious conflicts involving Muslim minorities attract military and political intervention by foreign governments considerably more often than conflicts involving other religious minorities. Foreign governments

Table 4.7   Binary Logistic regression of Multiple Factors That Influence the Decision to Intervene

Variables *(Values are logistic regression coefficients)*	*Political intervention*	*Military intervention*
Religious differences	0.4430*	−0.2125
Minority is Christian	0.1960	0.8808
Minority is Islamic	−0.0943	1.7529*
Ethnic differences	0.1037	0.3273
Cultural differences	−0.1988*	−0.0288
Protest 1990–1995	0.0655*	0.0655
Rebellion 1990–1995	−0.0054	0.1408***
Discrimination 1994–1995	0.1045***	0.0219
Democracy in 1994	−0.1634**	−0.0011
Separatism index	0.1478	−0.0194
Contagion of protest 1980s	−0.6569	−.1.4311
Contagion of protest 1990s	2.2131*	−0.4341
Contagion of rebellion 1980s	−1.2155**	1.2119
Contagion of rebellion 1990s	2.5967***	−.16196
N	241	241
% Correctly predicted, overall	72.61	89.63
% of Interventions correctly predicted	69.03	48.65

Notes
* = Significance (*p*-value) <.05;
** = Significance (*p*-value) <.01;
*** = Significance (*p*-value) <.001.

who intervene both politically and militarily are likely to be religiously similar to those minorities on whose behalf they intervene and this tendency is most pronounced for governments of Islamic states. Finally, these results remain significant even when controlling for other factors.

These results have some interesting implications. For instance, they have some bearing on accusations that Western states are more likely to intervene on behalf of minorities similar to them. Given that most of the increase in intervention on behalf of religiously differentiated ethnic minorities is probably due to interventions by members of the same religion as the minority group, there is some basis for this in the data. However, it is not just Christian groups that benefit from increased levels of intervention, Muslim groups also benefit. Furthermore, Christian governments, especially the United States, intervene on behalf of minorities religiously dissimilar to them in a greater proportion of cases than do Muslim governments, perhaps explaining why whether a minority is Christian is not a significant variable in the multivariate analysis. Thus, while Western governments are vulnerable to accusations of religious bias in their interventions, Muslim governments are even more vulnerable to this accusation.

Be that as it may, it is important to reiterate the limitations on these results. The information presented here on religion only shows whether or not conflicts involve groups of different religions and whether foreign government have religious affinities with those minorities on whose behalf they intervene. Any religious motivation on behalf of the interveners can only be inferred from their behavior. Thus, while the results are clearly consistent with and provide considerable support for the argument that religious affinities influence the decision to intervene in ethnic conflicts, the results cannot be considered absolute proof. However, it is fair to say that the facts that religious conflicts attract more intervention and the interveners in religious conflicts are more likely to have religious affinities with the minority on whose behalf they intervene strongly imply that religion is one of the stronger influences on the decision to intervene in an ethnic conflict.

Religious Conflict Crosses Borders

Another way religion can become an international issue is when religious conflicts cross borders. The habit of conflicts to cross borders is not unique to religious conflict. Rather, it is a potential result of most types of modern internal conflicts. Gurr (1993a,b, 2000) describes two ways in which ethnic conflicts can cross borders, both of which also apply to religious conflicts. The first, contagion, describes how conflicts can spill across borders to destabilize a region. This often occurs when groups with ethnic affinities reside in states bordering the one in which a conflict is taking place. These groups, whether they are minorities or majorities within the state in which they live are often influenced by the conflict by supporting the rebelling minority or can themselves be inspired to rebel. The second way in which conflicts cross borders, according to Gurr, is diffusion. This is the process where a rebellion in one place can inspire similar groups living elsewhere to do the same.

In practice these two methods for the spread of conflict overlap considerably. This is because many of the ethnically or religiously similar groups that may be inspired to engage in conflict live across the border from the conflict that inspires them. A good example of this is the rebellion by the ethnic Albanians in Kosovo against the Serbian government. The violence in Kosovo has recently spread to the sizable Albanian minority in bordering Macedonia. Also, there was considerable support for the ethnic Albanians from Albania itself as well as from numerous Islamic states and organizations.

To complicate matters further, if the kin groups living across the border control their state's government, domestic conflicts can become international conflicts. For example, the rebellion by Muslims in the Kashmiri province of India has contributed to sporadic military conflict between neighboring Pakistan, which is religiously and ethnically similar to the population in the province. The international ramifications of this dispute are even greater now that both Pakistan and India are nuclear powers.

Furthermore, violent conflicts tend to create refugees. Dealing with these refugees is by definition an international problem. While this most affects states bordering the state in which the conflict takes place, refugees from conflicts often travel thousands of miles looking for safe harbor. Refugees from Kosovo and the various conflicts in the former Yugoslavia during the 1990s can be found throughout Europe.

While many would argue that these examples of Kashmir and the various conflicts in the former Yugoslavia describe conflicts that are national rather than religious, it is indisputable that they are domestic conflicts that crossed borders and have considerable international implications. Thus, even if these conflicts are wholly un-religious, an assertion that we dispute, it is clear that they establish the principle that domestic conflicts can spread and there is no logical reason that this should not be true of religious conflicts.

As implied by Gurr's concept of diffusion, other conflicts do more than cross one or two borders to neighboring states. Some inspire, cause, or influence conflicts across much greater distances. For example, the Iranian revolution is credited with inspiring Islamic fundamentalists throughout the world. This is because the Iranian revolution demonstrated that a powerful Western-supported regime could be successfully opposed and that this could be done by Islamic fundamentalists.

Beyond this, the Iranian government has actively tried to export its revolution. This has alarmed a good portion of the Arab world, especially Saudi Arabia and other Persian Gulf nations (Fairbanks, 2001). One form these efforts have taken is Iranian support for militant Islamic terrorist and opposition movements. Iran is suspected to have connections to the

Lebanese factions that held U.S. and French nationals hostage (Fairbanks, 2001). After Israeli invasion of Lebanon, the Iranian Revolutionary Guard Core began the indoctrination and training of Lebanon's Shi'i, who eventually bombed U.S. Embassy and Marine barracks in Lebanon (Sadri, 1998). They continue to support Lebanon's Hezbollah faction that has continuously engaged in operations against Israel. One such operation occurred on October 7, 2000, ten days after the official beginning of the Al-Aqsa Intifada Hizballah forces penetrated the international border between Israel and Lebanon wounding and capturing three Israeli soldiers (Ben-Yehuda and Sandelr, 2002: 162). They are believed to have influenced the violent Islamic opposition movements in Egypt and Algeria (Ritcheson, 1995). During the 1980s, they supported the Islamic fundamentalists opponents to the Soviet supported rulers of Afghanistan (Sadri, 1998). They have provided military assistance to Sudan's Islamic government, which has been engaging in a campaign against the Christian and Animist population of southern Sudan (Ritcheson, 1995). They run training camps for Islamic militants in the Sudan.[15] They have also consistently supported opposition to the Arab–Israeli peace process by supporting Islamic opposition to this process including Palestinian Islamic terrorist groups such as Hamas and Islamic Jihad (Takeyh, 2000).

As a result of this, Iran has been on the U.S. state department list of those who support terror since 1984. Martin Indyk, the National Security Council's Senior Director for the Near East and South Asia during the Clinton administration described Iran as the world's "foremost" sponsor of terrorism (Indyk, 1999), an allegation that is echoed by the U.S. state department report on Patterns of Global terrorism.[16] This report states that the main focus of Iranian support for terrorism has been undermining the Arab–Israeli peace process. In order to accomplish this goal, "Iran has long provided Lebanese Hizballah and the Palestinian rejectionist groups—notably Hamas, the Palestine Islamic Jihad, and Ahmad Jibril's PFLP-GC—with varying amounts of funding, safe haven, training, and weapons."

To be fair, this desire to export revolutions is not limited to religious revolutions. The communist revolutions in Russia and Cuba attest to this. It can also be said that the U.S. desire to export democracy to the rest of the world is in a way the exporting of the American Revolution. Nevertheless, it is clear that this also occurs with religious revolutions.

The conflict in Afghanistan provides an example of another way conflicts can influence conflicts thousands of miles away. During the 1980s, thousands of Muslims from around the world came to Afghanistan to help fight against the Soviet occupation.[17] These people later returned to their own countries, as well as others, and became involved in conflicts and violent incidents across the globe. In August 1994, three French Muslims of North Africa who had been recruited by two Moroccan veterans of the Afghan war killed two Spaniard tourists in a hotel lobby in Marrakesh, Morocco.[18] Yemeni Islamic extremist leader Zain Abu Bakr al-Mehdar, who is responsible for the abduction of 16 Western tourists in December 1998 of which four were eventually killed, began his career as an Islamic holy warrior fighting the Soviets in Afghanistan during the 1980s.[19] One of the leading commanders of the Islamic resistance to Russian rule in Cechnya, who is known as Khattab, previously fought with Afghans against Soviet rule.[20] There is considerable evidence that many of the skilled Muslim guerrillas involved in the bloody campaigns in Algeria, Egypt, and Tunisia during the early 1990s were trained in Afghanistan during the 1980s.[21] In fact, veterans of the Afghan war were among the founders of the most radical of the Algerian groups, which have been waging a violent campaign against the Algerian government.[22] Those convicted of the 1993 bombing of the World Trade Center in New York were also Afghan war veterans.[23] These examples are only a few among many. Afghan veterans have also been involved in conflicts in Azerbaijan, Bangladesh, Bosnia, China, Egypt, India, Morocco, Iraq, Saudi Arabia, Sudan, Somalia, Tajikistan, Tunisia, Turkey, and Uzbekistan, among other countries.[24]

Osama Bin Laden, who is likely the most well known of Afghanistan's veteran religious warriors, represents the newest and perhaps the most international outgrowth of the Afghanistan conflict: the emergence of Islamic terrorism without borders. That is, while in the past terrorist groups, whether Islamic or not, were generally linked to a particular conflict or state, Islamists have since the late 1980s built a network that is truly international. This is because its members come from multiple states, and it targets not a single government but any government or nongovernmental body that is perceived to oppose their goal of establishing a worldwide Islamic Utopia and driving the foreign Western influences out of what they consider to be Islamic territory.

Osama Bin Laden comes from a rich Saudi family and has an estimated personal fortune of between $250 million and $1 billion dollars including agricultural, construction, transportation and investment companies in Sudan as well as an international network of honey stores that he uses to finance his organization. There is evidence that much of this fortune has been converted into precious gems and metals in order to avoid seizure. He also is said to have, over the years, given as much as $100 million in support to the Taliban. He claims to have begun to fight the Soviets in Afghanistan in 1979. In 1988 he established Al-Qaeda, an organization devoted to using whatever means necessary to achieve his goals of creating an Islamic Utopia and forcing the West out of the Middle East. In doing so he began to take militants, who had until this time pursued local goals, and forged them into an international organization. He has been linked to multiple terrorist incidents including both World Trade Center bombings (1993 and 2001), the 2001 bombing of the Pentagon, a 1993 attack on the UN relief operation in Somalia, a 1994 bombing of a Philippine airliner, a 1995 car bombing in Saudi Arabia, the 1996 attack on a U.S. military housing complex in Saudi Arabia, the 1998 bombings of the U.S. embassies in Nairobi and Tanzania, the 2000 bombing of a U.S. destroyer in Yemen, the 2002 car bombing of a Jordanian prosecutor in Amman, and the 2002 attacks on an Israeli-owned hotel and airplane in Kenya. He has also been linked to several unsuccessful operations including the 1996 attempted assassination of Egyptian president Hosini Mubarak, a 1999 attempted bombing of Los Angeles' LAX airport, a series of bombings of tourist sites in Jordan during the Millennium celebrations, and a planned 1999 attack on the U.S. embassy in India. Additional suspected Al-Qaeda members believed to be planning attacks have been arrested in Morocco, Saudi Arabia, and the United States. A large number of militants from about 55 to 60 countries have trained in training camps run by him,[25] estimates range between 5,000 and 70,000, and he is alleged to have published a manual for terrorists. The group has additional bases of operation in Algeria, Australia, Chechnya, Indonesia, Iraq, Kosovo, Lebanon, Malaysia, Pakistan, the Philippines, the Sudan, Syria, Uzbekistan, and the Palestinian-controlled territories as well as links with Iran. In addition to all of the aforementioned locales, operatives linked to him or who have trained in his Afghan training camps are known to have been in and/or come from Azerbaijan, Bangladesh, Belgium, Bosnia, Bulgaria, Cambodia, Canada, China, the Czech Republic, Dubai, Egypt, Eritrea, France, Germany, Hong Kong, Hungary, Israel, Italy, Kashmir, Kuwait, Kyrgyzistan, Libya, Morocco, the Netherlands, Russia, Singapore, Spain, Tajikistan, Turkey, Turkmenistan, the United Arab Emirates, the United Kingdom, Yemen, and the United States, including U.S. citizens and a former sergeant in the U.S. military. His organization also has links with other Islamic terrorist organizations including the Egyptian Islamic Jihad with which it merged in 1998, the Palestinian Islamic Jihad and Hamas, Lebanon's Hezbollah, the Libyan Jihad, the Abu Sayyaf separatist movement in the Philippines, Algeria's Gamat Al Islamiya, the Islamic Movement of Uzbekistan and Harkat ul-Ansar, the Pakistani group that changed its name to Harkat ul-Mujahadeen and has been linked to the killing of the American journalist Daniel Pearl. In addition, according to an Al-Qaeda booklet found in Afghanistan the organization also has links to unnamed militant groups in Jordan, Lebanon, Pakistan, Turkey, Kashmir, Indonesia, Somalia, Burma, Bosnia, Turkmenistan, and Tajikistan.[26]

The September 11, 2001 bombings of the World Trade Center and the Pentagon in particular show the international ramifications of the activities of religious terrorist organizations like that of Osama Bin Laden. Its operatives cross many borders in order to continue their struggle, requiring high levels of international cooperation in order to effectively fight them. Furthermore, the attacks had significant international economic impact, including a severe drop in world stock markets.

It is also clear that further attempts at mass killings within U.S. borders by Al-Qaeda are likely to occur. For instance a U.S. citizen, Jose Padilla, who converted to Islam and now calls himself Abdullah al Muhajir was arrested in May 2002 as part of a plot to explode a dirty bomb in the United States. A dirty bomb is a conventional bomb that flings radioactive material into the air. He apparently trained with Al-Qaeda in Afghanistan and Pakistan and was working with other U.S. citizens.[27]

Given all of this, it is clear that religious conflicts are no longer local matters. They can spread across borders both within a region and to kin groups to those involved in the conflict, as can most types of local conflicts. Successful religious revolutions can lead to the attempted exportation of that revolution. Participants of religious rebellions are no longer always indigenous to the state in which the rebellion takes place and often return to their home states with both their revolutionary ideologies and practical training and experience. Finally, Islamic revolutionary ideology, and the terrorism some of its adherents use, have become transnational phenomena that are no longer linked to a single state or particular conflict and whose fighters and operatives cross borders to participate in or even start multiple conflicts.

The Internationalization of Local Conflicts

Another way local religious conflicts can become international issues is through international political forums. This occurs when advocates for one or both groups involved in a local conflict use international forums such as the United Nations, other international organizations, or international political conferences to further their goals. Just as is the case with other parts of this chapter, it is clear that this phenomenon is not limited to religious issues. The many protests against world globalization and in favor of forgiving the debt of many Third World states testify to this. Yet, international forums are also often used to internationalize local religious issues and conflicts.

An excellent example of this is the UN-sponsored World Conference Against Racism, Racial Discrimination, Xenophobia and Related Intolerance held in Durban, South Africa from August 31 to September 7, 2001.[28] This conference was used by Arab and Islamic states to paint Israel as a racist state. While the ongoing conflict between the Palestinians and Israel also has national overtones, few would claim that it does not have religious elements. In fact, these religious elements are visible in the events surrounding the conference. The process for the conference began with several regional organizations meeting to prepare a draft agenda. The internationalization of the Israel–Palestinian issue arose from the meeting of the Organization of the Islamic Conference held in Iran. This draft agenda equated Zionism, Israel's nationalist ideology, with racism, calling it "a movement based on racial superiority" and characterized Israel's settlements as "crimes against humanity." It also referred to the "Jewish holocaust in Europe" spelling Holocaust with a lower-case "h" which, according to Jewish human rights groups diminished Jewish suffering under Hitler. This was not the first time such a resolution reached international prominence. In 1975 the U.S. General Assembly passed a similar motion equating Zionism with racism, which was later repealed in 1991. Additionally, the religious overtones of the Organization of Islamic Conference meeting was emphasized by the fact that Jewish and Bahai groups were banned even though they were theoretically entitled to attend the regional meeting because they live in the geographic region covered by the conference.

While this draft agenda itself mostly avoided religious rhetoric, the behavior and rhetoric surrounding the Durban conference more overtly revealed the religious overtones of this effort in a variety of ways. First, those supporting the efforts to paint Israel as a racist state were mostly from Arab and other Islamic states. The effort began at a meeting of Arab and Islamic states. The major advocates of the effort included Egyptian Foreign Minister Fayza Aboulnaga and Secretary General of the Arab League Amr Moussa. Second, at the conference Palestinian and Arab groups constantly disrupted protests and news conferences by Jewish groups and distributed overtly anti-Semitic literature including posters of Jews with big noses and bloody fangs.

Third, a meeting of nongovernmental human rights organizations at the conference submitted a proposal to include statements calling Israel "an apartheid regime" that had committed "racist crimes against humanity, including ethnic cleansing and acts of genocide." There was even a proposal at this meeting to remove a section protesting bias against Jews. Rabbi Abraham Cooper, the associate dean of the Simon Wiesenthal Center for Holocaust Studies in Los Angeles called the NGO proposal "the worst anti-Jewish document since the end of World War II."

Fourth, an American delegate, Representative Tom Lantos, stated, "if the conference fails, it will fail because the extremists are attempting to torpedo the conference . . . This inflammatory language . . . is reflective of the divisive, discriminatory and hostile climate created by the Arab extremists at this conference." This attitude was reflective of the U.S. government's sentiments that resulted in its sending a mid-level delegation rather than a high-level delegation including Secretary of State Collin Powell to the conference, despite considerable domestic pressure for him to attend, and eventually resulted in a U.S. and Israeli walkout from the conference. Fifth, even human rights groups such as Amnesty International and Human Rights Watch as well as U.S. human rights activist Jesse Jackson all of whom have been critical of Israel's treatment of the Palestinians opposed singling Israel out, especially when many of those singling it out have such dismal human rights records themselves.

Sixth, after lengthy negotiations between European governments and those supporting the anti-Israeli effort, a compromise statement was worked out that recognized "the plight of the Palestinians under foreign occupation" as well as "the right to security for all states in the region, including Israel." The agreement also recognized "the rights of refugees to return voluntarily to their homes in dignity and safety." Despite this

Pakistan and Syria made a last-minute effort to reinsert language calling Israel a racist foreign occupying power. While the compromise eventually prevailed, the concerted effort by Islamic and Arab states to internationalize the Palestinian–Israel conflict at the Durban conference and the religious overtones of many of these efforts highlight another way in which local religious issues can become international ones. This is especially so in that this was primarily an effort by Islamic states to demonize a Jewish state and those who defended the Jewish state were primarily from Christian states.

This was not the first time international forums have been used against Israel in this manner. As noted earlier the UN General Assembly passed in 1975 a resolution equating Zionism with racism, which was later repealed in 1991. Israel is the only state in the world to be denied membership in the International Red Cross and Red Crescent. Until recently, it was also the only state in the world that had been consistently denied membership in any of the UN's regional sections from which states are selected to serve on important UN organizations including the Security Council. Also, the United States has boycotted previous UN Conferences on racism due to the Zionism is racism issue. All these efforts to isolate Israel in international forums can be traced to Islamic and Arab states.

Holy Sites

Conflicts over the control of holy sites are generally, by definition, an international issue. This is because the religions that consider a site holy almost always have members who live outside of the state in which the holy site is located. In fact, in most cases, most of those who consider a site holy live outside of the state in which it is located. Thus, disputes over ownership and control of holy sites can easily become international ones.

Perhaps the most classic example of this phenomenon is the city of Jerusalem, which contains sites holy to three major religions which, combined, have billions of members. At different points in history Jews, Muslims, and Christians have conquered the city in what they considered to be a holy war and the dispute between these three religions, and often denominations within these religions, over control of holy sites there continues until today. Jews claim Jerusalem as their eternal capital and especially the Temple Mount that was the site of the *Beit Hamikdash*, the high temple of the Jewish religion. This site is currently occupied by the *Al-Aqsa* Mosque and it is believed that it is the location from which Mohamed rose to heaven and received instructions regarding the Muslim prayers. Finally, many of the events in the Christian Bible occurred in Jerusalem. Thus, all three religions make claims on parts of the city.

There are also denominational disputes within religions over holy sites within Jerusalem. The extent of these denominational disputes is exemplified by the Church of the Holy Sepulcher, the site of the crucifixion. The Church is jointly controlled by the Greek Orthodox, Roman Catholic, and

Armenian Churches with additional limited claims by the Coptic and Syrian Churches. Each of the three major sects controls certain areas and share other areas including the Holy Sepulchre and the Rotunda (Emmett, 1996). An example of the territoriality of the various sects in the Church is that when the Pope visited Jerusalem, the near-dead Patriarch Diodoros of the Greek Orthodox Church "dragged himself to the Church . . . to personally prevent the Pope from using the main door of the Church" (Walsh, 2001: 11).

Beyond this Muslims and Jews claim some form of control over the entire city. Many Muslims regard the entire city as a *Waqf*, an Islamic charitable trust that cannot change ownership (Talhami, 2000). The Israeli government claims sovereignty over all of Jerusalem. Many Christian states believe that the city should be an international one with joint or international sovereignty.

In the case of Jerusalem, the religious significance of the city also has considerable political significance in that it has become tied up in the Palestinian–Israeli conflict. Both Israeli and Palestinian leaders have claimed Jerusalem as their "eternal" capital (Emmett, 1996), a phrasing that intentionally invokes the religious significance of the city. This is very significant considering that the Israeli–Palestinian conflict itself has religious overtones. Given all of this, it is not surprising that the status of the city of Jerusalem has received considerable international attention by the media, governments, international organizations, advocacy groups, and religious groups.[29]

Another example of an international dispute over holy sites involves two giant statues of Buddha in Bamiyan Afghanistan. In February 2001, Mullah Muhammad Omar, the spiritual leader of the Taliban government that controlled Afghanistan at that time, ruled that these statues were idols and objects of worship and, thus, should be destroyed under Islamic law, along with all other statues that had been worshiped in the past. These statues, which may have been the world's tallest Buddhas (175 and 120 feet tall), along with many other smaller statues, are the remnants of a Buddhist civilization that existed in Afghanistan over a millennia ago (Barfield, 2001). In fact, over 2,750 statues in Afghanistan's National Museum were destroyed with axes and sledgehammers by a delegation led by the Taliban's minister of culture and information and by its finance minister.[30]

This destruction of the Bamiyan Buddhas resulted in an international outcry by government and religious leaders as well as scholars around the world. Keeping with a trend of growing international and interfaith recognition of the significance of cultural artifacts (Barfield, 2001), this outcry came not only from Buddhists. UN officials, including Secretary General Kofi Annan and Koichiro Matsuura, the head of UNESCO, were prominent in the unsuccessful efforts to halt the destruction. The Metropolitan Museum of Art in New York expressed a willingness to pay for the statues to be moved to another site. Even Islamic states such as Pakistan and Iran condemned the destruction. In fact, most Islamic scholars, including the chief Muslim cleric of Egypt Grand Mufti Nasr Farid Wasel, consider this interpretation of the law extreme and inappropriate. That these statues survived over 1,000 years of Islamic rule in Afghanistan is testimony to this fact. Thus, the efforts to stop the destruction of the giant Buddhas, as well as to preserve many of Afghanistan's other religious and cultural artifacts, while unsuccessful, was truly international.[31]

A Smaller World

A final reason that local conflicts are becoming international is that the world is becoming an increasingly small place. Information, money, goods, and people move across borders more easily, more swiftly, and in greater quantities than ever before.

The influence of modern communications technology on local events are well known. Local conflicts and events are often viewed in real time, with a prime example being the September 11, 2001 bombing of the World Trade Center in New York. Millions saw the second plane hit the building and later the collapse of both the main towers live on television and it is fair to say that few in the world did not know of these events within a day. The same is true to a lesser extent for most violent conflicts and events, whether or not religion is involved. This forces states which, in the past, would have been far removed from a conflict to officially react to the events of that conflict, if only to condemn an act, state support for a side or publicly express its neutrality.

In addition to simply having more knowledge of world events, states must often react to events on the other side of the world because they are economically impacted by them. The world's economy has become increasingly interdependent. This means that if a state's domestic political situation deteriorates to the extent that it's economy suffers, this has an economic impact beyond its borders. Foreign investors in that state will lose money. Banks, governments, and international organizations that loaned money to that state or businesses within it will likely see a decrease or halt of payment on those loans. Consumers in that state will be buying less, impacting on companies that export to that state. Less goods will be produced within the state impacting on the international market. In extreme cases such as the 2001 World Trade Center bombings, world consumer confidence can be affected impacting on sales and investment throughout the world as well as world stock markets. This, in turn, impacts on the wealth of anyone with investments in these markets, including those whose pension plans include investments in the stock market.

Finally, people are increasingly moving across borders. The most publicized population movements involve refugees from conflicts taking place throughout the world. These refugee flows can influence and often destabilize the politics of the states in which they arrive as well as those that they pass through. Refugees from a violent conflict often become the next generation of warriors in that conflict (Fein, 1993: 85), thereby, involving the state in which they reside in that conflict. They can often enter a peaceful state in great numbers and cause a radicalization of parts of its population, especially if that population is ethnically and religiously similar to the refugees (Kaufman, 1996a: 145). All these dangers are well known to states and states that are likely destinations for refugees are more likely to intervene in a conflict in hopes of mitigating that conflict and preventing the refugee flows (Regan, 1998: 763).

It is important to note that most of the world's population flows are not refugees from conflicts and are, rather people seeking better economic circumstances. Yet this type of population flow, while less dramatic, impact on a state's politics. Large-scale immigration can impact on a state's demographic balance, which can impact on a state's political status quo (Don-Yehiya, 2000: 90–91). Immigrant groups often overlap with economic classes, giving class struggles within a state additional fuel (Fenton, 1999: 142–169; Olzak, 1992: 19.32–37). In fact, the historical international migration of labor has often created large ethnic minorities within states that have since significantly impacted on those states' politics (Gurr, 1993a; Gurrand Harff, 1994). Some go as far as to blame most ethnic conflict on economic competition (Olzak, 1992; Olzak and Nagel, 1986).

One example of a manifestation of many of these problems is Europe's increasing Muslim population. Muslim immigrants from the Middle East, North Africa, and elsewhere have become significant and politically active populations in several European states. For example, France's Muslim population is over 2 million and is comprised mostly of North Africans who migrated to France during the twentieth century. Since the 1980s racist political parties like the National Front have blamed them for France's economic problems. The electoral successes of the National Front prompted the government to enact restrictive immigration laws that are targeted against North Africans. The government also has banned the wearing of headscarves by Muslim women in public schools. This, along with poor economic circumstances and grass-roots prejudice and discrimination against North Africans has led to numerous protests and riots by North Africans. This situation has been exacerbated by terrorist activities by Islamic fundamentalist immigrants of Algerian extraction who blame the French government for supporting Algeria's military government.[32]

Germany similarly has a population of over 2 million Muslim Turks as a result of immigration during the second half of the twentieth century. These immigrants cannot vote and federal law allows the state to restrict their freedom of association, assembly, choice of occupation, and movement. Most Turks in Germany wish to stay but getting citizenship is difficult, even for children of Turks born in Germany. Turks must also deal with social prejudice based on the belief that they are a foreign presence that cannot be assimilated into European society as well as with agitation by right-wing parties and violent and often fatal attacks by racist groups. However, it should be noted that the attacks take place within the context of violence against a wide variety of foreign groups in Germany and generally represent the actions of an extreme fringe who are overwhelmingly teenage or in their twenties and the police, with some success, have tried to prevent these attacks. Furthermore, there have been several large-scale demonstrations by Germans against this violence. Also, unlike France, which is tightening restrictions on immigrants, during the 1990s Germany slightly has made moves toward loosening its naturalization procedures. Nevertheless, this situation has prompted numerous demonstrations by Turks in Germany throughout the 1990s.[33]

Both of these cases demonstrate that even established immigrant populations can cause tensions within a society. This is especially true when the immigrants are culturally and religiously dissimilar to the host state.

Conclusions

This chapter has examined the various ways in which local religious conflicts can cross borders and, in doing so, become international issues. It is argued here that while nonreligious conflicts also cross borders, the potential for religious conflicts to do so is much greater. This is because while all of the factors that cause nonreligious conflicts to cross borders apply to religious conflicts, religious conflicts involve additional and unique factors that cause them to cross borders.

Perhaps, the most blatant manifestation of this phenomenon is the pattern of international intervention. The evidence described earlier in this chapter shows that while international intervention can occur in all types of conflicts, it is significantly more likely in religious conflicts. Furthermore, states who intervene in conflicts tend to share religions with those on whose behalf they are intervening. Thus while concerns like humanitarianism, security, and power politics no doubt play a role in the decision to intervene in a conflict, religion often tips the scales.

That the violence of local conflicts spills across borders to neighboring states and rebellions inspire rebellions by similar groups elsewhere is also not unique to religious conflicts. Yet many of the most well-known instances of these phenomena are religious. The conflicts that have inspired the most violence elsewhere in recent times have probably been the Iranian revolution and the civil war on Afghanistan. In fact, the Iranian revolution has, perhaps, had the impact on the Islamic world that the Communist revolution in Russia has on the West. Similarly, the veterans of the Afghanistan war, including but not limited to those organized by Osama Bin Laden's Al-Qaeda organization, are attempting, often successfully, to influence the politics of states throughout the world. Other than, perhaps, the movement toward decolonization it is hard to think of a post–World War II conflict that has either through the direct involvement of its veterans or through its demonstration effect has influences on as many people in as many places as these two religious conflicts.

While the sides of many local conflicts try to use international forums to further their goals, few have been as successful as the Palestinians.

The secret to the Palestinians' success seems to be that they are able to use the flag of religion to rally support. It is not just ethnically similar Arab states who support them in international forums, it is also religiously similar Islamic states such as Pakistan and Iran whose ethnicities are arguably no more similar to the Palestinians than they are to the Israelis, especially if one excludes the religious aspect of ethnicity.

Finally, conflicts over holy sites are by definition religious. Claims over religious sites are almost universally supported in cases where only one religion claims the site such as is the case with the Bamiyan Buddhas in Afghanistan. Even other Islamic states opposed their destruction by Afghanistan's Islamic fundamentalist government. Cases where holy sites are claimed by multiple religions, such as is the case with Jerusalem, are the focus of controversy and international attention. This stands in stark contrast to ethnic and national claims on historical sites. For example, the Serb claim that Kosovo is the birthplace of the Serbian people did little to deter NATO from intervening militarily against Serbia's violent campaign to maintain control of the region.

Given all of this, it is clear that while all conflicts can cross borders, religion causes them to do so more often. Realist concerns like balance of power and national security certainly motivate states as do humanitarian and economic concerns. Similarly economic interdependence makes it harder for states to fully avoid the fallout from many local conflicts. Perhaps these motivations can even explain a great deal of state behavior. Yet religion creates a measurably greater likelihood that a local conflict will be internationalized. Furthermore, as nonstate actors such as Osama Bin Laden become more involved in local conflicts as well as begin to develop an international agenda, traditional state-based understandings of international relations will become a less accurate description of international politics.

CHAPTER 5

TRANSNATIONAL RELIGIOUS PHENOMENA

Several domestic phenomena and issues that juxtapose with religion are becoming progressively global in that they are no longer bound by state borders. We qualify them as transnational. Religious fundamentalism is becoming an increasingly important factor in both domestic and international politics in most parts of the world and across religions with political Islam being, perhaps, the most obvious but clearly not the only example of this. Religiously motivated terrorism has an increasingly global agenda. International missionary movements often upset local governments and cultures. Human rights, including religious human rights, has become a global issue. Also many transnational issues like women's rights and family planning have religious aspects or overtones.

When we use the term transnational here, we are not referring precisely to the transnationalism school of thought that emerged in international relations theory in the 1970s (Keohane and Nye, 1970). We use it to refer to our argument that a number of religious phenomena are not limited by state borders. We adopt the world politics paradigm that Keohane and Nye tried to develop and see religious fundamentalism as a force that transcends the borders of the state and the nation-state.

Indeed, the development of these phenomena, including religious fundamentalism, human rights, and terrorism, occurs in an arena larger than any one state and the sphere of their impact is even greater. It often encompasses the entire world to some extent. Transnational religious phenomena also tend to have origins outside of traditional state policy-making circles. In fact, some of them like fundamentalism and terrorism are among the greatest challenges to a number of individual states and the international system that is largely based on the relations between sovereign states. Thus, these are not local phenomena that cross borders nor are these phenomena the result of state policies. Rather, they are transnational phenomena that recognize state borders only to the extent that they challenge the existence of these borders, at least in the form in which they now exist.

At the same time, this definition of transnational religious phenomena is not wholly incongruent with the transnational approach. Both religious and terror organizations were acknowledged by the contributors to the edited book on transnational relations (Vallier, 1970; Bell, 1970). So did more recent works (Enders and Sandler, 1999: 145–167). Nevertheless, although inspired by this school of thought, we do not feel bound by all its strictures. Hence, we do not intend to analyze the phenomena of religion as a transnational force according to all the features of world politics developed by Keohne and Nye and their successors.

Finally, it is important to point out that the transnational religious challenge to the state is not unique to the modern era. Rather, the tension between religion and state is an ancient one. We discover it already in the book of Samuel when the Israelites request a king to lead them in wars namely international politics, and the prophet is not totally satisfied with this request. While Islam was from the outset state oriented, Christianity ultimately could not stay apolitical and eventually took over the Roman Empire. However, Islam and Christianity did not stay confined to one state or nation. In fact, in Europe until the Reformation, the Catholic Church was a transnational actor that competed with the state for power. Hence, the inherent tension between transnational religion and the state has existed for millennia. This is because, many religious movements are simply not congruent with one state or nation and, thus, are global and hence transnational in nature. In this chapter we shall observe several facets of religion, almost all of them qualifying as transnational phenomena, and their implications for international relations.

Religious Fundamentalism

Religious fundamentalism is a transnational phenomenon. To a great extent clusters of fundamentalist movements in different states form transnational communities that exist without reference to state borders. For example, political Islam, which is described in more detail later, relies upon the ideas of thinkers from a number of states, has adherents in many states, and has goals that reach beyond individual states. As described in chapter 4, it also has a militant wing in which people from dozens of states engage in centralized training and fight for the movements goals, often in places very far from their home states. Similarly Christian fundamentalists try to spread their ideas, or as they might put it save souls, across the globe. For them spreading salvation knows no borders.

Beyond this, all fundamentalist movements share a number of similarities. The origins of fundamentalist movements throughout the world have in common many of the same transnational causes. Their organizational structures are similar across the globe. Their goals are also similar. In fact, it can be said that in many ways fundamentalist movements from different religions and different world regions more closely resemble each other than they resemble their non-fundamentalist co-religionists. These movements also have a significant impact on international politics.

The Origins and Goals of Religious Fundamentalism

In short, religious fundamentalism is a reaction against modernity, which is itself a transnational phenomenon. As discussed in detail in chapter 2, there are many aspects of modernity that social scientists thought would lead to the demise of religion. These include, economic development, urbanization, modern social institutions, pluralism, growing rates of literacy and education as well as advancements in science and technology. All of these factors helped to undermine the traditional community where religion held sway and replace it with a modern secular society based on secular principles. In addition, the Enlightenment and the scientific revolution that followed it created rational explanations for the world that displaced religious ones. Furthermore, the modern state, which makes use of secular scientific and rational principles, is run by a legalistic bureaucratic structure, and is based on secular ideologies like liberalism, fascism, socialism, and Marxism, was thought to have left religion behind or at least regulated it to the private sphere. These factors, and others, were expected to cause society to become more modern, advanced, and secular.

Yet, it is precisely these factors that gave rise to fundamentalism. This can be seen in the origin of the word fundamentalism itself. The term originated with a series of ten paperbacks published between 1910 and 1915 in the United States called *The Fundamentals*, which consisted of edited essays written by leading conservative theologians who defended biblical inerrancy and attacked what they perceived as the evils of secular, theistic modernism (Misztal and Shupe, 1992: 7). Thus, fundamentalists seek to counteract the influence of modernity on society in order to preserve religious values, identities, and communities. This argument is also inherent in the definition of fundamentalism used by Marty and Appleby's highly influential fundamentalism project. They define fundamentalism as

> a tendency, a habit of mind, found within religious communities and paradigmatically embodied in certain representative individuals and movements, which manifests itself as a strategy, or a set of strategies, by which beleaguered believers attempt to preserve their distinctive identity as a people or group. Feeling this identity to be at risk in the contemporary era, they fortify it by a selective retrieval of doctrines, beliefs, and practices from a sacred past. These retrieved "fundamentals" are refined, modified, and sanctioned in a spirit of shrewd pragmatism: they are to serve as a bulwark against the encroachment of outsiders who threaten to draw the believers into a syncretistic, areligious, or irreligious cultural milieu. Moreover, these fundamentals are accompanied in the new religious portfolio by unprecedented claims and doctrinal innovations. By the strength of these innovations and the new supporting doctrines, the retrieved and updated fundamentals are meant to regain the same charismatic intensity today by which they originally forged the communal identity from the revelatory religious experiences long ago. (Marty and Appleby, 1991: 3)

Thus the goal of fundamentalists is to protect their religious identity from modernity and secularism. Fundamentalist militance begins as a reaction to the penetration of their community by secular or religious outsiders. In particular, it is a response to the perceived marginalization of religion and the erosion of religious identities by modern ways of life (Appleby, 2000: 86–87, 101; Haynes, 1998: 186).[1] Consequently, fundamentalists tend to oppose both mainstream religion and secular power. They resist the state because it is perceived as the source of the secular and modern threat to religion as well as because the modern state often seeks to subjugate all antonymous forms of collective life, including religion. They oppose mainstream religions because these forms of religion tend to be in favor of modern ways of life and fail to express the religious, political, and social aspirations of most fundamentalists (Haynes, 1998: 717–718).

How do they do this? They tend to use a combination of techniques to accomplish their goals. They selectively interpret history and holy documents in order to justify their beliefs, especially their desire to gain political power and change their society. This selective retrieval, which is motivated by their fight against secularism and modernity, generally reaches the point where the changes they make in their religion can be more properly called innovations. While this process of retrieval and innovation grows in an atmosphere of religious conservatism, it can become militant when believers feel they must fight the unrighteous. This belief usually revolves around the belief that we are living in a special time where the exceptions to normal prohibitions of violence should be invoked. These movements generally revolve around charismatic male authoritarian leaders and recruit mostly among young educated unemployed or underemployed males (Appleby, 2000: 87–94).

Despite the fact that their ideologies focus on the past, fundamentalist movements are modern phenomena. Their reason for being is to defend and restore their religions from modernity. These movements also have many modern characteristics. They use modern communications, propaganda, political institutions and organizational techniques to attract and mobilize recruits as well as to reconstruct society through political action. They borrow from antimodern, anti-Enlightenment ideology to justify their cause. Also, even though most fundamentalist religions are patriarchal, they still mobilize women (Eisenstadt, 2000a: 601–603).

What do they hope to achieve by doing this? They hope to make their ideology the guiding principle in both personal and public life. That is, religious fundamentalism is concerned with defining, restoring, and reinforcing the basis of personal and communal identity that is believed to have been shaken or destroyed by modern dislocations and crises. They demand that this code of behavior be applied comprehensively in family and politics (Marty and Appleby, 1991: 602, 621). In fact, they believe that only through religion can we know what is best for society and because of this fundamentalists are not prepared to change their minds even in the face of empirical evidence that their political and economic policies often fail (Kuran, 1991). Furthermore,

> this conviction that the world is best knowable and livable through the lense of divine revelation is coupled with the fundamentalists' conviction that

their revelation is one that radically reframes all of life. All other knowledge, all other rules for living are placed in submission to the images of the world found in sacred texts and traditions. All other authorities and credentials are de-legitimized, or at least put in their place. (Ammerman, 1994b: 150)

In order to accomplish this, they focus on gaining control of the state. This is because the state is the final arbiter of disputes within its borders. The state regulates many aspects of social existence, thus, fundamentalists who also wish to regulate society inevitably become involved in modern politics (Marty and Appleby, 1991: 4). Their strategy to accomplish this is generally to capture the terms of public debate, define which issues are important, and define along what lines public debate over these issues will occur. If they are successful, this will legitimate both fundamentalist groups and their proposals. In order to achieve this goal, fundamentalist groups try to present themselves as the arbiters or religious legitimacy and moral authority. They try to gain control of society's religious institutions and make exclusive claims to the right to invoke religious symbols in political and moral discourse. If they succeed, this monopoly of religious and moral authority allows those who use it to align themselves with all that is good and moral and to present themselves as disinterested parties who involve themselves in politics in order to accomplish what is right and proper rather than out of any motivations of personal gain. This moral authority will often be acknowledged even by those who are not religious (Williams, 1994: 792–796).

Despite this macro-political agenda, the ultimate goal is to regulate the lives of individuals. Fundamentalists pay special attention to values, motivations, incentives, and ideals according to which the intimate zones of life are ordered. These include marriage, sex, family life, child rearing, education, morality, and spirituality (Marty and Appleby, 1991: 3). This represents an "intense preoccupation with individual conduct and interpersonal relations" (Marty and Appleby, 1993: 5). In fact,

with a few important exceptions, fundamentalists have expended the greater portion of their energies, and have enjoyed greater success, in reclaiming the intimate zones of life in their own religious communities than in remaking the political or economic order according to the revealed norms of the traditional religion. (Marty and Appleby, 1993: 5)

Despite this, they persist in their political activism that is intended to expand their sphere of control (Marty and Appleby, 1994: 3).

The Transnational Linkages and Agendas of Fundamentalist Movements

While, in the short term, the political goal of fundamentalist movements are generally to influence or take over state governments, their origins, agendas, and resources tend to be transnational. The modern social, political, and economic processes to which fundamentalists are reacting are transnational. They especially thrive when the masses are dislocated by rapid and uneven modernization that causes haphazard change in economic and cultural patterns and the modern education and social welfare systems that are meant to deal with these problems fail (Appleby, 1994: 40). Thus the processes to which fundamentalists are reacting are transnational. In addition, because they in many ways constitute, by definition, an illegitimate polity in a Westphelian international system, they often prefer the transnational arena of world politics.

For the fundamentalists, transnationalism is not only a process it is also a goal. The solution they present to the perceived problems of modernity is a return to the traditional moral practices of the past, though as discussed earlier this vision of the past is a very selective one. Because of these similarities, "fundamentalists seem to have more in common with one another across traditions than they do with their non-fundamentalist coreligionists, at least with regard to seminal questions such as the role of revealed truth in guiding human inquiry" (Marty and Appleby, 1993: 5). More specifically, they are linked in their belief of the primacy of religion as the final authority in all spheres of human life (Mendelshon, 1993: 32).

Most of their efforts to accomplish this are local. Typically, they establish education, health, employment, and welfare systems in places where the government systems are inadequate or nonexistent. In doing so they build up a base of support and educate the young to believe in their worldview. Yet even these efforts have transnational linkages. For example the education, health, employment, and welfare institutions run by Hamas, a Palestinian fundamentalist organization that also supports terrorism, operate with funds donated by individuals from around the world including contributions from the United States, Canada, Belgium, Germany, Italy, France, Israeli Arabs, Saudi Arabia, and other Arab states.[2] Also, this model for gaining influence locally is used across the globe by most fundamentalist movements.

Furthermore, the movements themselves are transnational in that they attempt "to establish a new social order, rooted in the revolutionary universalistic ideological tenets, in principle transcending any primordial, national or ethnic units and new socio-political collectivities" (Eisenstadt, 2000b). Thus, their message is international and they desire to spread this message across international borders. While this is often done peacefully through attempts to gain adherents across the globe, it can also result in a violent international campaign such as that of Osama Bin Laden's Al-Qaeda organization.

In short, the goal of fundamentalist movements does not stop at influencing or taking over state governments. When they succeed at this, like other messianic movements or ideologies such as international Communism, their next step is to use the state apparatus in order to spread their ideology. This success can come in the form of replacing a state government with a religious one as occurred in Iran and Afghanistan. It can also come in the form of influencing political leaders either by converting those leaders to their cause or using domestic political pressure to influence policy. In either case, the result is a state foreign policy which, in part or in full, is motivated by the transnational goals of fundamentalist movements. Thus, influencing the state is simply one step toward accomplishing a transnational agenda.

However, despite fears that fundamentalists will take over a state and use it to further their agenda, it is probably their successes in framing public debate and convincing many individuals to, in whole or in part, accept their ideologies that will have the most lasting influence on politics, both domestic and international. Their successes at taking over governments and replacing them with religious regimes have been few. While clearly these exceptions, especially Iran and Afghanistan, have significantly influenced international politics, these successes have been few and flawed. The rule of the Taliban in Afghanistan proved to be unpopular and fell apart due to domestic pressures and the consequences of their international agenda. The rule of religious fundamentalists in Iran is also becoming increasingly unpopular. This is because while fundamentalist movements have, thus far, been very successful at exploiting the failures of modernity, they have been relatively unsuccessful at solving or mitigating the problems caused by these failures.

In addition, when fundamentalist movements take over states, it is often easier for other states to marginalize or counter their impact. For example, the United States has managed to at least partially isolate Iran using a containment strategy similar to the one used against Eastern Europe during the Cold War. It also successfully removed the Taliban government of Afghanistan. However, countering the impact of the anti-American aspects of Islamic fundamentalist ideologies on the thoughts of people in the Muslim world is considerably more difficult.

For this reason among others, a more lasting and more common influence of fundamentalism on international politics is the result of their gaining converts to their ideologies. This influences both domestic and international politics in two ways. First, these ideologies influence the belief systems of policy makers. That is, if a policy maker is influenced by a fundamentalist ideology, this ideology will play a part in policy making whether or not a government is a religious one or not. Second, if a substantial portion of a state's population is influenced by fundamentalist ideologies, this, in turn, influences the policies of that state's government. Even in autocratic governments, policy makers would be unwise to make a decision that runs directly counter to some belief, moral, or value that is widely and deeply held by their constituents. Thus, the influence of fundamentalists on the domestic and international policies of a state is roughly in proportion to their ability to convert that state's population to their way of thinking. This can occur also with respect to a specific issue when fundamentalists succeed in convincing a state's population and/or its policy makers that their view is the correct one on this issue even if they fail to convert many to their ideology as a whole.

Political Islam

Perhaps the most visible international manifestation of religious fundamentalism of late has been political Islam. Like fundamentalist movements in other religions, political Islam is a reaction against modernity. Adherents of political Islam feel that traditional identities and morals are under attack and must be defended. They have the political aim of making religion more relevant in politics. And, they selectively interpret the religion to accomplish these tasks. This begs the following question: if political Islam is similar to other fundamentalist movements, why is it so much more visible than the others?

Islam and Politics

There are several answers to this question. The first, and probably most popular answer among analysts is that Islam from its inception has been a political religion. In its extreme, this argument posits that the role of religion in Islam is said to have fossilized in the seventh century where religion and politics were inseparable (Dalacoura, 2000: 879).

While it is arguable that this is an overstatement of the situation, Islam and politics are clearly linked. The concept of separation of religion and state is, at the very least, considerably weaker in states populated by Muslims than it is in the West. In fact, within Islam itself this separation is nonexistent. In Islam, secular law is superseded by divine law and there is no church–state dualism (Gellner, 1992: 6–9).

This means that Islam is not meant to be an institution separate from the state, not even as a major political actor. Rather, it is inseparable from the state both as a source of law and as an influence on all decisions by rulers. Thus, even medieval Europe can be said to have had more separation of religion and state than Islamic doctrine is willing to accept. Furthermore, Islam is comparatively resistant to public–private distinction (Appleby, 2000: 106). Thus, the trend found in the West of leaving religious decisions to the individual is considerably rarer in the Islamic world. In fact, Islamic fundamentalists often have little in common with even conservative Christian fundamentalists. It is seen as a way of life in which followers may see no division between the spiritual and secular. Christianity, in contrast, has a long history of separation between religion and politics (Haynes, 1994: 4–5). This major difference between the Western and Islamic worlds can be traced to the fact that the West experienced a Reformation and Enlightenment and the Islamic world did not. Thus, the historical processes that allowed the West to form a concept of separation of religion and state never occurred in Islam (An-Na'im, 2002: 31).

However, a distinction must be made between the doctrine of Islam and the reality of Islam's historical role in government. Despite the fact that doctrinally Islam is inseparable from politics, true unity between the two is rare, if it can be said to have ever happened at all, and the general rule is pragmatism. That is, historically the Islamic clergy have been close to those who wielded power but rarely ruled themselves (Haynes, 1998: 128–129). Thus, religious states like Iran are the exception, rather than the rule.

Rejection of the Modern Secular State

Ironically, it can be said that it is precisely this lack of an ideal unity between religion and politics that is fueling political Islam. Islamists, those who follow the doctrines of political Islam, are dissatisfied with the religious credentials of most states in the Islamic world. In fact, this rejection of the secular and corrupt nature of these states can be said to be the second reason why political Islam has been more visible on the world scene that other types of fundamentalism. Furthermore, most Islamists would prefer a single Islamic state that encompasses the entire Islamic world, and eventually the entire world, over the many individual Islamic states that exist today.

Islamists' dissatisfaction with secular regimes in the Islamic world, or at least with regimes that they consider not religious enough, exists along three fronts: that these regimes do not sufficiently follow Islamic principles; that they are corrupt and inefficient; and that they are unduly influenced by the West. Since World War II, and to a great extent even before this, governments in the Islamic world have followed secular ideologies including, but not limited to, liberalism, Communism, socialism, and fascism as the basis for their political regimes. All these ideologies have in common the fact that they de-emphasize the role of religion in society and politics and emphasize various secular principles. This pursuit of these Western-styled bases of governing and modernization has greatly frustrated Islamists. In fact, Islamism is, in part, characterized by a rejection of the lifestyles that are based on these ideologies and a desire to replace them with Sharia, Islamic law, as the basis for society (Haynes, 1994: 64, 1998: 146).

The reason Islamists have had considerable success at convincing people that this is the case is that they have been successful at blaming the socioeconomic failures of most governments in the Islamic world on the fact that these governments are too secular. Most states in the Islamic world have been experiencing socioeconomic disequilibrium. This disequilibrium is common to many Third World states and is the result of a number of transnational causes. Urbanization has undermined the traditional community. These states have become more dependent on the world economic system, undermining peoples' sense of control, over their fates. To make matters worse, governments have remained authoritarian, and often corrupt, with little voice in politics being given to the common man. Finally, the traditional non-fundamentalist religious leadership has, perhaps correctly, been associated with the failures of the political leadership (Appleby, 2000: 106, 361–365). Thus, the obvious solution is for a religious regime to replace the existing secular ones.[3] That Islamic charitable organizations have often had more success at alleviating the plight of the poor only adds to the credibility of Islamist organizations (Appleby, 2000: 107).

Despite this widespread agreement among Islamists that a transnational Islamic state is the solution to the socioeconomic problems of the Islamic world, there is no consensus as to the nature of the Islamic state, and especially on how to translate this concept into the complex modern political arena (Haynes, 1994: 65–66). This is because there is no real basis for an Islamic state in tradition. Under the Caliphate, an era in early Islam that Islamists consider to be the basis for the Islamic state, Islamic law was used more for governing civil affairs and was never the law of the Caliphate (Tibi, 2000: 852). Islamists also have had difficulty in dealing with the issue of who should hold power and how it should be exercised (Appleby, 2000: 368–369).

It is also important to note that, while Islamists take advantage of the economic failures of governments, individual poverty is not correlated with who is most likely to become an Islamist. In fact, those most likely to join these movements are upwardly mobile young men from the middle or lower middle class with professional degrees. This includes those that become suicide bombers. Thus, it is more likely that those who become Islamists are motivated by a desire to change the world, rather then by dire economic circumstances. More specifically, these people are often potential elites who are for some reason prevented from turning their economic success into political clout and feel that Islamism may be a vehicle for accomplishing this (Pipes, 2001–2002).

Many politicians in the Islamic world agree with this assessment. For instance, Kuwaiti Politician Sheikh Saud Nasser Al-Sabbah (2002: 13) argues that Kuwait "is now hijacked by groups calling themselves 'Islamic' while in reality they are only using Islam as a cover to hide their political agenda. They are trying to climb to the top and dominate the political process under the banner of Islam." Malaysian former Deputy Prime Minister Anwar Ibrahim (2002: 10) similarly argues,

> Bin Laden and his proteges are the children of desperation; they come from countries where political struggle through peaceful means is futile. In many countries, political dissent is simply illegal. Yet, year by year, the size of the educated class and the number of young professionals continues to increase. These people need space to express their political and social concerns. But state control is total, leaving no room for civil society to grow.

Thus, it is not the uneducated poor who are the driving force behind political Islam. Rather it is educated elites who are not allowed access to political and social power.

Finally, despite its rejection of modern secular ideas, many modern ideas prevail even within the context of political Islam. For example (Zubadia, 2000: 75–76) notes,

> The Islamic thrust in recent decades has been in large part a reaction against secularization and its ostensible aim was to reverse and stop that process. It succeeded in this respect in many visible ways: veiling of women and segregation of the sexes; the prohibition (in practice re-shaping) of interest on loans; and, in the case of Egypt and Iran, the introduction of Sharia, [Islamic law], in different ways, into the legal system. But have these measures halted the inexorable socioeconomic processes which are difficult to control or plan? Take the question of women and the family. It was the stated aim of all Islamic movements to keep women at home as mothers and homemakers, the cornerstone of the Muslim family. Yet everywhere women are going out of the home to work in ever increasing numbers. Families cannot afford home-bound mothers, and the occupational structure offers increasing opportunities. Paradoxically, the veil has facilitated rather than inhibited this much wider social and economic participation by women, in bestowing respectability, and modesty on female public appearance. Or take for example women's political participation: one of the planks of Khomeini's rise . . . was in opposition to granting political rights to women, including the vote. Yet, at the inception of the Islamic Republic, there was no question of not granting women these rights. In Egypt, and other Arab lands, it is only the most backward conservatives who object to women's political participation, and they are losing. We have seen an about-turn of the Iranian regime on family law and family planing in the face of modern sensibilities and pragmatic considerations. I have noted that Khomeini's ruling in 1988, authorizing the bypassing of Sharia in favor of the interests of Islamic government. This is the clearest step in the interests of pragmatism, opening the gates wide for the adjusting of policy and legislation to current imperatives. In the area of crime and punishment, it is noted that although Sharia penalties are on the law books, they are seldom applied, and then for political motives . . . The greatest challenge to the Sharia, however, is not the push for modifications of its provisions, but the fact that it is just irrelevant to the great bulk of legislation in modern society.

Be that as it may, the dissatisfaction by Islamists with the secular regimes of the modern Islamic world and their attempts to alter or replace these regimes are a large part of the reason that this form of fundamentalism is more visible than other forms of fundamentalism.

Rejection of the West

A third reason that political Islam has become so visible in the West is precisely because an essential element of political Islam is its opposition to the West and Western values. That is, like fundamentalists elsewhere, the current manifestation of political Islam is a reaction against modernity, but it is also a reaction against the West. Thus, these Islamic groups do not only seek to counteract what they see as the evils of modernity, but they also seek to replace the Western interpretation of modernity with their own as the dominant view in the world (Eisenstadt, 2000a: 608–609). In short, they feel they are taking part in a transnational struggle to determine which worldview will guide the Islamic world's views on how modernity should be realized. This struggle is not only between clusters of states, it also occurs to an extent within these states.

Osama Bin Laden's February 23, 1998 declaration in *Al-Quds al-Arabi* provides a good example of an extreme form of this opposition. This declaration accuses the United States of occupying Saudi Arabia, stealing its riches, cowing its rulers, humiliating its people, and using it as a base to attack its Islamic neighbors. The United States, as part of its continuing Crusader-Jewish campaign, is said to be continuing this slaughter through the blockade of Iraq that was in effect at the time of the declaration. The war serves the purposes of the Jewish state and its occupation of Jerusalem by distracting attention away from its crimes against Muslims. All this constitutes a clear declaration of war by the United States against "God, his prophet and the Muslims" thus justifying jihad against them. Because of this, Bin Laden feels justified in issuing a Fatwa, or Islamic decree, that killing Americans and their allies, civilian or military, is a duty of all Muslims (Lewis, 1998). While some of the specific facts have changed since this declaration, such as the U.S. blockade of Iraq ending with Iraq's occupation, it is clear that Bin Laden, among others, still holds by the more general assertion that Western crimes against Muslims justify a religious ear against the West.

Although this particular version of the vision of the West as a threat to Islam is an extreme one, its basic elements are in line with the feelings of many Muslims toward the West. The theme of colonialism, for example, is an important element of how the Islamic world views the West. European powers did, in fact, rule much of the Islamic world as colonial powers. During this period of Western rule, the colonial powers tried to impose Western political ideas and concepts on the territories they ruled. Thus, it is easy to see how many of these ideas are seen as foreign and illegitimate. In fact, this legacy of colonialism can be said to have led to an Islamic feeling of weakness and vulnerability (Fuller and Lesser, 1995). These feelings exist to the extent that many acts by Western states are seen as attempts to continue the Western control of the Islamic world through other means. Western support of secular regimes is seen as an attempt to continue colonialism by proxy. The Western support for Israel is seen as an attempt to maintain a foreign and illegitimate colonial entity in the Islamic world. In short, colonialism is seen as a transnational tool of the West, which is used to dominate the Islamic world.

Similarly, the preponderance of Western sources of entertainment, including television shows and movies, are seen as part of a transnational

Western campaign to undermine Islamic values and traditional society. An example of such an argument is made by Akbar (2002: 47–49)

> Nothing in history has threatened Muslims like the Western Media . . . It is the American mass media that have achieved what American political might could not: the attainment of world domination. Hollywood succeeded where the pentagon failed . . . Muslims ask: Now that the Western Media have helped conquer communism, who will be their next opponent? It is not difficult to guess: Islam.

While it is debatable that there is a conscious attempt by Hollywood to undermine the Islam of the Islamists, there is truth in the argument that this is the result of the incursion of Western media into the Islamic world. For instance, Fischer (2002: 63) notes, "Far more powerful than either fax or audiocassette have been the visual and music media, which have been reworking the lifestyles of Iranians and other Muslims."

This anger against the West is directed, in particular, at the United States

> A wide consensus [among Islamists] exists that Washington and Hollywood have joined forces to establish a hegemony over the world (the "new world order"). In the words of Ayatollah Khomeini, perhaps the most influential modern interpreter of Islam: "The danger that America poses is so great that if you commit the smallest oversight, you will be destroyed. . . . America plans to destroy us, all of us." (Pipes, 2002: 43)

This vision of threat is mirrored in the West by a fear and distrust of Islam. This is most obvious in Samuel Huntington's (1993a, 1996a) clash of civilizations thesis that the post–Cold War world is divided among several civilizations and that the greatest threat to the Western civilization is the Islamic civilization. While, clearly there are many Muslims who wish ill on the West, as is substantiated by the many violent terrorist incidents including the events of September 11, 2001, it is unclear whether this is truly the view of all Muslims. Yet the feelings on both sides by some that a basic enmity exists between the West and Islam can potentially create the situation where the enmity between minorities within each civilization becomes real for all. Huntington himself argues that this is occurring. "Undeniably, the terrorist actions of Osama bin Laden have reinvigorated [western] civilizational identity. Just as he sought to rally Muslims by declaring war on the West, he gave back to the West its sense of common identity in defending itself" (Huntington, 2002: 5).

In any case, the divide between the West and Islam runs deeper than a clash between two power blocs of states, and hence must be analyzed in transnational terms. It also includes a basic clash between two sets of values. This constitutes the final, and perhaps most important, reason that political Islam is more visible on the world scene than other forms of fundamentalism.

Is Islam Compatible with Democracy and Human Rights?

There can be said to be a transnational conflict between the Islamic world and the West over values, with each side simultaneously trying to defend its values as well as spread them. Modern Western values and especially those of the United States include the concepts of democracy, separation of religion and state, and human rights as core values. The argument that all of these basic values are foreign to Islam is a common one. This is due to the link between religion and politics in Islam. Because Islamists consider Islamic law to be the only legitimate basis for governing, there is little room for concepts like democracy and human rights and clearly no room for separation of religion and state. Nor is there room for any opposing viewpoint. Thus, the concept of political freedom is alien to Islam (Jaggers and Gurr, 1995: 478; Lewis, 1993: 96–98). In fact, many argue that the very idea of secular authority and jurisdiction is an impiety in Islam (Juergensmeyer, 1993: 19–23). In the words of Bernard Lewis (1987: xvi–xvii), "The true and sole sovereign in the Muslim view was God, from whose mandate the Prophet derived his authority and whose will, made known by revelation, was the sole source of law."

Most who study human rights argue that Islamic states have a poor human rights record. This is because Sharia law, de facto, results in discrimination against members of other religions (Van der Vyver, 1996). Most Islamic states, especially those in the Middle East, have prohibitions against proselytizing and conversion away from Islam. Some states actually outlaw minority religions. Iran, for example, has outlawed the Bahai religion. In addition to banning the Bahai religion, Saudi Arabia bans all non-Islamic public worship, and sometimes private worship. Violation of this law can result in arrest, lashes, and deportation (Boyle and Sheet: 1997). The Saudi government also severely restricts the religious practices of Shi'i Muslims, who follow a different branch of Islam than does the Saudi government. These restrictions include bans on the public practice of religious rituals, building private mosques, the entrance of foreign Shi'i clerics into the country, censorship of public speeches by Saudi Shi'i clerics and scholars, and a ban on the importation of Shi'i religious books and audiocassettes (Boyle and Sheet, 1997).[4]

This pattern of discrimination against religious minorities is not limited to Iran and Saudi Arabia. Rather, it is the norm for all Islamic states in the Middle East. Algeria, even while fighting Islamic extremists, declares Islam to be the only legal religion in the state, though in practice some minority religions are allowed to practice in private.[5] Bahrain is comparatively moderate and both in law and practice guarantees religious freedom but nevertheless declares Islam to be its official religion and prohibits proselytizing by other religions.[6] Saddam Hussein's Iraq, also an officially Islamic state, similarly prohibited proselytizing as well as conversion away from Islam.[7] In addition to general restrictions on the religious practices of religious minorities[8] it also treated them harshly, but much of this is due to political, and not religious, motivations. In Kuwait non-Muslims are barred from citizenship and many nonrecognized religions including Buddhists, Hindus, Sikhs, and several Christian denominations are not allowed to worship publically.[9] Lebanon is a multiethnic, multireligious state and thus guarantees religious freedom. However religion colors the country's politics at all levels. Its 18 religious communities control all issues of personal status, and marriage between Christians and Muslims is prohibited.[10] The law in Libya is based on Mu'ammar Al-Qadhafi's interpretation of Islamic law and the number of churches permitted in the country is limited to one per city.[11] Oman's basic charter designates the Koran as the major source of legislation. The country prohibits proselytizing by minority religions, conversion away from Islam, and the printing of non-Islamic materials. Also, minority religions are required to register with the government.[12] Qatar forbids the public worship of all non-Muslims and officially permits private worship only by Christians and Jews, though some other religions are unofficially allowed to operate privately. Furthermore, it only recognizes some Christian denominations.[13] Though Syria has no official religions, its leader must be a Muslim. It discourages proselytizing and has banned the Jehovah's Witnesses.[14] Tunisia is an officially Islamic state and, while comparatively tolerant of other religious minorities, bans the Bahai faith.[15] The United Arab Emirates only recognizes specific Christian religious denominations, and even this recognition is only in some of the individual Emirates.[16] Yemen is comparatively tolerant but maintains a ban on proselytizing by non-Islamic faiths and conversion away from Islam.[17] Even those Islamic states that are considered more moderate have little tolerance for religious minorities. For example, Egypt, which guarantees religious freedom in its constitution, severely discriminates against its Coptic Christian minority (Fox, 2000e). Jordan recognizes only the three major monotheistic religions of Islam, Christianity, and Judaism as legitimate religions. Even the recognized non-Islamic religions in Jordan are restricted. Proselytizing by non-Muslims is illegal and in order to have official recognition, religious institutions must obtain a government permit, which is often denied.[18] Morocco similarly recognizes only Christianity and Islam, outlaws proselytizing, confiscates bibles written in Arabic, and severely restricts its Bahai minority.[19] Turkey, an officially secular state, officially recognizes only those minority religions mentioned in the Treaty of Lusanne (1923), which are Judaism and the Greek Orthodox and Armenian Apostolic churches. Furthermore, the Greek Orthodox are not permitted to construct new churches and the publishing of Greek Orthodox books is restricted.[20]

Many Islamic states outside of the Middle East also exhibit considerable intolerance for religious minorities. The behavior of the Afghan government when it was ruled by the Taliban is well known. However, even before the Taliban came to power it was an Islamic state based on Sunni Islam, which caused strong objections from the country's Shi'i Islam minority. In addition proselyting by non-Muslims was illegal.[21] Many attribute the ongoing civil war in Sudan to the imposition of Islamic law by the country's government on the Christian and Animist population of the country's southern regions. Indonesia recognizes only Islam, some denominations of Christianity, Buddhism and Hinduism. Other religions are not banned but must register as social organizations rather than religious ones and must obtain permits to hold public events. While the government must approve the building or expanding of all places of worship, in practice this has been used to restrict only minority religions. There are also numerous reports of attacks by civilians on Christians and forced conversion to Islam, which the government does little to prevent.[22]

Malaysia is an officially Islamic state. Proselyting by non-Muslims is prohibited and the government restricts the building of non-Islamic places of worship and the allocation of land for non-Islamic cemeteries. The government monitors the activities of the country's Shi'i minority, and periodically detains members of what it considers Islamic "deviant sects" without trial or charge.[23]

Pakistan is also an officially Islamic republic. Any speech or action considered derogatory to Islam or its prophet Mohammed is illegal and the number of such "blasphemy" laws is increasing. The country's courts apply different standards of evidence for Muslims and non-Muslims. Members of minority religions can be prosecuted for breaking Islamic law. Such arrests and prosecutions are common. Even when there is little evidence against the accused, conviction is common because judges fear retaliation by religious extremists. Religious minorities, which account for 5 percent of the country's population, constitute about 25 percent of the prison population.[24]

As can be inferred from the aforementioned discussion, one of the most common forms of restrictions on minority religions in Muslim states is restrictions on proselytizing. This form of restriction goes beyond the different views of human rights that exist in the West and Islamic world. Missionaries, especially those from the West, are seen, perhaps correctly, as purposely trying to undermine Islam. They are also seen as part of a concerted effort by the West to force its values on the Islamic world.

When considering this pattern of intolerance it is important to keep several facts in mind. First, the brief description provided here of the situation in the Middle East and other Islamic states constitutes only a terse and condensed summary of the situation in each state. Second, the description is limited to religious rights. Most religious minorities in the Middle East and other Islamic states also have severe restrictions placed on their political rights. Third, most of the states described here are not ruled by Islamist governments. Rather, many of them, in fact, are fighting Islamist challenges to their rule and, accordingly, are likely more tolerant than their Islamist challengers would be if they ever rise to power. This confirms Gurr's (2000: 282) assessment that "few states in the Islamic world are prepared to grant full political and cultural rights to religious minorities."

All of this makes it clear that the contradictions between Islam and the Western concepts of human rights and equality run very deep both in theory and in practice. These contradictions are recognized by many Islamists who, rather than address the tension between the two, prefer to question the validity of those elements of the concept of human rights that clash with their concept of Islam (Van der Vyver, 1996). In an era where international intervention in state affairs is justified by human rights concerns and universal jurisdiction for prosecuting human rights offences is being asserted, this transnational clash of views on religious human rights is becoming an increasingly international issue.

The link between Islam and autocracy is less clear than is its link with intolerance. While many scholars argue that Islam is inherently undemocratic, many others argue that there is room for democracy in Islam (Appleby, 2000: 255–263; Midlarsky, 1998: 486–488). However, the concept and practice of democracy in Islamic states, such as it is, diverges significantly from Western concepts and practices (Esposito and Voll, 1996). As demonstrated earlier, democracy in the Islamic world is most often only for Muslims and not for religious minorities. This clearly diverges from the Western concept of liberal democracy that includes the ideas of equality for minorities and the same civil rights for all citizens.

The empirical evidence is also mixed. Some studies find that Islam is strongly linked to autocracy. Jaggers and Gurr (1995) found that few Arab states have taken part in the trend toward democratization that took place in the late twentieth century. Fisch (2002) found that even when controlling for economic and social factors, Islamic states are more autocratic during the 1990s. Also, Fox (2000a, 2001c) found that Middle Eastern states as well as Islamic states outside of the Middle East were disproportionately autocratic during the 1990s. Midlarsky (1998) found that the correlation between democracy and Islam depends on how you measure democracy. If you focus on political institutions, Islamic states are undemocratic; however, if you focus on political rights there is no positive or negative correlation between Islam and democracy. However it should be emphasized that the political rights scale used in Midlarsky's study focuses on political and not religious rights. In another study Price (1999) also finds that Islam neither undermines or supports democracy and/or human rights.

In all, Islamic states have very poor record with regard to human rights and tolerance of religious minorities. They are among the least democratic in the world and, given their poor record on civil rights, even those that tend to be more democratic are certainly not liberal democracies. More importantly, this description is accurate not only for states run by fundamentalists, it also applies to states run by governments considered moderate, pro-Western, and sometimes even ideologically secular. Thus, this intolerance and tendency toward autocratic rule is not unique to political Islam, rather it is a trait common to governments in most Islamic states.

Clearly the implications of the clash of regimes and values are very pertinent for international relations. The Western, and particularly U.S., policy of encouraging the spread of liberal democracy and human rights is likely to cause friction with the Islamic world. There is simply an incongruence between Western and Islamic values. This also implies that those who believe that the opposition in the Islamic world to the West is based on economic deprivation or anger at a particular U.S. or Western foreign policy, such as the U.S. support for Israel, are in error. Those in the Islamic world who hate the West, hate it not for what it does but what it is. Western wealth may provoke envy and Western support of Israel may be considered an unwanted intrusion into the Islamic world, but even if the West were poor and Israel did not exist, the basic contradictions between Islamic and Western values would still exist and still provoke conflict.

Similarly, the threat many Muslims believe is posed by the Western media is not primarily because the intrusion of this media into the Islamic world is seen as a conscious attack on Islamic values by the West, though clearly many feel this is the case. Rather, it is a threat because of the fact that the Western media successfully brings Western ideas and values to the non-Western world and plays a role in transforming these societies. That this occurs is undeniable, the issue of intent is besides the point. In other worlds, while there is no Hollywood conspiracy to undermine proper Islamic values as defined by the Islamists, Hollywood's activities nevertheless have this result. It is simply a practical manifestations of the friction between Western and Islamic values.

Furthermore, while the more pro-Western Islamic governments may be content to pay lip service to Western values when possible and to otherwise resist change, it is unlikely that Islamists will be content to resist the West passively. Their rhetoric and past behavior shows that Islamists consider the West an enemy that is a threat to their way of life and that this enemy must be fought with any and all means available to them. Thus, to the extent that they control state policy or can otherwise act on the international scene as non-state actors through tactics including terrorism, Islamists will continue to be significant actors in international politics.

It is important to remember that while much of this discussion has referred to the behavior of individual states, the basic topic at hand is beyond any single state or coalition of states. Rather, it is a clash between two transnational ideologies. Militant Islam, and to a lesser extent other strains of Islam, promote a set of values that in a number of ways contradict Western values. While the venues for this clash may often be the state and some of the actors in this clash, both domestically and internationally, may be state governments, the true battleground and motivating force behind these actors know no borders. The United States may be among the strongest promoters of Western values but Western values influence thinking across the Western world as well as the thinking of many outside of it. Islamic values also have their adherents across the globe and do not even have a single dominant avatar, though some states like Iran and

Saudi Arabia are more prominent than others in defending and spreading these values.

Islam is not Monolithic

Many scholars who study the topic correctly note that Islam, like most religions, is not monolithic, that Islamism is just one interpretation of Islam, and that it is an interpretation held only by a minority of Muslims. Many Muslims practice traditional Islam that is more conservative and passive than in political Islam. Most states populated by Muslims tend to promote a more state-centric version of Islam where the oppositional trends of the religion are de-emphasized in favor of emphasizing support for the state (Akiner, 2000; Haynes, 1994: 67–70). There are many Islamic thinkers who believe that dialogue with the West is both necessary and will strengthen Islam (Esposito and Voll, 2000: 617). Finally, many argue that there is a nonpolitical, modernist version of Islam, which is "a liberal, political and social Islamic ethos of human rights, pluralism, and democracy; a religious individualism; and a rejection of the presumed authoritative status of traditional schools of Islamic law and theology" (Nettler, 2000: 50).

Furthermore there are many who are reinterpreting the concept of jihad. Traditionally jihad is a holy war to conquer and subjugate non-Muslims or to replace a secular state with an Islamic one. Many now argue that there is no justification for jihad against a state where Muslims enjoy religious freedom (Gopin, 2000: 82–83). Others go further arguing that "The notion of aggressive jihad has become morally untenable as a means of conducting international relations; and the rise of the modern human rights movement has tumbled the moral foundations of segregation and discrimination against women and non-Muslims" (An-Na'im, 2002: 33). Some are even reinterpreting jihad to mean a personal internal struggle for self-improvement. While it is unclear how many Muslims support these newer interpretations of jihad, it is clear that a good number do not support the use of the concept to justify terrorism. There is a consensus that jihad, at its most violent, refers to conventional warfare against infidels and apostates and the rules for behavior in war that do not allow for murder and terrorism or even consider the random slaughter of uninvolved bystanders (Lewis, 1998).

Similarly, in the context of Samuel Huntington's predictions of a civilizational war between the West and Islam, many argue that there will be more clashes within Islam than between Islam and other civilizations. There are several versions of this argument. First, many claim that the true basis for post–Cold War conflict will be nonreligious factors like national, political, cultural, psychological, postcolonial, modernity, and strategic issues, all of which divide the Islamic world (Ajami, 1993; Bartley, 1993; Esposito, 1995; Fuller and Lesser, 1995; Monshipouri, 1998). Second, many posit that Islam is not the threat many believe it to be for a variety of reasons. These include arguments that the Islamic world is secularizing (Fuller and Lesser, 1995), that political Islam is controversial within the Islamic world (Pfaff, 1997), and that it is more of a threat to authoritarian regimes within the Islamic world than to any entities outside of it (Esposito, 1995; Halliday, 1996). This is because the rhetoric of political Islam is really more about how these societies will organize themselves internally, though this may have some implications for the West. Thus the real question is whether Islam can provide answers for problems facing Muslim societies (Halliday, 2000: 130–131). Third, many believe that rather than rejecting it, the West is being embraced by other civilizations (Kirkpatrick et al., 1993; Mahbubani, 1993). Fourth, it is arguable that the clash of civilizations is a self-fulfilling prophecy brought on by Western fear of Islam and not any aggressive actions by Muslims (Esposito, 1995: 253). Finally, several quantitative studies show no basis for a post–Cold War clash between the West and Islam. Fox (2000a, 2001b) found that Islamic ethnic minorities are no more violent than are minorities of other religions and that the extent of Islamic participation in ethnic conflict has not changed with the end of the Cold War.

On the other hand, many agree with Huntington's arguments.[25] Even some of Huntington's critics like Hassner (1997a,b) and Heilbrunn (1998) believe that there may be something to Huntington's arguments with regard to clashes between the Western and Islamic civilizations.

Be that as it may, it is clear that Islam, like most other long-standing religions, is a diverse tradition with many different trends that includes adherents of many nationalities. Its adherents, from Islam's earliest years, have continued to engage in lively debate of the proper interpretation and application of the religion. It is also clear that many within the Islamic world do not always get along with each other, with the Iran–Iraq and Gulf wars being just a few of the most obvious examples of this. Furthermore, political Islam is not accepted by all Muslims, and probably is not accepted by most of them. Many governments of Islamic states have been actively repressing political Islam because they correctly see it as a threat to their regimes. None of this is in question.

What is in question is the role of Islam in general and political Islam in particular in world politics. The events of September 11, 2001, as well as the numerous terrorist incidents that have occurred before and after this watershed event show unambiguously that Islamists intend to make their mark. The events of September 11, 2001 have caused the United States to replace the governments of Afghanistan and Iraq and aggressively look for international support for its war on terrorism. It is too early to tell whether this will become the new paradigm for U.S. foreign policy as did its war on Communism or whether it will become just one element of its foreign policy as did the war on drugs or the war on poverty. Whichever of the two eventually turns out to be the case, it is undeniable that the international efforts of political Islam have caused major shifts in the foreign policy of the world's most powerful state and has similarly influenced the policies of many other states. Thus, political Islam is already impacting international relations, regardless of whether most Muslims support this ideology.

More importantly there are some deeper questions. What do political Islam and mainstream Islam agree upon? If such agreement exists, to what extent does this influence international relations? There are several points of agreement among most Muslims. First, Islamic concepts of tolerance and the proper form of government diverge from those of the West. As discussed earlier, even those states that are somewhat democratic and those that repress Islamists (with the two not being mutually exclusive) are also intolerant of religious minorities. Yet tolerance of religious minorities is an essential element of the Western concept of liberal democracy. As spreading this concept is an essential element of U.S. foreign policy, as well as of many other Western states, this will inevitably cause tensions between Western and Islamic states.

Ironically, the U.S. efforts to fight terrorism in the wake of the events of September 11 may have had the effect of harming democracy in the Islamic world. Repressing terrorism gives autocrats in the Islamic world an excuse acceptable in the West for repressing their populations (Ibrahim, 2002: 9).

Second, there is considerable agreement among Muslims over the issue of Israel. While the range of official policies ranges from getting Israel to make major concessions to the Palestinians to calls for the total destruction of the "Zionist entity," it is fair to say that few, if any, Islamic states will take the Israeli side in any dispute with the Palestinians. The attempts by Islamic states to declare Israel a racist state at the UN-sponsored World Conference Against Racism, Racial Discrimination, Xenophobia and Related Intolerance held in Durban South Africa described in chapter 4 is a good example of this.

Third, most Islamic states resent Western efforts to influence their domestic policies. This is often seen as a continuation of European colonialism in the Islamic world. To be fair, this view is shared by much of the non-Islamic Third World. However, Islam has a more particular historical grievance with the West. Until about 1800, Islam's history was a successful one in the realm of world politics. It managed to spread its political control throughout much of the known world. However, for the past two centuries, the West has emerged as more powerful on the world scene than the Islamic world. This has caused considerable resentment against the West (Pipes, 2002).

The phenomena of a political movement that transcends the political borders of a state and crosses nations suits the transnational model of international politics as developed by Keohane and Nye already in 1970 (Keohane and Nye, 1970). The pattern of political Islam exceeds the state-centric paradigm of international relations promoted by the West in both organizational terms and also issues. Political Islam, as well as Islam in general, presents not only a challenge to the West's organization of international politics but also over basic issues. The Islamic world in general differs with the West over fundamental issues like the proper form of government, the proper role of religion in government, and tolerance of religious minorities. It has historical grievances against the West. It also differs with the West on more specific, but nevertheless important, policy issues such as the Palestinian–Israeli conflict.

Political Islam shares all of these differences and grievances and, in contrast to most of the Islamic states, advocates a violent war with the West in which the only limitations appear to be the limits on their resources. The killing of noncombatants and civilians is considered justified. Also, the behavior of groups like Al-Qaeda indicate that the use of weapons of mass destruction are not out of the question. Furthermore these groups are simultaneously trying to undermine and replace governments within the Islamic world, which they consider to be not sufficiently religious. The examples of Iran and Afghanistan are enough to demonstrate the potential impact on international relations, should these efforts be successful.

Terrorism

Religious terrorism is also becoming a transnational issue. While religion has always been a motivation for terrorism (Rapoport, 1984) religious terrorism is becoming the dominant form of terrorism in the international system. In a series of studies on Terrorism, Weinberg and Eubanks (1998) found that terrorist activities shifted to a more religious pattern during the early 1980s, primarily attacks by Islamic groups on Western targets. Furthermore, Weinberg et al. (2002) found that most terrorist groups formed during the 1990s, as well as most of the terrorist groups active in the late 1990s were religious-based Islamic groups.

The event that has thus far most probably been the strongest influence on world politics in the twenty-first century, the events of September 11, 2001, was a series of religiously motivated terrorist attacks. Furthermore, these attacks were perpetrated by an international terrorist organization that operates in as many as 60 countries and has an international agenda. These attacks have significantly altered the international relations agenda of the United States, the world's most powerful state.

Religious terrorism is also an issue on a smaller scale. That is, local religiously motivated terrorist groups are taking part in conflicts that have relevance to the international community. Resolving the Palestinian–Israeli conflict, for example, has for many years been an important foreign-policy goal for many Western and Islamic states, though it is fair to say that the opinions as to what is an appropriate resolution to this conflict vary. The conflict has drawn mediation efforts from heads of state, including several U.S. presidents and the leaders of several European and Arab states, as well as from more than one secretary general of the United Nations. One of the most difficult issues in the conflict is how to stop the terrorism perpetrated by Palestinians against Israeli citizens. Much of this terrorism is at the hands of Islamist groups like Hamas and Islamic Jihad, who are non-state actors.

Israel's difficulties with Hizbullah, a Shi'i Muslim Islamist terror organization in Lebanon is another transnational facet of the Arab–Israeli conflict with international implications. Israel's conflict with Hizbullah was a large part of why Israel until recently occupied southern Lebanon. One of Israel's stated goals was to create a buffer zone between Hizbullah and Israel in order to prevent terror attacks including rocket attacks.

Islamist movements challenge many Arab states including Algeria and Egypt. While Egypt has successfully repressed its Islamist challengers, the Algerian government continues to fight a civil war with them. This war threatens to destabilize the region and has caused numerous terrorist incidents in France. Other Islamist terror organizations like those in the Philippines and Chechnya have also drawn international attention and mediation efforts. In Pakistan, an Islamic Republic, terror acts were not directed only against Hindu Indians over the Kashmir issue but also against Shiites Moslems by Sunni Moslems (e.g. 48 people killed in a Mosque on Friday July 4, 2003. The next day 19 Russians were killed by two Chechnian suicide bombers in a rock concert in Moscow).

More importantly, all of these individual terror organizations have many transnational linkages. They share ideologies, often drawing inspiration from each others' spiritual leaders. To a lesser extent they also share resources. They have cooperated with each other in aspects of training. Also, in many instances they draw volunteers from nonlocal sources. The Chechens and the Taliban government of Afghanistan have both received a significant number of volunteers from throughout the Muslim world. Also, Muslims with British passports have become suicide bombers for the Palestinian cause.

This growth of religious terrorism on the international scene is related to the growth of fundamentalism and political Islam. This is because most religious terrorists are fundamentalists in general and Islamists in particular. The question is why do these groups tend to engage in terrorism?

The answer is simple. Fundamentalists wish to affect political change and terrorism is one tactic among many available to those who wish to affect political change. Thus the question is why do many fundamentalist groups choose this tactic rather than others? The answer is twofold and involves the nature of fundamentalism and the limited options available to fundamentalist organizations.

Fundamentalism is a reaction against modernity. They feel threatened by the political, social, and economic entities that advocate modernization. These entities pose a threat to their morals, belief systems, and traditional lifestyles. Thus, it is imperative to protect themselves from these influences. They have two options, to shield themselves from the world or to remake the world around them in accordance with their religious beliefs. While many groups choose the former option, many also choose the latter.

It is this predisposition of fundamentalists to try and reorder the world that causes them to opt for terrorism. While most fundamentalist movements would likely prefer to use nonviolent means to achieve their goal to recreate the perfect religious society, this is generally not possible. Much, if not most, of the world prefers modernity and secularism and cannot be convinced or persuaded to change their political, economic, and social systems to ones more acceptable to fundamentalists. That few states have done so peacefully is proof of this. Many would argue that even in fundamentalist states like Iran and Afghanistan under the Taliban, the majority, if given a free choice, would choose a more secular system. Thus, fundamentalists who wish to remake their state into a more religious one have no choice but to use violence.

Why does this violence take the form of terrorism? Mostly because this is the most effective form of violence in which fundamentalist organizations are able to engage. If they had the numbers and resources to achieve a revolution within a state, it is likely that they would not need to use violence in order to achieve their goals. In addition, even if fundamentalist organizations have the numbers to achieve their goals through peaceful means like the ballot, governments of modern states have a significant advantage in resources.

For example, when in 1992 Algerian fundamentalist political parties seemed to be poised to take control of the government through free elections, a bloodless military coup cancelled the elections and installed a government that continues to rule at the time of this writing. Until the elections, most Islamist opposition to the state was through peaceful means. Only when that avenue was closed did the violence and terrorism begin.

These same limitations are the reason why most fundamentalist groups who engage in terrorism use this tactic. Palestinian fundamentalist groups like Hamas and Islamic Jihad may have the support of a large part of the Palestinian population, but against the military might of the Israeli Army, terrorism is the best they can do, as under the current circumstances there is no way they could win a conventional war against the Israelis. Even Osama bin Laden who has at least hundreds of millions of dollars and thousands of recruits at his disposal has very few resources compared to the United States alone, much less the entire West combined. The world system is simply set up to favor state power. Another unique facet of religious terrorism is that of suicide bombing, a tactic that religious movements are more able to use than are secular states. Religion and especially Islam can promise a reward to the suicide bomber in the world to come. The secular state cannot.

Thus, the international trend of religious terrorism has international causes. First, the international political, social, and economic trends that helped to create fundamentalism also gives fundamentalists their motivation to remake the world order. Second, the nature of the international system constrains the political options of these fundamentalist organizations, leaving them few effective options other than terror.

Religious terrorism is also qualitatively different from secular terrorism in a number of ways. First, the classic goal of secular terrorists is to use violence in order to motivate a political audience to agree to the terrorists' demands. Thus terrorism is a means to an end. While this is also true of religious terrorists, they often also see the violence as an end in itself (Hoffman, 1995: 272–273). For instance, the September 11 attacks were clearly intended to alter U.S. policy, but they were also seen as a means to punish the United States for the perceived sins it had committed.

Second, religious terrorists operate under less constraints than do secular terrorists. Secular terrorists need to appeal to sympathizers, thus some acts are often beyond the pale. In contrast, religious terrorists often "execute their acts of terror for no audience but themselves" (Hoffman, 1995: 273). Third, while the goal of secular terrorists is most often to change an existing system, religious terrorists generally feel that they must replace the system itself. This alienation from the system enables "far more destructive and deadly" operations (Hoffman, 1995: 273).

Fourth, religious terrorists feel that they have divine justification for their acts. Thus, religious terrorism "assumes a transcendental dimension, and its perpetrators are thereby unconstrained by the political, moral, or practical constraints that seem to affect other terrorists" (Hoffman, 1995: 272). Thus, the terrorist is absolved of guilt for his actions due to the guilt of his victim (Drake, 1998: 57). Religious ideologies are one of the most effective ways to dehumanize victims. The victims are evil sinners and deserve what they get. Due to this, mass killings of civilians such as the thousands of victims in the World Trade Center can actually be considered praiseworthy. Similarly, the antiabortion activists who kill those who work for abortion clinics can justify these actions as killing murderers.

Fifth, while most religious traditions constrain the use of violence on civilians, many religious terrorists feel that they are living in special times that allow them to make exceptions to the normal prohibitions against such violence (Appleby, 2000: 88). This phenomenon is strongly linked to messianism, the belief "that there will be a day in which history or life on this earth will be transformed totally and irreversibly from the condition of perpetual strife which we have all experienced to one of perfect harmony that many dream about" (Rapoport, 1988: 197). Terrorists who believe that they live in a messianic age often feel that they must either take action to cause this age to come about, including provoking a war to rid the world of unbelievers. Also, when the expected messianic age or event does not occur, which has generally been the case until this point in time, believers often seek to attack those they blame for the failed messianic event (Rapoport, 1988).

Sixth, religious terrorists feel that their actions are righteous to the extent that these actions can earn them a place in the afterlife. Thus, religious terrorists are more willing to die for their cause, making suicide bombings a viable tactic.

Finally, terrorism by definition is the antithesis of a territorial-state based international order. Transnational religion in certain cases aspires to undermine the state especially the modern state. Hence, it is only natural for a transnational movement opposed to a state-centric international system to adopt a strategy that is designed to undermine the rules of international order.

In all, religious terrorism is a very serious challenge to the existing world order. Its goal is to change the modern secular order into a religious one. It is also motivated by an ideology that has little room for compromise or quarter. Thus, U.S. President Bush's "war on terrorism" was most likely inevitable. Both terrorists and their choice of terrorism are products of the world system and their goal of changing that system are one of the many ways religion is becoming a transnational issue. Furthermore, the West and the United States in particular are seen as the guardians of the world system. Given this, it was only a matter of time before the United States was forced to deal with the issue.

Proselytizing

Proselytizing is a significant source of international tension. Proselytizing is also a clear example of a transnational interaction between societies that evades the interstate level of interaction. Missionaries from many religions travel internationally to find converts for their religions. However, their efforts are often not welcome. For example, nearly every Middle Eastern state prohibits proselytizing and many of them even ban conversions away from Islam.

A number of Western European states also restrict proselytizing. France bans proselytizing in schools and in 1998 created the "Inter-ministerial Mission in the Fight Against Sects/Cults." France also does not recognize all branches of Jehovah's Witnesses, or the Church of Scientology, as qualifying religious associations for tax purposes, and therefore subjects them to a 60% tax on all funds they receive. Germany also persecutes members of what it perceives are religious cults, especially Scientologists. Members of the religion are essentially blacklisted. They are barred from renting halls and spaces in some cities and towns, they are barred from political parties, and there are some banks that will not allow them to open an account in their bank. Many local governments in Switzerland also prohibit the handing out of fliers in public and door to door religious solicitations by religious groups, laws aimed primarily at the practices of Scientologists.[26]

This type of prohibition is more extensive in Greece. According to the Greek constitution, proselytizing is prohibited for all religions, including the Greek Orthodox religion. However the law is only forcefully implemented toward minority religions (Pollis, 2002). Local Greek Orthodox bishops have been known to warn parishioners not to visit clergy or members of minority faiths and neighbors, and request that the police arrest missionaries for proselytizing.[27]

These efforts at proselytization and the government efforts to control and limit them are part of larger transnational clashes between worldviews. In local contexts, these clashes manifest in two ways. First, they are local manifestations of clashes between two transnational ideologies. For example, as noted earlier, Christian missionaries are often seen in Islamic states as trying to undermine Islam on behalf of the West. Second, these transnational religious efforts at gaining adherents are often also seen as a threat to more specific local cultures. For example, the restrictions in France on proselytizing and what it calls "cults" noted earlier seem to be targeted at religions that are not indigenous to France, including some Christian groups. It is arguable that this is part of France's well-known tendency to actively protect its local culture.

Human Rights

The issue of human rights in general, and religious rights in particular is becoming an increasingly international issue. The U.S. state department, for example, has written a yearly human rights report that includes a section on religious rights since the 1970s and has recently begun to issue a separate yearly report on religious rights. Human rights are also an important element of the foreign policies of many European states.

Religious rights are also enshrined directly and indirectly in a number of international treaties, declarations, and documents:

Article 18 of the 1948 UN Universal Declaration of Human Rights includes the right to "freedom of thought, conscience, and religion." This includes the freedoms to change religion or belief, worship alone or with others in private or in public, and to teach one's religion, as well as to observe, practice, and worship according to one's religious beliefs. The 1966 International Covenant on Civil and Political Rights, also sponsored by the United Nations, repeats this language on religion. The 1948 UN Convention on the Prevention of Genocide includes religion as one of the bases for identity that define a group which can be the object of genocide.

The 1981 UN Declaration on the Elimination of All Forms of Intolerance and Discrimination Based on Religion or Belief adds to these previous documents with a long list of rights including: freedom of worship and assembly; freedom to maintain places of worship; to establish and maintain religious charitable organizations; freedom of access to religious articles necessary for worship, rites, and observance; freedom to write, publish, and disseminate religious documents; freedom to teach as well as establish and maintain places for this purpose; freedom to choose religious leaders; freedom to solicit and receive voluntary contributions; freedom to observe holidays and days of rest, and to maintain communications with others of one's religion at the national and international levels.

In addition to the United Nations, many regional international organizations have also passed similar declarations. For example, the Article 9 of 1950 European Convention for the Protection of Human Rights and Fundamental Freedoms contains language identical to that of the 1948 UN Universal Declaration. Article 12 of the 1969 American Convention on Human Right also contains similar language. Article 8 of the 1969 African

Charter on Human and People's Rights contains a simpler clause guaranteeing "freedom of conscience, the profession and free practice of religion." In 1990, the Nineteenth Islamic Conference of Foreign Ministers adopted the Cairo Declaration on Human Rights in Islam, which states in Article 10 that "it is prohibited to exercise any form of compulsion on man or exploit his poverty or ignorance in order to convert him to another religion or to atheism."

Thus, human and religious rights are the topic of international treaties and declarations that are often given the force of law in countries that adopt them. However, from the declarations of the regional organizations, it can be seen that different parts of the world have different views on the extent to which religious rights should be protected. Western organizations and the United Nations include a comprehensive list of rights. The only analogous Islamic declaration promises only protection against forced conversion. In fact, the discussion earlier in this chapter listing the various restrictions on religious rights in Islamic states demonstrates that nearly all of the protections contained in the 1981 UN Declaration on the Elimination of All Forms of Intolerance and Discrimination Based on Religion or Belief are violated by at least some Islamic states.

In addition to being a source of tension between the Islamic and Western worlds, this disparity between Western and Islamic concepts of religious human rights is a potential source of military conflict. This is because, in the wake of the Cold War violations of human rights is becoming a more acceptable reason for military intervention. It is possible that this doctrine will evolve to include religious human rights. The religious repression in Afghanistan was one of the justifications used by the United States in legitimating its recent incursion into that state. Also, the continuing "war on terrorism" will likely create situations where the United States may wish to invade or intervene in a country and find it convenient to use violations of religious rights as a justification. As is documented earlier in this chapter, this justification could be potentially applied to most Muslim states.

All of this is part of a larger trend of sovereign governments becoming more accountable to "external legitimating audiences." That is, states must often justify actions taken within their own borders to other states as well as to NGOs (Clark and Friedman, 2000).

Other International Issues That Overlap with Religious Ones

There are a number of international issues that themselves are not religious issues but are impacted upon by religion. One obvious example is the issue of women's rights. It is an essential element of modern Western values that women deserve equal rights and treatment to men. Pursuing these rights is an important part of the agenda of international human rights organizations, international organizations such as the United Nations, and to a lesser extent many Western states.

The treatment of women worldwide is strongly correlated with religion. In particular, in many Muslim states women both legally and in practice have a status far inferior to those of men. In most Middle Eastern states, for example, laws governing personal status are based on the Sharia, Islamic law, which generally gives women an inferior status. Many applications of this religious law, which are codified as state law, violate what Westerners consider the human rights of women.

There are several restrictions that are common to many Middle Eastern states. First, many states restrict the ability of women to leave the country without the permission of their husband, or in the case of an unmarried women, male relative. In some cases women actually need permission, in others the permission is only needed to obtain a passport. In other states the husband must make a specific request to the government not to let his wife out of the country. Second, inheritance laws strongly favor men. Women heirs tend to get smaller inheritances from parents than their brothers. Even a sole female heir will often get only half of parents' estate with the rest going to other male relatives. Also, if a widow is not a Muslim there is often no inheritance at all. Third, many Middle Eastern states forbid Muslim women to wed non-Muslim men. In Saudi Arabia, a woman needs the consent of the government to even marry a non-Saudi. Fourth, in many states only males can pass their citizenship to their children. Fifth, it is much harder for a woman to obtain a divorce than it is for a man. In many states the man needs to state no reason for divorcing his wife but women must give a valid reason. Sixth, in the case of a divorce, custody laws tend to favor men. Seventh, in many states the Sharia law concept that two women's testimonies are equal to that of one man is applied in civil courts. Eighth, many states require females to cover their hair and wear modest clothing, though these restrictions are often not nearly as strict as they are in states like Saudi Arabia where the woman must be completely covered from head to toe in a loose fitting robe. Ninth, female genital mutilation occurs in several of these states. Finally, many Middle Eastern states permit polygamy, but the current wives generally must consent to their husband taking any additional wives.

There are also some more severe restrictions that are found in some specific states. For example, in Kuwait women may not vote or hold public office. In Qatar a woman must get the permission of her husband before obtaining a driver's license. In Yemen it is a matter of civil law that a wife must obey her husband.

Perhaps the most extreme case of restrictions on women is Saudi Arabia. Saudi women suffer from almost all of the restrictions listed here, usually in their most extreme form. This includes the restrictions on inheritance, child custody, and court testimony described earlier. In addition it is nearly impossible for a Saudi woman to get a divorce against the will of her husband. They cannot travel anywhere without a male chaperone.

They cannot check into a hotel and even foreign women cannot make a hotel reservation without special permission from the government. They may not operate motor vehicles or even ride a bicycle. Furthermore, they are segregated from men in all aspects of society, including schools, the workplace, buses, and hospitals. Consequently their freedom of movement as well as their ability to obtain education and employment is severely limited. Also, the death penalty can be given as punishment for giving birth to a child out of wedlock.

These types of laws are not limited to the Middle East and exist in other Muslim states. The treatment of women in Afghanistan under the Taliban is well known. Indonesia has laws similar to those mentioned earlier in the areas of polygamy, divorce, and transfer of citizenship. In Malaysia, laws that require a woman to obey her husband make domestic violence claims difficult to file and spousal rape is not considered a crime. Malaysia also has laws similar to those described earlier in the areas of polygamy, divorce, and inheritance. In Pakistan most women who are raped often do not file charges because if they cannot prove that they did not consent they can be executed on charges of adultery. As Pakistan's courts do not give women's testimony the same weight as that of a man, the rapist can testify that there was consent and escape punishment while the woman is punished for adultery. Marital rape is not a crime and men who mutilate or kill their wives over accused adultery are rarely convicted. Female genital mutilation is practiced in Pakistan. Pakistan also has laws similar to those described earlier in the areas of divorce and inheritance.

Attempts to convince Muslim states to change this treatment is met with resistance, though several Muslim states like Morocco, Turkey, and Tunisia, have made some steps at improving the status of women. Other Muslim states and some Muslims in all of them consider the inferior status of women wholly appropriate as this is what they believe is mandated both by Islamic law and long-standing tradition within their states. Given this and the Western agenda of improving the status of women worldwide, this issue is likely to remain a significant one in international relations for some time to come.

Another issue on the international agenda is the issue of family planning. Unlike women's rights, this issue is not a particularly West vs. Islam issue. Rather it pits secular and economic concerns against the religious sentiments of several religious movements. Many consider family planning important, especially in the Third World, because population growth is a serious threat to a state's economic stability and its ability to modernize.

It is clear that population growth can offset development. If population growth occurs faster than growth in GNP, per capita GNP actually decreases. Thus, it can make a country even less able to provide for its people. Rising populations also increase the cost to the government for providing health care, sanitation, education, and other necessary social services. It also increases the amount of resources that must go to food supply and distribution. It increases the size of the workforce, often faster than jobs are created thus increasing the economic drain of welfare programs. All of this also reduces the resources available for investment in economic development. Thus population growth is not the primary source of economic hardship but it is a contributing factor.

One solution to this problem is family planning, to make available the information and means for people to use contraception and abortion. However, contraception and abortion are against the tenets of several religions. Thus, a diverse group of actors on the international scene oppose attempts by international organizations at promoting family planning. These include factions within U.S. politics, the Catholic Church, and many Islamic states and organizations. A common denominator of all of the aforementioned factions is that these issues are not only raised at the interstate level but also at the society level and hence are more transnational in character.

Conclusions

The purpose of this chapter has been to demonstrate that there are religious forms of organizations, institutions, and issues that are larger than any one state and are, thus, transnational. The phenomena of a political entity that transcends the political borders of a state and crosses nations suits in general, if not exactly, the transnational model of international politics as developed by Keohane and Nye already in 1970 (Keohane and Nye, 1970). Religious fundamentalism by definition exceeds the state-centric paradigm of international relations promoted by the West in both organizational terms and also issues. Fundamentalism or religious extremism because of its inherent contention with the modern state is an international phenomenon that has been playing a central role in both domestic and international politics. It also has its roots in processes inherent in the international system. Among the major religions because of several factors analyzed earlier, the Islamic manifestation of fundamentalism, political Islam, has been particularly active both within the Islamic world and in its confrontation with the West. Hence, political Islam in particular presents a challenge to the West's organization of international politics. Religious terrorism, especially since September 11, 2001, has played a part in reshaping the foreign policies of a number of states. Missionary movements often offend local governments and cultures. Finally, issues on the international agenda like human rights, women's rights, and family planning often overlap with religious issues.

CHAPTER 6

THE CLASH OF CIVILIZATIONS DEBATE

Ever since Huntington (1993a, 1996a,b) proposed his clash of civilizations thesis there has been a vigorous debate over its validity. Since Huntington's concept of civilizations considerably overlaps with religion, this means that, in essence, this debate has been over the role of religion in international relations. However, this discussion of religion is a very odd one in that most of those engaged in the debate, not in the least Huntington himself, went to great lengths to avoid the term religion. Rather, the focus was on culture, which just happened to be predominantly defined by religious identification.

This debate has also taken on a larger meaning because it is essentially over what, if anything, will define the nature of conflict in the post–Cold War era. According to Huntington civilizational conflicts will be the most common and intense forms of conflicts in the post–Cold War era. Yet, many others disagree arguing that other traits including religion and nationalism will define conflict in the post–Cold War era. Some even argue that conflict will decrease.

Be that as it may, any discussion of the role of religion in international relations would be incomplete without a discussion of the civilizations debate. This discussion proceeds in several stages. First, we assess the overlap between religion and Huntington's concept of civilizations. Second, we evaluate the debate over whether civilizations will be the basis for post–Cold War international relations. Third, we examine the comparative influence of civilizations and religion on ethnic conflict using a quantitative analysis of the MAR dataset.

The Overlapping Concepts of Ethnicity, Religion, and Civilizations

While Huntington's concept of civilizations strongly overlaps with religion, the two are not the same thing. This discussion is intended to assess the extent of this overlap. Although this discussion includes definitions of ethnicity and Huntington's concept of civilization, it does not include a detailed definition of religion. This is because religion is a difficult concept to define and involves complex theological issues that are beyond the scope of this discussion. Instead, for the purposes of this discussion the term religion refers to religious similarities and differences between individuals groups. That is, religion is defined here as a basis of identity. While, clearly, identity is only one aspect of religion, this simplification of the term is useful in that it allows us to proceed with our discussion of the overlap between religion, ethnicity, and civilizations while avoiding many difficult issues that are beyond the scope of this study.

Huntington's concept of civilizations includes elements of both ethnicity and religion from his definition of a civilization as

> the highest cultural grouping of people and the broadest level of cultural identity people have short of what distinguishes humans from other species. It is defined by both common language, history, *religion*, customs, institutions and by the subjective self identification of people.[1] (Huntington's 1993a: 24)

The extent of the overlap between Huntington's concept of civilization and religion is made clearer by an examination of the list of civilizations he provides. It is important to emphasize that many take Huntington to task over his division of the world into civilizations, both in principle and with the specifics of these divisions.[2] This discussion is limited to the inclusion of religion into the concept of civilizations by Huntington himself. This is because, the object here is, among other things, to compare Huntington's concept of civilizations to religion and the only way to do so is to understand and operationalize Huntington's definitions.

Huntington (1993a, 1996a: 45–48) divides the world into eight major civilizations: Western, Confucian/Sinic, Japanese, Islamic, Hindu, Slavic-Orthodox, Latin American, and "possibly" African. All of these civilizations, save one, include some aspect of religion in their definition and some of them appear to be wholly defined by religion. The Islamic civilization appears to be defined solely by religion and any Islamic group, whatever other cultural traits they may possess, are included in this civilization. The Hindu civilization seems to also be defined wholly by religion, but Hindus tend to be less culturally diverse than Muslims. The Confucian/Sinic civilization includes Confucianism, and by inference Buddhism,[3] as a "major component" (Huntington, 1996a: 45). The West is uniformly Christian and is differentiated from other civilizations by religious factors including "the effects of the Reformation and . . . [its] combined Catholic and Protestant cultures" (Huntington, 1996a: 46) as well as its adherence to the concept of separation of Church and state (Huntington, 1996a: 70). The Slavic-Orthodox civilization is differentiated from the West in that it is based on the Orthodox branch of Christianity developed separately from Western Christianity and had "limited exposure" to important Western religious and historical events including the Renaissance, Reformation, and Enlightenment (Huntington, 1996a: 45–46). The Latin American civilization is distinguished from the West, in part, by the fact that it is primarily Catholic (Huntington, 1996a: 46). The Japanese civilization has a distinct religious tradition including Shintoism.

The African culture is the only civilization that is not religiously homogeneous. The civilization's members belong to various Christian faiths and animist religions. Rather, Huntington defines this civilization based on a common sense of identity. Using self-identity as the basis of group definition has considerable precedent in the literature on ethnicity. In fact, many definitions of ethnicity are based on the concept of self-perception and definition. For example, Gurr (1993a: 3) defines ethnicity as follows:

> . . . in essence, communal [ethnic] groups are psychological communities: groups whose core members share a distinctive and enduring collective identity based on cultural traits and lifeways that matter to them and to others with whom they interact.
>
> People have many possible bases for communal identity: shared historical experiences or myths, *religious beliefs*, language, ethnicity, region of residence, and, in castelike systems, customary occupations. Communal groups—which are also referred to as ethnic groups, minorities and peoples—usually are distinguished by several reenforcing traits. *The key to identifying communal groups is not the presence of a particular trait or combination of traits, but rather in the shared perception that the defining traits, whatever they are, set the group apart.*[4]

Thus, Gurr's definition of ethnicity is based on ascriptive traits that build the perception among a group that they are a group. Carment and James (1997b: 2), Deutsch (1981: 55), Horowitz (1985: 68), and Romanucci-Ross and DeVos, (1995), among others, similarly argue that self-perception and identity are the most important components of ethnicity.

Interestingly, this definition is markedly similar to Huntington's definition of civilizations. There are only two significant differences between the two definitions. First, Gurr, while including it in his definition of ethnicity, in practice places considerably less emphasis on religion than does Huntington in his definition of civilizations. While for Gurr, religion is just one of many traits that can contribute to a common identity, for Huntington it appears to be a major defining trait that is an essential part of all of his civilization save one. Furthermore, Huntington is unsure of whether the African civilization, the one civilization with no obvious religious character, is, in fact, a civilization. Second, Huntington's and Gurr's definitions differ in the broadness of the identity groupings that they address. Huntington's civilizations are the "highest cultural grouping of people and the broadest level of cultural identity" (Huntington, 1993a: 24). In contrast, Gurr's definition of ethnicity defines a much more narrow base of identity. In fact, Huntington's civilizations can be said to be amalgamations of many similar ethnic and national groups. Thus, he predicts that the more narrow ethnic identifications described by Gurr will become less relevant in the post–Cold War era and will be replaced by broader civilizational identities.

This view of civilizations as based on identity supports Huntington's inclusion of the African civilization in his list of civilizations. However, that Huntington qualifies his inclusion of this civilization, which is the only one based fully on nonreligious identification, in his list of civilizations implies that religion truly is the basis for his concept of civilizations.

There is no shortage of additional evidence that Huntington's concept of civilizations is based on religion. First, he argues that the process of social and political modernization has weakened local identities as well as the nation-state. As a result, in much of the world, religion is filling this gap and is becoming the basis for identity (Huntington, 1993a: 25–29, 1996a: 95–99). Second, Huntington (1996a: 100–101) similarly argues that the failure of Communism, socialism, and other Western (economic) ideas have created an ideological vacuum, which religion has begun to fill. This argument is echoed by many others, especially Mark Juergensmeyer (1993) who argues that the failure of governments in the Third World based on Western ideologies like liberalism, Communism, socialism, nationalism, and fascism to provide political justice and economic prosperity has resulted in a crisis of legitimacy for these ideologies. Consequently religion is growing stronger as a local and more authentic basis for legitimacy. Third, he makes a number of explicit statements that he bases his definition of civilizations on religion. When he discusses the history of civilizations he argues, "the major civilizations of human history have been closely identified with the world's great religions" (Huntington, 1996a: 42). When listing his civilizations in his book he states, "religion is a central characteristic in defining civilizations" (Huntington, 1996a: 47). When discussing civilizational wars he notes, "since religion . . . is the principle defining characteristic of civilizations, fault line wars are almost always between peoples of different religions" (Huntington, 1996a: 253).

Thus, when Huntington uses the word civilizations, to a great extent he is also invoking religion. Yet the two are not exactly the same. For instance, he divides the Christian world into three civilizations based on various denominational and historical differences. Yet he ignores similar differences within the Islamic civilization. The most important, but by no means the only, such difference is the split between the Sunni and Shi'i branches of the religion. It is also arguable that the cultural differences between Arab and Asian Muslims are at least as broad as the differences between the West and Latin America. Thus, while Huntington bases his definition of civilizations to a great extent on religion, he is inconsistent in the extent to which he applies religious differences in constructing his list of civilizations.

The overlap between ethnicity and civilizations is more straightforward. Ethnic groups are groups that define their identities more narrowly than do civilizational groups. Most civilizations contain several ethnic groups. Based on this, any conflict between groups of different civilizations (civilizational conflicts) will also be between two different ethnic groups. However, conflicts between two different ethnic groups may or may not also be civilizational conflicts.

The Debate Over the Clash of Civilizations Hypothesis

Since the appearance of Huntington's 1993 article in *Foreign Affairs*, there has been a spirited debate over his argument that future conflicts would be between civilizations. One reply, also published in *Foreign Affairs*, was actually written in the form of a poem (Tipson, 1997). Since his later book and articles basically elaborate on the argument made in the *Foreign Affairs* article, this discussion here will evaluate this debate based on the arguments that are made regarding the subject, rather than on a chronological basis. Also, given the considerable volume of discussion on this issue it is beyond the scope of this work to assess all of Huntington's critics and supporters. Accordingly, the sources cited here are meant to be representative of the debate as a whole, rather than an exhaustive discussion of the debate.

Huntington's clash of civilizations thesis is relatively simple. With the end of the Cold War, the old basis for international relations and conflict based on East–West rivalry has ended. It is to be replaced by conflict between the major world civilizations that are described earlier. There are three types of conflict that will occur. The first type is core state conflicts. This type of conflict is based on the assumption that most civilizations have a core state or core states that are the vanguard of that civilization. These states tend to be the most powerful states in their civilizations and are often the origin of the civilizations culture. For example, the United States is the core state of the Western civilizations and China is the core state of the Sinic/Confucian civilization. These core states are expected to compete in the world arena leading to tensions between them.

The second type of conflict are international fault-line conflicts. These conflicts occur between states of different civilizations that happen to border each other. For example, the tensions between India and Pakistan can be considered a fault-line conflict between states belonging to the Hindu and Islamic civilizations. The final type of conflict is a domestic fault-line conflict. This type of conflict is between groups belonging to different civilizations within the same state. This includes tensions caused by the Islamic immigrants in many Western states.

Huntington further argues that the most violent of the civilizations is the Islamic civilization that is said to have "bloody borders." He expects that tensions between the Western and Islamic civilization will be particularly intense.

It is important to note that many of the criticisms of Huntington's theory that are described here contradict each other and, in fact, some of the individual critics contradict themselves and many attack Huntington's theory along several different lines. While it is possible to divide the criticisms of Huntington's theories into several schools of thought, this is avoided here because of the overlapping of critics and criticisms. Rather, the debate is presented in the form of the types of arguments that are posed in criticism of Huntington's clash of civilizations theory.

First, many argue that conflicts will continue to be fought along traditional lines. While most of these arguments, such as those of Ajami (1993), Gray (1998), and Pfaff (1998) focus on international conflict, their arguments are applicable to domestic conflict. That is, most of these authors argue that traditional realpolitik theories still provide the best explanation for international conflict but their arguments can be generalized to apply to domestic conflict if one focuses on their most basic argument: that those factors that caused conflict during the Cold War will continue to do so after it. Similarly, many like Beedham (1999), Kirkpatrick et al. (1993), Halliday (1997), Heilbrunn (1998), Hunter (1998), Kader (1998), Kirth (1994), Rosecrance (1998), Tipson (1997), and Yamazaki (1996) argue that the civilizations Huntington describes are not united and most conflicts, both international and domestic, will be between members of the same civilizations. These conflicts will be based on the same historical, national, and economic issues that were the basis for conflict in the past. Walt (1998) combines these two arguments stating that nationalism remains the most important factor in the post–Cold War era, making conflicts within civilizations as likely as conflicts between them.

Interestingly, most of those who argue that civilizations will not be the basis for post–Cold War conflict do not argue that post–Cold War conflicts will not be religious ones. In this case the difference between civilizations and religion is important. Much of the conflict within the Islamic world, for example, is between Sunni and Shi'i Muslims. Also, conflicts between Protestant and Catholic Christians, such as the conflict in Northern Ireland, would be considered to involve religious but not civilizational identity. While, by no means is it claimed here that any of these critics claim that religion will be the basis for post–Cold War conflict, it is posited here that the contentions of these critics do not necessarily contradict the argument that a significant portion of these conflicts will be between groups who belong to different religions.

Second, many argue that the world is becoming more united and interdependent, thus causing a general reduction of conflict in the post–Cold War era. Anwar (1998) and Tipson (1997), for example, argue that factors like economic interdependence, communications, and world integration will lead to a world civilization that will rise above conflicts. Ahari (1997) makes a normative version of this argument, saying that the only culture that should occupy the world is the human culture. Ikenberry (1997) believes that the process of globalization does not even need to reach a very high level, arguing that "a belief in universalism and global cultural homogenization is not necessary to pursue an order that goes beyond the West. All that is needed are states with commitments to democracy, free markets and the rule of law." Also, Halliday (1997) notes that there has been a historical borrowing and mixing among cultures, making it difficult to argue that the civilizations Huntington describes are distinct. Unlike the previous type of criticism, if this one is correct, religion will become less important on the world scene, except perhaps as a basis for dialogue among different groups.

Third, many argue that Huntington ignored an important post–Cold War phenomenon that will impact on conflict, thereby making his theory irrelevant. That is, many argue that some factor other than civilizations will be the basis for world conflict or the lack thereof. Viorst (1997) argues that Huntington ignores the fact that the world is better at managing conflict than it used to be. He also believes that population and environment issues will define world politics in the future. Ajami (1993) argues that Huntington underestimates the power of modernity and secularism and that people are more interested in economic prosperity than maintaining their traditions. Barber (1998) argues that power in the post–Cold War era will be defined by control over information technology. Senghass (1998) argues that most ethnopolitical conflicts result from protracted discrimination rather than cultural roots. Rosecrance (1998) points out that military power overshadowed civilizations in the past and there is no reason it cannot do so in the future. He also argues, as do Hunter (1998) and Nussbaum (1997), that economic power is the most important type of power today. Kirkpatrick et al. (1993) believes that since other civilizations want to be like the West, the predicted West vs. non-West conflicts will not occur. Similarly Mahbubani (1993) argues that the non-West wants Western leadership and is, in fact, afraid that the West is weakening. Howell (1997) argues for an opposite trend of the West becoming easternized.

Fourth, many argue that Huntington has his facts wrong. Some, Anwar (1998), Hassner (1997a), Heilbrunn (1998), Kader (1998), Neckermann (1998), and Walt (1997), simply argue that the facts do not fit Huntington's theory. Pfaff (1998) accuses Huntington of ignoring facts. Some, like Hassner (1997b), even go as far as to accuse Huntington of bending the facts to fit his theory.

Fifth, nearly every empirical study on the topic found Huntington's theory to be incorrect. These studies include: a study of militarized international disputes which shows that intra-civilizational conflicts were more likely than inter-civilizational conflicts, civilizational conflicts, if anything, waned as the Cold War ended and that Huntington's West vs. the rest and Islamic threat to the West predictions were unfounded (Russett et al., 2000);[5] another study found that trade interdependence, economic growth, relative material capabilities, alliance membership, and territorial contiguity provide better explanations for international militarized disputes than Huntington's concept of civilizations (Henderson, 2002); two studies of international war found that cultural factors do not have any consistent impact (Henderson, 1997, 1998); another study of international war shows that, if anything, civilizational differences make states less likely to go to war (Henderson and Tucker, 2001); a study found that UN General Assembly voting behavior is better explained by East–West alignments, realism, interdependence, and political similarity than by civilizations; a study of civil wars found political factors to be more influential than cultural ones (Henderson and Singer, 2000); another study of civil wars found that civilizational conflict has dropped since the end of the Cold War and there is no evidence of a change in the relative intensity of violence in civilizational and noncivilizational civil wars (Fox, 2003b); and several studies of ethnic conflict found that there was no change in the dynamics of ethnic conflict, not in the ratio of civilizational to noncivilizational conflicts with the end of the Cold War, including the extent of conflicts involving Muslim groups, and that post–Cold War ethnic conflicts were not particularly civilizational (Ellingsen, 2000; Fox, 2001b, 2002b; Gurr, 1994).

However, not all quantitative studies are wholly inconsistent with Huntington's theory. For instance, a series of studies shows there to be a connection between international ethnic alliances and international conflict (Davis and Moore, 1997; Davis et al., 1997). However, while these studies are consistent with the clash of civilizations theory, they do not directly test it in that they focus on ethnic and not civilizational conflict and in that they do not compare the Cold War and post–Cold War eras.

Also, a series of studies on terrorism, found that in the 1980s and 1990s terrorism was becoming more civilizational in that most terrorism was by Islamic groups against non-Muslims and most new terrorist organizations were Islamic (Weinberg and Eubanks, 1998; Weinberg et al., 2002). While these studies do directly test Huntington's theory they are also not conclusive because terrorism is one tactic among many available to groups engaged in conflict. Thus, this study shows that Muslim groups disproportionally select terrorism as their preferred tactic but cannot directly speak to whether this is reflective of all violent domestic conflict including guerrilla warfare and high-intensity civil war.

The many studies mentioned earlier that focus on a broader range of civil and ethnic wars are more broadly focused and most likely represent the true disposition of civilizational versus noncivilizational war. Thus, the preponderance of the empirical evidence indicates that the facts do not fit Huntington's clash of civilizations theory.

A fifth type of critique of Huntington's theory focuses on his methodology. Hassner (1997a) and Pfaff (1998) accuse Huntington of oversimplification. Beedham (1999), Pfaff (1998), Smith (1997), and Tipson (1997) question Huntington's assessment of what are the world's civilizations. Ikenberry (1997) similarly argues that the features that Huntington feels make the West unique are, in fact, not cultural factors nor are they unique to the West. Heilbrunn (1998) notes that Huntington, in his various writings, contradicts himself. Gurr (1994) and Halliday (1997) note that Huntington's evidence is completely anecdotal, leaving room for many to cite counterexamples. Similarly, Senghass (1998), Rosecrance (1998), and Walt (1997) argue that Huntington provides no systematic analysis of the link between civilizational controversies and political behavior. That is, a quantitative, or at least a more systematic, analysis of Huntington's is necessary before it can be properly evaluated. This is the same argument made here and, as noted earlier, the vast majority of quantitative studies contradict Huntington's theory. However, Pfaff (1998) accuses Huntington of the opposite. He argues that political science in general, and Huntington specifically, have wrongly made the behavioral assumption that political behavior can be explained scientifically.

Sixth, many argue that because of his popularity among policy makers, Huntington's theory is a self-fulfilling prophecy (Hassner, 1997a; Pfaff,

1998; Singhua, 1997; Smith, 1997; Tipson, 1997 and Walt, 1997). Similarly, Anwar (1998) and Gungwu (1997a) accuse Huntington of making unwarranted doomsday predictions. That is, Huntington's theory is said to have caused policy makers to expect clashes with other civilizations, especially the Islamic civilization. If these predictions, combined with the activities of groups like Al-Qaeda succeed in convincing Western policy makers that Islam is a threat, it will be treated as one. If this occurs, conflicts between the West and Islam would probably be given more attention and provoke a more conflictive response from the West making escalation more likely and peaceful resolution less common than may otherwise have been likely.

Seventh, Aysha (2003) argues Huntington himself does not believe his own theory and Huntington's true intent was to address four problems in U.S. domestic politics. First, Huntington sees multiculturalism as a threat to America's commitment to individualistic liberalism. Creating culturally based enemies is a way to counteract this trend. Second, during the Cold War, U.S. identity was to a great extent based on its fight against Communism and Communism's collapse led to an identity crisis in the United States. Huntington's theory gives the United States an enemy in order to shore up its identity. Third, an international crisis is a good way to strengthen the ties between citizens and the federal government to counter a rising tide of anti-federalism. Finally, economic globalization is eroding U.S. nationalism. Getting people to believe in the clash of civilizations theory will help to counter this trend.

Despite all this, Huntington is not without his supporters. Gregg (1997), Gungwu (1997a,b), Hardjono (1997), Harris (1996), Murphey (1998), Naff (1998), and Seamon (1998), and Walid (1997), among others, agree with his argument and use it to make policy prescriptions. Marshall (1998) agrees with Huntington's thesis, arguing that the majority of conflicts are occurring along religious divides. Even some of Huntington's critics, including, Anwar (1998), Hassner (1997a), Heilbrunn (1998), agree that it may be true for at least part of the world, especially Huntington's West vs. Islam predictions.

Even many of Huntington's detractors admit that if he is wrong, he is brilliantly wrong. For example, Hassner (1997a), who is among Huntington's most vehement critics (his review of Huntington's book is titled "Morally Objectionable, Politically Dangerous") admits that Huntington "is perhaps the most brilliant, articulate, versatile, and creative living political scientist." Similarly, Heilbrunn (1998) states, "Huntington may be America's most distinguished political scientist. He is certainly the most exasperating."

Huntington's (1993b) reply to some of these critiques can be best summed up by his statement: "got a better idea?" He cites Kuhn's (1970) famous work on scientific paradigms which, among other things, argues that a paradigm need only be better than its competitors, it doesn't have to explain everything. Huntington argues that the Cold War paradigm was not perfect, and neither is the Civilizations paradigm. There were anomalous events that contradicted each paradigm. However, both paradigms have strong explanatory power for the era that they explain, and, more importantly, this explanatory power is greater than any competing paradigm. He responds to the arguments that post–Cold War conflicts will occur on a level more micro than civilizations by restating his argument that groups of states have strong bonds of history, culture, language, religion, and location that bond them into civilizations. He also responds to what he calls "one world theories." He notes that the argument that all of the world will become liberal democracies is deterministic and assumes only one historical alternative. He responds to the assumption that communications make the world smaller, thus causing unification, by arguing that the increased level of interaction will only cause more conflict. He asserts that the argument that modernization will lead to homogenization does not fit the facts.[6] Finally, he argues that a universal civilization can only be the result of a universal power, which, as of yet, does not exist.

In his book, Huntington (1996a: 29–40, 59–78, 128) further elaborates on this theme of "got a better idea?" He argues that the four competing paradigms of world unity, that the world will be divided in two along economic or cultural lines, realism, and anarchy, cannot be both parsimonious and at the same time have good explanatory power to the extent to which the civilizations paradigm can. That is, he argues that the civilizational paradigm is the simplest theory that has the ability to explain real-world events. He also addresses the argument that the world will coalesce into one civilization in more detail. He argues that the major components of a civilization include language and religion, both of which serve to divide the world, rather than unite it. The end of the Cold War has not united the world, rather it has released the forces of "the more fundamental divisions of humanity" including civilizational conflicts. He repeats the aforementioned argument regarding increased interaction causing increased opportunity for conflict. Finally, he argues that modernization does not necessarily mean Westernization. It is possible for other civilizations to modernize economically without adopting Western culture. He also admits that balance of power considerations can also play a role in political alliances but in the long run they are subordinate to civilizational considerations.

In all, the aforementioned discussion establishes, if nothing else, that there is considerable debate over the nature of conflict in the post–Cold War era. Huntington predicts a rise in civilizational conflict. However many have opposing predictions. These include that things will continue as before and that there will be a drop in conflict due to the world's growing interdependence. In addition, many dispute Huntington's assertion that civilizations as opposed to more conventional explanations for conflict are the key to understanding conflict on the post–Cold War era.

More importantly, many of the criticisms that apply to Huntington's theory do not apply to the major argument of this book, and to our main concern in this book, namely that religion continues to have an influence on international relations. The first argument that the bases for conflict during the Cold War will continue to be important after it, as noted earlier, does not contradict the argument that religion can influence conflict. This is because religion was one of the bases for conflict during the Cold War. Furthermore, while Huntington claims that civilizations will be the primary basis for conflict in the post–Cold War era, it is not claimed here that religion will be the primary driving force behind international relations. Rather, it is argued here that though religion is an important factor in international relations, it is only one among several important factors. This argument regarding religion is considerably less ambitious than Huntington's arguments regarding civilizations and it is arguable that many of Huntington's critics would not dispute this more humble claim.

The second argument that the world is unifying posits that conflict as we know it is ending. Thus, it is unlikely that religion will be a basis for this conflict. However there is no reason to believe that if world unification actually occurs, religion will not be a part of this process. In fact, there is a growing literature that argues that religion can be a basis for conflict resolution,[7] thus it can also be part of the process of bringing people together.

The third argument that Huntington ignored some aspect of international relations that makes his theory irrelevant can also be applied to religion. Although his theory incorporates religion, it does so in a distorted manner. Thus, it is arguable that he also ignores religion in its true form.

The rest of the arguments apply to Huntington's methodology and motives in constructing and proving his specific theory. None of this contradicts the argument that religion is an important influence on international relations.

The Comparative Impact of Religion and Civilizations on Ethnic Conflict

Until this point the focus of this discussion has been on the overlap between the concepts of civilization and religion. The basic elements of this discussion can be summarized in the following two points. First, while there is an overlap between the concepts of religion, ethnicity, and civilizations, they are not the same thing. Second, there is considerable debate over whether Huntington's predictions are correct.

The purpose of this section of the discussion of the civilizations debate is to make use of empirical data from the Minorities at Risk (MAR) dataset in order to assess whether Huntington's predictions of an increase in civilizational conflict in the post–Cold War era are correct.[8] This analysis attempts to answer several questions. First, what is the overlap between religious and civilizational conflict? Second, has the amount of civilizational and religious conflict changed since the end of the Cold War? Third, are civilizational and/or religious conflicts more violent than other types of conflict? Fourth, do more conventional theories of conflict provide better predictors of which conflicts will be more violent? Fifth, is there any truth in Huntington's predictions that the Islamic civilization will be the most violent and the greatest threat to the West in the post–Cold War era?

Definitions and Parameters

It is necessary at this point to clarify the parameters of this analysis and to define what is meant by several key terms. This analysis is based on the MAR dataset that uses ethnic minorities as a unit of analysis. This means for every ethnic conflict there is a majority group that controls the state and a minority group that lives within that state. Because this dataset focuses on ethnic conflict, all of the civilizational conflicts analyzed fall into the category of fault-line conflicts within states.

For the purposes of this analysis, conflict is defined as the combined level of protest and rebellion in which an ethnic minority engages in a given year. This is achieved by adding the protest[9] and rebellion[10] scales provided in the MAR data, which are available at the time of this writing on a yearly basis between 1985 and 1998.

A conflict is a religious conflict if the two groups involved belong to different religions. This does not include groups belonging to different denominations. A conflict is separatist if the minority group currently expresses a desire for some form of separatism or in the past expressed such a desire.[11]

A conflict is a civilizational conflict if the two groups involved belong to different civilizations. While this definition is a simple one, applying it to ethnic conflict is problematic for several reasons. First, Huntington is unclear as to whether he includes Buddhism in his list of civilizations. While, in his book, Huntington (1996a) hints that Buddhism may constitute a separate civilization, he appears to include it as part of the Confucian/Sinic civilization. The Buddhist civilization appears on his map of "The World of Civilizations: Post-1990" (26–27). He also infers that there is a Buddhist civilization on page 257 table 10.1 where he argues that the Chinese–Tibetan conflict is intercivilizational "since it is clearly a clash between Confucian Han Chinese and Lamaist Buddhist Tibetans." Otherwise, one would assume, as did Gurr (1994), that Buddhists were included in the Sinic/Confucian civilization. This is mainly because Huntington does not include it in his listing of civilizations. Also, on page 45, Huntington includes "the related cultures of Vietnam and Korea," which are countries with Buddhist majorities, in the Sinic/Confucian civilization. Finally, Huntington, on page 48, concludes, "Buddhism, although a major religion, has not been the basis of a major civilization." Based on this final statement and the fact Buddhism is not included in his listing of civilizations either in his book or Huntington's (1993a) article, this study operationally includes Buddhist groups in the Sinic/Confucian civilization.

Second, it is unclear to which civilizations certain states belong. Israel, for example, is a Jewish state. This is problematic because Huntington's definitions are based largely upon religion and he does not discuss Judaism.

For the purposes of this study, Israel is included in the Western civilization because, other than religion, Israel exhibits most of the characteristics of the Western civilization and because the Islamic states in the region consider it a Western intrusion onto the region. Likewise in the Philippines, the majority group is Asiatic but they are mostly Westernized and Christian. In this case, religion was the deciding factor and they were coded as Western.

Third, many minority groups are similarly difficult to categorize due to the vagueness of Huntington's definitions. The Afro-Americans in the United States and several Latin American countries could be considered either Western due to their religious affiliations or African because the African civilization is based on identity. For operational purposes, these groups are considered part of the African civilization because there are many indications, especially in the United States, that many Afro-Americans consider themselves to have a distinct identity which is, in part, tied to their African origins. Black Moslem groups in Africa are similarly difficult to categorize. They can be considered part of either the African or Islamic civilizations. Since Huntington seems to be ambivalent about the African civilization and defines the Islamic civilization wholly on the basis of religion, these and all other Moslem groups are considered part of the Islamic civilization. The Druze, Bahai, and Sikhs, like the Jews, are groups that do not fit well into any of Huntington's categories. Since the Druze and Bahai religions are considered Islamic offshoots and the Sikh religion combines elements of the Islamic and Hindu faiths, ethnic groups of these three religions are considered here part of the Islamic civilization. Another problematic group are the Gagauz in Moldova. They are Orthodox Christian but not European in origin. For operational purposes, religion was the deciding factor and they are included in the Slavic-Orthodox civilization. Finally, there are many minority groups that are of mixed origins. An excellent example are the Roma minorities in Europe. These groups were coded as "mixed" and clashes between them and other groups are considered non-civilizational conflicts.

Fourth, a major category of minority group does not fit into any of Huntington's civilizations. This category is indigenous minorities like native Americans or the Aborigines of Australia. While the religion, race, and culture of these groups vary widely, indigenous peoples have a common historical experience that in many ways makes them more similar to each other than to any of Huntington's civilizations. For this reason, these groups are not considered here to be part of any civilization and conflicts involving them are considered not civilizational.

Finally, the MAR3 dataset is designed to assess the relationship between majority and minority groups within a state. The majority group is operationally defined as the group that controls the state. Accordingly, in cases of civil war, there is no such majority group. This only affects three cases: Afghanistan, Bosnia, and Lebanon. All cases in Afghanistan are coded as not civilizational because all four ethnic groups are Islamic. In

Bosnia, the three ethnic groups, the Serbs, Croats, and Moslems belong to three different civilizations (Slavic-Orthodox, Western, and Islamic respectively). Accordingly, these three cases are coded as civilizational conflicts. Similarly, Lebanon is ruled by a combination of Moslems and Christians. Accordingly, all of the cases in Lebanon are considered civilizational clashes.

This exercise of placing groups into Huntington's categories reveals a major weakness of his theory: that it is too vague. That a good number of ethnic groups are difficult or impossible to place into specific civilizations proves, if nothing else, that Huntington's theory is not sufficiently rigorous. As the analysis describe later shows, it is also not a very accurate theory.

Analysis

The first question asked in this analysis is what is the overlap between religious and civilizational conflict? The analysis in table 6.1 shows that while there is considerable overlap between the two, they are not the same thing. During the Cold War 26.2 percent of ethnic conflicts were either only civilizational or only religious, after the Cold War this percentage dropped slightly to 23.7 percent. Thus, in about one-quarter of ethnic conflicts civilization and religion do not coincide. If conflicts between ethnic groups of different denominations are included as religious conflicts, religion and civilization do not overlap in about one-fifth of ethnic conflicts. Thus, at least for ethnic conflict, civilizations and religion, while similar, cannot be considered the same thing.

The second question asked in this analysis is has the amount of civilizational and religious conflict changed since the end of the Cold War? Huntington predicts a significant increase in civilizational conflict. The analysis in table 6.1 shows that this did not occur. In fact, the distribution between Cold War years (1945–1989) and post–Cold War years (1990–1998) ethnic conflict is nearly identical. In no category was there a change of more than a few percentage points. Such a small change is to be expected

Table 6.1　Comparative Number of Religious and Civilizational Conflicts During and After the Cold War Era

	Cold War era		Post–Cold War era	
	N	%	N	%
Conflicts neither religious or civilizational	114	48.9	139	50.5
Conflicts civilizational only	28	12.0	34	12.4
Conflicts religious only	33	14.2	31	11.3
Conflicts both religious and civilizational	58	24.9	71	25.8
All civilizational conflicts	86	36.9	105	38.2
All religious conflicts	91	39.1	102	36.1

because of the many changes in ethnic conflict that occurred at the end of the Cold War. One reason for this is that the breakup of several states in the former Soviet bloc caused many minority groups to become majority groups, and vice versa. For example, many former minorities in the USSR, including the Azerbaijanis, Belorussians, Estonians, Georgians, Kazakhs, Kyrgys, Latvians, Maldivians, Tajiks, Turkmen, Ukrainians, and Uzbeks all now have their own states. Furthermore, many of these states have large ethnic Russian minorities. Also, the end of the Communist dictatorships allowed many formerly quiet ethnic minorities to become more politically active. Thus, it is expected that there would be some minor changes in the distribution of ethnic conflicts. That these changes are so minor show that, at least for ethnic conflict, there has been no significant change in the extent of religious and civilizational conflict with the end of the Cold War.

The third question asked in this analysis is are civilizational and/or religious conflicts more violent than other types of conflict? The answer to this question, shown in figure 6.1, is no for civilizational conflict but yes for religious conflict. Throughout the 1985–1998 period, the average level of violence in civilizational conflicts is lower or roughly equal to that of non-civilizational conflict. Religious conflicts, however, are consistently more violent than nonreligious conflicts throughout this period. They are also more violent than both civilizational and non-civilizational conflicts. Thus, religion is a better predictor of which ethnic conflicts will be violent than is civilization.

The fourth question asked in this analysis is do more conventional theories of conflict provide better predictors of which conflicts will be more violent? In the case of ethnic conflict, the most important conventional predictor of violence is separatism. In fact, no single factor is more important in determining whether an ethnic minority will engage in violence

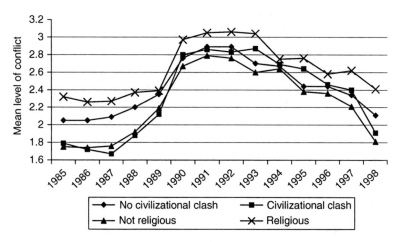

Figure 6.1　Mean Levels of Religious and Civilizational Ethnic Conflict, 1985–1998

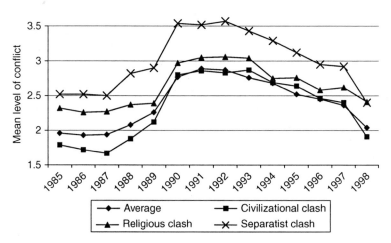

Figure 6.2   Comparative Levels of Civilizational, Religious, and Separatist
Conflict, 1985–1998

than whether it is separatist and seeking some form of self-determination (Gurr, 1993a,b). Accordingly, figure 6.2, compares the impact of separatism, civilizations, and religion on ethnic conflict.[12] While civilizational conflicts are near or below the average level of violence and religious conflicts are slightly above the average level of violence, separatist conflicts are considerably above the average level of violence. Thus, separatism is an even better predictor of those conflicts that are most likely to be violent than is religion. Also, civilizations has no value whatsoever as a predictor of violence in ethnic conflicts. This means that those critics of Huntington who argue that those factors which in the past cause conflicts will continue to so do in the future are correct, at least with regard to ethnic conflict.

The analysis in figure 6.3 further examines the relationship between religion and separatism with regard to ethnic conflict. It shows that, the most violent form of ethnic conflict is combined religious-separatist conflict. That is, ethnic minorities are most likely to be violent when they are both separatist and religiously different from the majority group in their state. However, it is important to note that the most important of these two variables is separatism. This is demonstrated by the fact that few ethnic minorities engage in rebellion unless they are separatist. Thus, it can be said, that a major cause of ethnic violence is separatism and religion is a strong exacerbating factor. Civilizations, in contrast, do not enter into the equation.

The final question asked in this analysis is whether there is any truth in Huntington's predictions that the Islamic civilization will be the most violent and the greatest threat to the West in the post–Cold War era. The analysis in table 6.2 shows that there has been little change in Islamic participation in ethnic conflict since the end of the Cold War with one exception. This exception is that conflicts within the Islamic civilization have

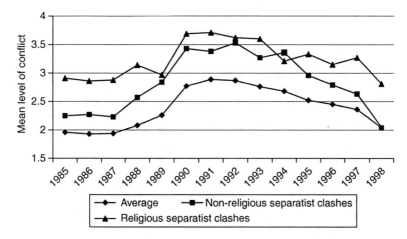

Figure 6.3 Religious versus Nonreligious Separatist Conflicts, 1985–1998

Table 6.2 Islamic and Western Involvement in Civilizational Conflict*

Type of conflict	Groups involved	Cold War era		Post–Cold War era	
		N	% of all ethnic conflict	N	% of all ethnic conflict
Civilizational conflicts	Islam vs. West	13	5.6	18	6.5
	Islam vs. non-West	41	17.6	50	18.2
	Other civilizational conflicts	32	13.7	37	13.5
	Total	86	36.9	105	38.2
Non-civilizational conflicts	Within Islam	25	10.7	38	13.8
	Within West	9	3.9	11	4.0
	Other noncivilizational conflicts	113	48.5	121	44.0
	Total	147	63.1	170	61.8
All conflicts involving Islamic groups		79	33.9	106	38.5
All ethnic conflicts		233	—	275	—

Note
* This table appeared previously in Fox (2001b).

increased significantly. This type of conflict rose from 10.7 percent of all ethnic conflict during the Cold War to 13.8 percent of all ethnic conflict after the Cold War. This is a rise of about 29 percent. In fact, this is the only significant change of any kind in the pattern of ethnic conflict since

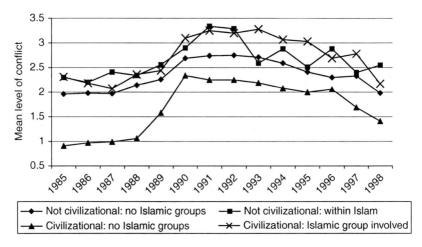

Figure 6.4   Mean level of Conflict Involving Islamic Groups, 1985–1998

the end of the Cold War. Thus, Huntington was correct in that the Islamic civilization would become more bloody with the end of the Cold War but he was wrong in predicting that this blood would be between them and other civilizations.

The analysis in figure 6.4 compares the levels of violence in conflicts involving Islamic and non-Islamic groups. The results show that conflicts involving Islamic groups are more violent than conflicts not involving Islamic groups, but that it seems to make little difference whether these conflicts are civilizational or not. In fact, if anything, the conflicts within Islam are slightly more violent in that they are more violent in 8 of the 14 years examined in this analysis. This provides further evidence for the finding that while Islamic groups may be bloody, there is nothing particularly civilizational about this blood.[13]

One potential reason for the level of violence exhibited by Islamic groups is that they are very likely to have separatist tendencies 73.2 percent of Islamic groups in Islamic states and 70.6 percent of Islamic groups in non-Islamic states are separatist as opposed to 44.6 percent and 38.9 percent, respectively, of non-Islamic groups. Thus, even among Islamic groups, more traditional explanations for ethnic conflict are more effective then Huntington's clash of civilizations theory.

In all, Huntington's clash of civilizations theory does not hold up well for ethnic conflict. There has been no real increase in civilizational ethnic conflict since the end of the Cold War. Civilizational conflicts are not more violent than are non-civilizational conflicts. Also, while Islamic groups are disproportionally violent, this has little to do with Huntington's concept of civilizations. It is arguable that since this analysis is limited to ethnic conflict, it does not disprove Huntington's theory. However, as discussed earlier, the results of nearly every other empirical study of the theory on both international and domestic conflict also contradict the theory.

Despite this failure of Huntington's concept of civilizations to account for post–Cold War conflict, religion does appear to have an influence. However, it is important to remember that this is only an influence, and religion is not the major driving force behind conflict in the post–Cold War era. Rather other factors like separatism seem to be more important. Nevertheless any understanding of ethnic conflict in the post–Cold War era, and for that matter during the Cold War as well, would be incomplete without taking religion into account.

Conclusions

In all, the civilizations debate can be paradoxically described as both the most important debate in international relations during the 1990s and as the biggest waste of time in that decade. It is an important debate in that it got people to begin to ask important questions including, but by no means limited to, what will be the nature of the international system and the basis for conflict within it now that the Cold War has ended, but history has not? Many of Huntington's critics were forced to provide an alternative to Huntington's proposed paradigm. This discussion continues to be a lively one and though no consensus has been reached, or is likely to be reached any time soon, it provides an important forum for a better understanding of the world system in which we live. Huntington also introduced nonrealist factors like culture into this debate, though many of his critics took exception to this, and he himself seems to be a realist. His main contribution, as far as this book is concerned is that he brought religion into international politics even if he did not call it by its real name.

However, it is unfortunate that the basis for this debate has been the clash of civilizations thesis. This has detracted from the discussion on several levels. First, the theory has so far not passed the empirical test. Most academics and nearly all empirical studies of the topic contradict the proposition that future conflict and competition in the world arena will be between civilizations as Huntington defines them. Clearly, much energy and time has been wasted on refuting Huntington, when it could have been used more productively toward examining more promising avenues of research.

More specifically, Huntington's theory has caused the academic community to focus on an odd artificial construct when more traditional concepts like nationalism, ethnicity, and religion are certainly more useful and accurate concepts in the understanding of international relations in the post–Cold War era. For example, the empirical results presented in this chapter show that religion and ethnic separatism have considerably more explanatory value than does Huntington's concept of civilizations. Similarly, the results presented in chapter 4 show that religion is an important factor in international intervention. In fact, in nearly every major empirical study of Huntington's theory, other factors prove to be important and civilizational factors prove to be unimportant.

It is probable that both Huntington's theory and the debate surrounding it are products of two long-term trends in the study of international relations. The first is its tendency to ignore religion. While it is argued here that religion has always been an important factor in international relations, this fact became even more obvious during the 1980s and 1990s. Events like the Iranian revolution, the rise of the Christian right in the United states, the growth of religious-based opposition movements and conflicts throughout the Islamic world, and the increasing prominence of ethnoreligious conflict all contributed to this. Yet it was the dogma of Western international relations scholars that religion was not relevant.

Then, along came Huntington with a theory in large part based on religion that somehow avoids using the term religion. It allowed a discussion of this increasing realization that the world was changing that was nevertheless less threatening to many of the sacred cows of the discipline. It is telling that many of those who criticized Huntington denied that religion was a factor in international relations, even in the distorted guise of civilizations.

The second factor that explains the civilizations debate is Western-centrism. Fox (2001b) demonstrates, as is demonstrated here, that from a global perspective there has been little change in civilizational conflict with the end of the Cold War. However

> From the perspective of the Western civilization . . . there is some justification for some, but not all, of Huntington's arguments. The majority of ethnic conflicts involving the West both during and after the Cold War have been civilizational. Also, the majority of post-Cold War civilizational ethnic conflicts involving the West are with Islamic groups and . . . this is new to the post-Cold War era. Thus, while Western involvement in civilizational ethnic conflicts has risen at about the same rate as other civilizations, much of this rise has been an increase in civilizational ethnic conflict with Islamic groups. (Fox, 2001b: 466)

This means that only when viewing the world from the viewpoint of a Westerner is there any reason to believe in the truth of Huntington's predictions regarding the Islamic threat to the West. If one looks at the situation from a more global perspective, or even from the perspective of another civilization, his theory does not hold up. That the one aspect of his theory that has gained some acceptance among Western academics is precisely his predictions regarding Islam further shows the extent to which his theory is Western-centric. This is especially the case when considering that academics in the Islamic world vigorously disagree with this prediction.

Yet, as discussed in chapter 5, there are tensions between Western and Islamic states for a variety of structural reasons including that Islamic doctrines and culture are not fully compatible with Western concepts of democracy and human rights. Another source of tension between the two cultures is the history of colonialism and the current distribution of power in the world system. Yet none of these factors are new to the post–Cold War era. Rather they represent processes and tensions that are centuries old. Furthermore, the most violent manifestations of these tensions, including but not limited to the attacks of September 11, 2001, are at the hands of a minority of Muslims who follow political Islam. Thus, we do not need a new theory to understand these phenomena, rather we need a better understanding and interpretation of more classical concepts. Furthermore, this clash of worldviews is present within the Islamic world with many relatively secular states fighting off fundamentalist challenges. Though, to be fair, the worldviews of those who rule secular Islamic states are also different from those of the West.

Thus the general situation with regard to the Islamic world mirrors the results presented here with regard to ethnic conflict. Conflict is common both within the Islamic world and between it and members of other religions. Also, none of this is new to the post–Cold War era, and scholars who study the Islamic world were writing about these tensions well before the end of the Cold War. The only reason it has now become more obvious to Westerners like Huntington, is that they are no longer preoccupied by the East vs. West ideological conflict of the Cold War.

In sum, it is not possible to discuss the current understanding of the role of religion in international relations by international relations scholars without addressing the civilizations debate. However, the debate is, perhaps, a better example of the failures of international relations theory than of its accomplishments. The clash of civilizations theory itself is, at best, a fatally flawed theory that is based on two of the greatest insufficiencies of international relations theory, its failure to directly address religion and its Western-centrism. Yet, the debate was successful in getting international relations scholars to at least indirectly address religion. It also forced a rethinking of old paradigms and how, if at all, they applied to the world after the Cold War. For these reasons alone the debate is an important one, even if it may be based on flawed premises. It is at this juncture that we turn from a global phenomena to a local dispute that also has a mixture of religious and ethnonational features.

CHAPTER 7

THE PALESTINIAN–ISRAELI CONFLICT: A CASE STUDY OF RELIGION AND INTERNATIONAL POLITICS

To examine the claims of our book and to explain them, we chose to analyze a case where religion played or conceivably could have played a most important role—the Israeli–Palestinian conflict. A salient event that demonstrates the importance of religion in recent times is the title or name given to the outburst of violence at the end of September 2000—"the Al-Aqsa intifada." Al-Aqsa is the name of the mosque situated on the Temple Mount in the middle of Jerusalem, holy both to Jews and Muslims. The official reason to this title was that on September 28, 2000, then Israeli opposition leader Ariel Sharon visited the Temple Mount in Jerusalem, an event considered by the Palestinians as the provocation to the second Intifada. A prelude to the outbreak of violence occurred in September 1996 when the right-wing Netanyahu government (1996–1999) authorized the opening of a tunnel in Jerusalem that led to the Haram al-Sharif as the Temple Mount is called by the Muslims. To the Jews the place was holy since it was the location of the first and second Temples, and the Western Wall was the only remnant left from those holy shrines. Two Mosques are located on this domain, Omar and Al-Aqsa, the latter built at the spot where, Islam's founder, the prophet Mohammed is believed to have risen to heaven. Religion and international relations are tied up in this conflict because of the worldwide religious lookouts toward the Holy Land. The convergence of the three monotheistic faiths in this part of the world added to the bond between religion and international politics. Yet the penetration of nationalism in the Middle East and the strategic and economic importance of the region transcend the sacred and complicate our investigation.

A full understanding of the tension must start with Mandatory Palestine (1917–1948), a period in which the basic motifs of the future conflict had been constructed. Here we shall highlight several outbreaks of violence that contained religious motifs. Subsequently, we shall analyze the evolution of the conflict from international and interethnic perspectives. The purpose of this chapter is to examine our contention on the relative weight of religion as an intervening factor in a national conflict.

Mandatory Palestine

The religious tones of this conflict had commenced immediately after the conquest of Palestine by Britain in 1917, a period known in Jewish Arab historiography as Mandatory Palestine. This period continued until the 1947 UN resolution to partition Palestine into two states. These religious tones were accompanied by national sentiments, and as we shall see, it is not always clear which one is the predominant one. Two events occurred at the outset of the intercommunal conflict in Palestine. The first one was the November 1917 Balfour Declaration, a document in which the British government promised a national home in Palestine for the Jewish people and convinced the Arab community that the Zionist aspirations for a national home were politically achievable (Sykes, 1967: 11). The second was the outbreak of intercommunal disturbances in 1920. The 1917–1947 period witnessed three major waves of violence, of which two had religious features. In the first wave of violence during the early 1920s anti-Jewish themes played a central role in the rhetoric of the incitement. Most of the instigation did not differentiate between Jews and Zionists. Similarly the Jews were blamed for importing permissiveness, Communism, and Western civilization values (Porath, 1976: 45–50). Religion played a role and accompanied the struggle over Palestine henceforward.

The trigger to the second wave of violence was also religious. It started in 1928, during Yom-Kippur day of atonement—the holiest Jewish holiday of the year—during Jewish prayers at the Western Wall when rumors spread that the Jews were altering the Temple Mount or Haram al-Sharif Mosques. While the issue of the placement of benches at the Western Wall was not new to the growing presence of Jews in Palestine this issue generated an outbreak of violence during the Ninth of Av, the Jewish mourning day for the destruction of the Temple in ancient times.

Violence at the sites of worship and on religiously significant days manifested the religious character of confrontations. The fact that the leader of the Palestinian community was the Jerusalem Mufti—the Muslim religious authority—who assumed also the position of head of the Muslim community in Palestine bestowed a religious attribute to the struggle (Porath, 1976: 149–158). Similarly the establishment of the Supreme Muslim Council presided by the Mufti, eventually very active in promoting riots along religious lines, added to the religious themes of the conflict (Porath, 1976: 158–168; Sykes, 1967: 110–111). Still we cannot ignore the fact that it was the penetration of nationalism into the Middle East and the awakening of a secular Jewish national movement that activated the Arab awakening (Antonius, 1965: 389–398).

Religious and National Factors in the Arab Attitude

The religious significance of Palestine in Islam in general and Palestinian nationalism in particular is indeterminate. One source for Palestine's religious significance is the doctrine of *dar al-Islam* (the home of Islam) that consigns land occupied by Islam to the Muslim nation. But contemporary Islamists preferred to give a special status to Palestine and chose the Caliph al-Khattab tradition (638 C.E.) that designated Palestine as a *waqf*, namely religious endowment. By this they promoted the status of Palestine above that of regular lands that were once occupied by Islamic rulers such as the Arabic or the Ottoman Empires to that of a religious trust for all Muslims (Frisch, 1994: 52–53; Litwak, 1998: 153–154).

Another source of sanctity of Palestine emanates primarily from the holiness of Jerusalem dubbed in Islam as Al-Quds (the holy), applying a holy status to the city. It was toward Jerusalem that the Muslims in the beginning directed their prayers (qibla) (Litwak, 1998: 153). The competition with Mecca and Medina—the two holiest cities in Islam and connected more than any other place to the Prophet's life—however, cancelled this custom thus reducing Jerusalem's status in Islam. The Muslims very soon directed their prayers toward the Ka'ba, a stone located at the center of the main mosque in Mecca. In turn, the city received its status from the two mosques built on Temple Mount—Dome of the Rock built in 688–691 and the Al-Aqsa (the furthest) Mosque. The Mosque was built on the spot from which according to Islam's tradition the prophet Muhammad ascended to heaven, based on a phrase in the Qur'an. This structure linked Jerusalem to the Qur'an that does not mention the city even once. This tying of Jerusalem to the Prophet's life ascended the status of Jerusalem.

In general, over the years the status of Jerusalem ascended when it came under threat of occupation by competing religions. This was the case following the conquest of the crusaders in the Middle Ages, and repeated itself when the Zionists revealed their aspirations in Jerusalem and Palestine. It is no accident that the Arabs compared the two invasions. This analogy while making a distinction between religion and politics very difficult, nevertheless is useful in stressing the mobilization power of religion. When weighing the contribution of Palestine against that of Jerusalem as religious motifs it seems that the latter was the more powerful.

To be sure, at the outset the reaction of the Islamic world to the conquest of Jerusalem by the Crusaders was one of compliance. The pragmatic policy of the Muslim rulers to the Franks, as the crusaders were dubbed by the Arabs, started changing with the ascendance of Zangi, the Kurdish ruler of Syria and especially his son Nur al-Din the rulers of Damascus. These rulers tried to infuse a religious motif in the struggle against the Franks. Since the capital of the Crusader Kingdom was Jerusalem, the religious sentiment and the significance of Jerusalem blended together. But the zenith of the religious awakening occurred with the conquest of Jerusalem in 1187 C.E. by Salah al-Din. In the subsequent years the religious dimension accompanied the jihad against the crusaders extending to all of Palestine. The Islamic world approached sternly the conquest of Jerusalem in 1229 by the crusade and the Ayyubids conquered Jerusalem in 1245 under a religious banner. This was the beginning of the end of the Crusaders' Kingdom in Palestine. The Mamluks, the heirs of the Ayyubids in ruling the region, fearing a new Christian conquest continued in strengthening the Islamic character of Jerusalem and its environs (Porath, 1976: 2–3; Perry, 1983: 78–81).

This pattern repeated itself in the modern era with the British and Zionist occupation of Palestine following World War I. As pointed out earlier the importance of Palestine as an independent national unit materialized following the emergence of Zionist intentions to establish a national home in Palestine. The command of the struggle by the Jerusalem Mufti who stressed the Jewish threat to Haram al-Sharif (sacred precinct), the former Temple Mount, and especially to the Dome of the Rock and Al-Aqsa Mosques located there infused potent religious tones into the Jewish–Arab struggle in Mandatory Palestine. Historical evidence supports the premise, however, that the Mufti mobilized religion for the sake of the national cause. This elevation of the religious character of the conflict with the Jews promised broader external support from other Muslim states for the Arab–Palestinian cause. It suited the nascent character of the emerging nations in the Middle East who were just becoming independent at this time, and were unable yet to militarily support the Palestinian Arabs. Moreover, the buildup of the religious aspect of the violence had the potential of widening the conflict from a local ethnic dispute to a transnational religious confrontation, thereby altering the structure of the conflict and its balance of power.

In was this rationale that motivated the Mufti in December 1931 to convene an Islamic conference in Jerusalem with representatives from 22 countries. At this opportunity he called upon Muslims elsewhere in the British Empire to agitate for a change in Britain's Palestine policy. One outcome of the conference was the mobilization of the Muslims of India behind the Palestinian cause, an important consideration for the British government that controlled both Palestine and India (Porath, 1976: 216–222, 247–250). By doing this the Mufti also helped to actualize the potential of the conflict to become a transnational issue.

While the 1929 crisis subsumed a strong religious rudiment, the Arab strike and rebellion of 1936–1939 testified that it was the national motifs as far as the Arab community in Palestine was concerned that now inspired the struggle. Significantly, this was the most severe crisis of the three major outbreaks of violence in Mandatory Palestine. While religious slogans continued to flourish, what motivated the riots and the strike was a change in the balance of power between the national communities in Palestine. A rise in Jewish immigration levels from 5,000 a year in 1929–1930 to over 37,000 in 1933 and over 66,000 in 1935, as well as increased Jewish land purchases during that period, stimulated the 1936 crisis (Porath, 1978: 58).

International political developments as well as transnational ones such as the rise to power of Hitler in Germany, and the growth of anti-Semitism in East Europe induced the immigration to Palestine that caused the crisis in the mid-1930s. Alarmed by the sudden flood of European Jews into Palestine and the rapid disappearance of land from Arab control, the Arab community perceived it as the materialization of the Balfour Declaration. Bands of Arab irregulars formed to battle the Jewish settlers, provoking the reciprocal rise of armed Jewish forces. The discovery of smuggled weapons in the hands of the Jews and the slaying by the Mandate police of Az-a-Din al-Kasam, a popular Palestinian commander, triggered the mass mobilization of the Arab community behind its national leadership. Arab demands included the cessation of Jewish migration and land purchases, and the establishment of a representative legislative council reflecting the Arabs' majority status. These protests also crossed borders to other Arab states. Demonstrations and riots by Egyptians and Syrians against their European Mandate powers also encouraged the Arabs in Palestine. The broad support expressed for their strike and the generation of collective action exhibited the capability of the Arab leadership to mobilize the Arab masses in support of advancing Palestinian national goals. A major vehicle in carrying the message across borders was Islam.

Significantly, Britain reacted rapidly to the rebellion in Palestine. It was the Mandatory power that, whether because of fear of religious inspired disturbances or out of international responsibility and considerations, reacted to the continued violence. London established a Royal Commission headed by Lord Robert Peel to investigate Arab complaints. The Peel commission produced a plan to partition Palestine into two states—Arab and Jewish—thus highlighting the ethnonational dimension of the struggle. The rationale behind this plan was to provide the Jews with space and land, thus to be able to build a viable state. Denying them Jerusalem and the central mountains area (Judea and Samaria) illustrated disregard for their religious aspirations. The Arab side totally rejected this proposal while the Zionists accepted it, in principle but with qualifications (Zionism, 1943: 471–480; Porat, 1978: 271–276; Dothan, 1979; Aroian and Mitchell, 1984: 236–237; Gal-Nor, 1991: 211–239). The reaction of both sides indicated that the political motif was predominant. Attempts to end the crisis via negotiations continued. But while the Peel Commission Partition Plan was at least partially accepted by the Zionist side, both the Jews and the Arabs rejected the Woodhead Commission (appointed in November 1938 by the British government to correct the findings of the Peel Commission report (Katz, 1992: 401–439)).

Another indication of the international-secular direction the conflict took was the mobilization of the Arab states behind the Palestinian cause. In February–March 1939 the British convened the St. James Palace Conference in London. Besides representatives of the Jewish and Arab communities of Palestine, delegates from Saudi Arabia, Iraq, Trans-Jordan, Egypt, and Yemen also participated. During the conference the Arab representatives refused to meet their Jewish counterparts and the deliberations ended without any agreement. Lacking formal or semiformal accords, the British government issued in May 1939 a new White Paper, essentially a unilateral act to be imposed on the parties. In this White Paper, the British government promised an independent Palestine within ten years, clarified that it did not see itself committed to the building of a Jewish state in Palestine, restricted Jewish land purchases, and limited Jewish immigration to 75,000 over the next five years (Laqueur and Rubin, 1991: 64–75, Document 17). Ironically, both sides rejected the White Paper for being too conciliatory to the other (Laqueur and Rubin, 1991: 76; Porat, 1978; J.C. Horowitz, 1968). The policy implications of the White Paper were circumscribed, however, by the outbreak of World War II in fall 1939. But both the idea of partition and the involvement of the Arab states did not fade away.

World War II witnessing the Holocaust put the solution to the Jewish problem on the agenda of the international community leading to an international movement to find a homeland for Jews. Britain had to abandon its 1939 White Paper. In 1942, the Zionists adopted the Biltmore Program demanding openly for the first time the establishment of a Jewish state in Palestine (Laqueur and Rubin, 1991: 77–79). The outbreak of the Jewish rebellion by the United Resistance Movement in September 1945, ultimately brought Britain to transfer the Palestine Problem to the United Nations (Hoffman, 1983: 18–40).

The November 29, 1947 UN Partition Resolution while different from the 1937 plan as far as geography was concerned essentially accepted the principle of two nation-states for two peoples. The rationale in effect was like in the Indian–Pakistani 1947 partition namely that ethnic communities separated by religion cannot share power in one polity. The Arab reaction to the UN Plan resulted in clashes during the period prior to May 1948 between the Jewish militia—the *Haganah* and the *Irgun* underground—and the Palestinian–Arab irregular forces. Clashes and atrocities took place primarily in the major Arab–Jewish cities as well as in the North. In essence a civil war, more severe than that of 1936–1939 year, erupted between the Arab and the Jewish districts of Jerusalem, Jaffa-Tel Aviv, Haifa, Safed, and Acre (Avigur et al., 1978: 32–33; Khouri, 1966: 73–81). The Arab exodus served as further evidence of the interethnic existential threat. What started as an elite phenomenon—the middle and upper classes leaving the big towns and their immediate environs—spread to the countryside. Together with those Arabs that were forced off their land by the Jewish militias that now turned into the Israeli Defense Force (IDF), these refugees became the substance symbol of the Palestinian problem (Bachi, 1974: 53–54; Morris, 1987: 57–60, 128–131).

Palestine Partition and the Decline of the Religious Motif

One outcome of the religious dimension of the conflict was the vote at the United Nations of the Muslim states against the partition plan. On the over all, however, the secular-international trend continued and the religious dimension gave way to the national. The UN General Assembly Resolution of November 29, 1947 calling for the establishment of two states in Palestine was the first step in an attempt to transform the Arab–Israeli conflict into an interstate relationship. This transformation was accelerated by the transition of the region into an interstate system. By the end of 1946, all of the countries surrounding Palestine had achieved sovereignty. In the ensuing years the new states' protection of their national independence were the central features of Middle Eastern politics.

The regional reaction to the establishment of the Jewish state was also primarily an Arab one rather than a Muslim one. On May 14 following the British evacuation from Palestine, all the Arab states declared war on Israel and the bordering states entered Palestine. Thus, the Israeli war of independence that started as an intercommunal war changed into an international war. In the years following the establishment of the Jewish state, the Arab states took over the struggle from the Palestinians against Israel. Similarly, in the ensuing years the struggle against the Jewish state became the responsibility of the Arab states rather than the Muslim world. But most of the Muslim world showed solidarity with the Arab states by boycotting Israel diplomatically (formal relations) and economically (the Arab boycott).

The period 1948–1967 can be defined as the interstate period in the Arab–Israeli conflict (Sandler, 1988; 58–64). In many of the Arab countries surrounding Israel in addition to being sovereign states, the military unseated the traditional land aristocracy and religious leadership. Trying to advance modernization these military elites saw traditional religion as representing the old regime. While cooperating at the outset with religious radical organizations like the Muslim Brothers (al-Ikhwan al-Muslimun) the officers in Egypt soon tried to control them (Lewis, 1981: 14–15). Their main objective was not to dismantle them but rather to steer them toward a reformist direction (Kantori, 1981: 80–81). Also the Socialist B'ath parties in Syria and Iraq in their attempt to modernize their societies and redistribute wealth in their countries brought religion under the control of the state.

Among the Arab states, during the first two decades, Egypt played the preeminent role in the crises between Israel and the Arab states (Ben-Yehuda and Sandler, 2002: 60–61). The wave of Pan-Arabism, a movement that emphasized a trans-state Arab nationalism, that spread throughout the Arab world, originating in Egypt and led by Gamal Abdel Nasser as an ideology by definition demoted the Islamic identity and hence the religious factor in the conflict. The conflict during those years was fueled by the national objection to Israel as a state. Israel's illegitimacy as a state served as a rallying point for Arab unity and its destruction was a maxim of Pan-Arab identity. In the post–Suez War years, Egyptian-oriented Pan-Arabism strengthened, reaching its peak in the 1960s.

Another factor that eclipsed the Islamic identity was the entry of the Cold War into the Middle East. The USSR and the United States replaced the old colonial powers and further overwhelmed the relevance of traditionalism in the region (Kerr, 1971; Taylor, 1982; Khouri, 1966). The growing involvement and influence of the Soviet Union in the Middle East influenced the status of religion. Stalinist Russia epitomized a model of fast industrialization without the clergy, which attracted many regimes in the Third World, thus rejecting the alternative bourgeois model (Organski, 1965: 214–218). Egypt under Nasser loomed as one of the pivotal countries of the Third World, aspiring to proceed with fast modernization and an agrarian revolution, while downgrading the traditional elites. The combination of ideologies of socialism and nationalism as well as a revolutionary spirit induced secularization.

The second most active Arab state in terms of crises in the 1948–1967 period was Jordan (Ben-Yehuda and Sandler, 2002: 88–89). The primacy of Jordan was obviously related to the demographic strength of the Palestinians in the Hashemite Kingdom. But the Hashemites also exhibited a less ardent Pan-Arabism, a fact that made them suspect among Palestinian nationalists who then identified their cause with that of Pan-Arabism and Egypt (Sayigh, 1997; Be'eri, 1978). It was the ethnonational Palestinian cause rather than religious aspirations that activated cross-border violence. The weight of the Palestinians in Jordan and the weakness of the regime following the 1951 assassination of King Abdullah allowed for Palestinian activity from Jordan against Israel. Yet, despite the Palestinian factor and despite the conservative fabric of the regime the Jordanian–Israeli relationship was the least hostile in comparison to that of other Arab states.

Indeed, despite Jordan's control of the Old City in Jerusalem, including Judaism's holy places, Israel was selective in its retaliations for insurgency activity originating in Jordan because of its common interest with the Hashemites in containing the Palestinians, and tried to avoid direct confrontations with the Arab Legion (the Jordanian army). Two incidents, the Qibya (October 14, 1953) and Qalquilya (October 10, 1956) operations, both against Jordanian targets in response to a series of cross-border provocations, escalated beyond the original plans into international crises (Ben-Yehuda and Sandler, 2002: 183–185). Significantly, neither Israel nor Jordan, in contrast to the Israeli–Egyptian border, allowed the crises to escalate into a war. The second Arab–Israeli interstate war broke out in 1956 with Egypt, a country that did not control any religious sites or parts of the biblical Land of Israel. Following the Sinai 1956 War, for a decade no crisis erupted between the two neighbors. In 1958, Israel allowed British troops to fly over its territory into Jordan in an operation aimed at bolstering the Hashemite regime against domestic pro-Nasserite and Palestinian radical forces.

Another indication to the international climate that dominated the region and the secondary role of religion during that period was the status of Jordanian-controlled East Jerusalem. The Jordanians adopted a deliberate policy of downgrading East Jerusalem while enhancing the capital city of Amman. Despite its attraction as a tourism center, Jerusalem failed to develop economically. Prior to the 1948 war Jerusalem functioned as the administrative center. In the years following the war all of these functions shifted to Amman. Notwithstanding the fact that it was surrounded by Bethlehem, a major attraction to Christian tourists and Ramallah a summer attraction to rich Arab tourists, Jerusalem failed to emerge as a major metropolitan hub. Undoubtedly what guided the Hashemite dynasty, which prides itself on being of direct lineage to the prophet Mohammed, were political interests of state and nation building in a country where most of its population was Palestinian on both sides of the Jordan River (Sandler and Frisch, 1984: 34–38).

Alongside the Arab states the Palestinians played a secondary role. Following a failed attempt to establish the all Palestine government in Gaza under the auspices of the Egyptian government and the leadership of the exiled Jerusalem Mufti, the Palestinians disappeared as an international actor. In Jordan, with the exception of the Tahrir, a conservative Islamic party, all the Palestinian parties were either Pan-Arabist or Communist oriented (Cohen, 1980). In the 1964 Cairo summit, the Palestinians reappeared as a political actor with the establishment of the Palestine Liberation Organization (PLO). Four months later a Palestinian Conference convened in East Jerusalem and ratified a constitutional document known as the Palestinian National Covenant (al-Mithak al-Kawami al-Filastini). This document defined the Palestinian community, asserted the imperative of destroying the state of Israel and replacing it with a "secular democratic state," and detailed the strategy of struggle (Yaniv, 1974; Hamid, 1975: 90–109; Harkabi, 1979). In 1968 the title in Arabic used for national in the Covenant was changed from *Kawmiyya* to *Wataniyya*, which implies a territorial patriotism instead of Pan-Arabic nationalism. This move was accompanied in 1969 by a takeover of the PLO by the Fatah— a secular guerrilla force under the leadership of Yasser Arafat. The failure of the Arab states to liberate Palestine in 1967, despite the boasting of Egyptian leader Gamal Abdul Nasser, and their devastating defeat in six days of war boosted the PLO and its guerrilla strategy as the only way to accomplish the Palestinian goals (Harkabi, 1977: 14–16). In the ensuing years the PLO became an umbrella organization of all the ideological guerrilla groups, most of them representing also different radical Arab states, all of them secular and radical (Sahliyeh, 1968; Cobban, 1984).

In the years ensuing the June 1967 War the PLO ascended primarily in Jordan. Despite the plans to fight a "war of liberation" against Israel from across the Jordan River PLO growth eventually posed a political threat to the Hashemite regime. In September 1970, following a hijacking of three commercial airliners by the Popular Front for the Liberation of Palestine (PFLP) a radical group within the PLO, King Hussein of Jordan decided to crush the armed Palestinian groups within his country. Hussein's decision on September 15 to put Jordan under martial law triggered threats from Syria and Iraq to intervene on behalf of the Palestinians. Syrian tanks moved closer to the Jordanian border, crossing it on September 18. Jordan turned to the United States, and agreed that the Americans would ask Israel to try and deter the Syrian invasion via a mobilization of its forces. Washington in turn promised to deter both an Egyptian or Soviet retaliation against Israel. Syria pulled out of Jordan on September 22. Left to its own devices, the Hashemite regime destroyed the PLO infrastructure over the next ten months.

PLO forces and their families fled Jordan for a new sanctuary in Lebanon, whose central government was too weak to resist their presence. Lebanon bordered Israel and hence conformed with the guerrilla warfare strategy by which the PLO could continue its fight against the Jewish state from Arab states bordering Israel. The PLO's relocation to Lebanon also had religious implications. The PLO presence in Lebanon helped to transform the sectarian balance of power in that country in favor of the Muslim communities triggering an interreligious civil war. But this awakening could not detach itself from the Arab–Israeli conflict, thus ultimately leading to the 1982 Lebanon War. In this war that started on June 6, 1982, Israel's official goal was to remove the PLO from Southern Lebanon following its continued bombardment of the Galilee. In reality, because of the Syrian military presence in Lebanon Israeli forces fought both the Palestinian irregular forces and the Syrian army thus introducing a pattern of a mixture of ethnic and international conflicts. This type of war was reminiscent of the 1947–1948 war that also involved both intercommunal and interstate violence, entitled by Sandler as a compound conflict (Sandler, 1988: 55). The 1982 Lebanon War was further compounded by the Israeli struggle in the West Bank and Gaza against PLO supporters and Lebanese Christian, Muslim, and Druze militias (Sandler and Frisch, 1984: 149–163).

Religion Ascendant

The period between 1967 and 1973 constituted a "twilight zone" between the interstate dominant and the interethnic dominant eras. The 1970s witnessed the emergence of the PLO as the representative of the Palestinians in the West Bank and the Gaza Strip. In October 1973 Israel was attacked by Arab states and the Palestinians hardly played any role. Nevertheless, following the war, representatives from the Arab states gathered at the 1974 Rabat conference and officially recognized the PLO as the sole representative of the Palestinian people. The Hashemites of Jordan who had ruled the West Bank from 1948 to 1967 and aspired to reclaim it were losing ground. In 1974 the PLO gained observer status at the United Nations and the General Assembly received a speech by Arafat warmly. The PLO was further, empowered by the landslide victory of PLO-affiliated candidates a year later in the West Bank municipal elections. In 1982, Israel under the leadership of a nationalist-led government headed by Menahem Begin tried to eradicate the PLO both in the West Bank and Lebanon (Sandler and Frisch, 1984: 149–163).

The 1982 Lebanon War epitomized as we said earlier the compound structure of the Arab–Israeli conflict and hence a return to the pre-1948 era. Besides the international domestic mix it also indicated a future trend—the emergence of religious forces that would make the conflict even more complex. The collapse of the religious balance of power and hence the clerical power-sharing structure mobilized the Shiite minority that had been acquiescent until then. In the continuation of this development the local Shia established a contact with the clerical regime in Iran thus creating a radical religious militia named Hizbullah—the party of God. This new phenomenon paralleled evolutions among the Palestinians.

Five years after the outbreak of the Lebanon War the first Palestinian territory-wide violent uprising dubbed as Intifada erupted. The trigger for the Intifada was a December 8, 1987 road accident between an Israeli truck and a car carrying Palestinians laborers. As word of the death of four Palestinian passengers spread, Gazans gathered for spontaneous and violent demonstrations. In retrospect, early indications of increasing tension during the preceding year signaled that a crisis was developing. In both the Gaza Strip and in the West Bank the number of violent incidents and disturbances more than doubled from 1986 to 1987. Almost every indicator of violence, such as the number of incidents, scope of disturbances, and casualties on both sides, increased over 100 percent throughout the months preceding the Intifada, in comparison to the previous year (Shalev, 1990: 45, 209; Schiff and Yaari, 1990: 26).

Religious elements that emerged in the territories were the main forces to incite the uprising. Neither the PLO nor Arafat had planned or even anticipated the uprising, or its strength, persistence, and violence. In the past, the Palestinians inside the territories (the insiders) had never sought to usurp the mantle of leadership held by the PLO. In the wake of the PLO's defeat in Lebanon, the continuation of the status quo presented a threat to the Palestinians. The first Intifada thus constituted a structural change within the Palestinian community in that the inside segment emerged as the vanguard of the Palestinian revolution, thereby threatening the PLO (Sandler and Frisch, 1984: 79–99). The uprising nevertheless benefited the PLO, but to a larger extent the religious groups of the uprising. Hamas, the Palestinian wing of the Muslim brethren emerged during the first months of the Intifada (Litwak, 1998: 149). Besides Hamas, the smaller but even more extreme splinter group, the Islamic Jihad perceived itself as the match that had ignited the Intifada. It was thus not an accident that Gaza was the main source of instigation.

The PLO suffered a defeat in Lebanon by the Israeli Army resulting in Yasser Arafat's removal from Beirut in September 1982. The weakness of the PLO in the wake of its expulsion from Lebanon to Tunis and the resulting despair of the inhabitants of the West Bank and Gaza convinced the West Bank and Gaza Palestinians and especially the religious cells in Gaza that it was upon them to initiate the struggle against Israel. Another threat to the Palestinians was Israel's 1979 settlement drive, advanced by the national religious coalition headed by the Likud, that came into power in 1977, which ushered thousands of new Israelis into the territories, many of them motivated by religious vigor. The religious claim to the land inspired Palestinians to adopt a parallel theology (Frisch, 1994: 49). Israel's appointment of pro-Jordanian mayors in the territories following the PLO's exit from Lebanon signaled a renewed partnership between Israel and the Hashemites, an alliance that posed yet another threat to the Palestinian cause. The PLO tried to squelch the Jordanian-inclined Palestinian leadership via assassinations of "collaborators" with Jordan and Israel. One of the goals of the Intifada was obstructing a Jordanian–Israeli regime in the territories.

The situation in which the Palestinians found themselves was ripe for a religious awakening. While the Arab states all expressed their customary verbal support none came out to actively help. The first Gulf War then going on between Iraq and Iran contributed to the minimal attention and lack of involvement on the part of the Arab states toward the Palestinian uprising. In addition to supporting Iran in that war, Syria was also expending considerable resources in Lebanon, where it supported factions in the PLO contesting Arafat's leadership. Egypt used the crisis to restore its leading role in the Arab world and return to the Arab League, a task accomplished in March 1989. At the same time, Cairo was careful not to escalate the confrontation between the Palestinians and Israel to such a level that it might be drawn into the confrontation. The distribution of forces between the two sides favored Israel. The religious awakening intensified the intensity and amplification of the demonstrations, thus expanding the range of riots to women and youth participation and the spreading across the territory. With time the unprecedented violence in the 20-year control of the territories convinced the Israeli leadership that a new situation has developed in the territories and a religious element has entered the scene.

While religious movements and sentiments were in the background of the Intifada the political dimension was present throughout the uprising. From an early point in the crisis, both sides used a mixture of violence and diplomacy in their efforts to manage the conflict, a relatively new combination of crisis-coping modes. On the Palestinian side, the internal command of the Intifada designated the PLO its official representative, even though the initiative for the uprising originated from within the territories. In allowing the PLO to speak for them, the inside Palestinians indicated that they contemplated a political solution to their plight. The shift toward assimilating negotiations with violence was not a sudden event: the PLO had already begun modifying its strategy in the mid-1970s (Sandler and Frisch, 1984: 58–70; Cobban, 1984: appendix 1).

On November 15, 1988, one year after the eruption of the Intifada, the Nineteenth Session of the Palestinian National Council (PNC) declared the establishment of a Palestinian state, called explicitly for the settlement of the Arab–Israel conflict, and endorsed an international peace conference.

The PNC also echoed the internationally heralded campaign to eliminate nuclear arms and settle regional conflicts by peaceful means, without giving up its claim that the crux of the Middle Eastern conflict was the Palestinian question. At the end of a long paragraph listing all the Palestinian rights invoking the appropriate UN resolutions and announcing the establishment of a Palestinian state, the Declaration also stated that the desired political settlement will provide "security and peace arrangements for all the countries in the region." In order to attain these goals, the PNC emphasized the need to convene an effective international conference under UN supervision with the participation of the UN Security Council permanent members. The conference, with the Palestinian cause as its essence, would include all the parties to the conflict in the region and its basis would be the PLO's acceptance of Security Council Resolutions 242 and 338 (Shalev, 1990: 245–246). The PLO behavior here represented the norms of the international system.

The Arab states' reaction was also political. The mass participation in the Intifada was so threatening that it induced King Hussein to utter a declaration on July 31, 1988, in which he severed administrative and legal relations between Jordan and the West Bank. Fearing the spread of the Intifada to his Kingdom, King Hussein decided to cut his loses and sanctify the PLO's role as the sole representative of the territories, as recommended by the 1974 Rabat Conference (Brand, 1990: 501–527). Jordan also recognized the proclamation of the PNC on November 15, 1988 of an independent Palestinian State in exile (Brand, 1990: 509). Also the Egyptians initiated an international response to the Intifada. In September 1989, President Mubarak came out with a ten-point plan that included inter alia three principles which worried the national-religious wing of Israeli national unity government at the time: that Israel must accept the principle of "territories for peace," halt further settlement establishment, and allow the participation of East Jerusalem residents in the West Bank elections (Laqueur and Rubin, 1991: 551).

The Intifada waned as a result of the outbreak of a secular international crisis—the conquest of Kuwait by Saddam Hussein. For the next nine months, from August through March 1991, the Intifada fell dormant. The Intifada came to further halt in the interval between the end of Desert Storm in March 1991 and the Madrid conference of October 1991 (Eisenberg and Caplan, 1998: 75–81). Arafat and the PLO officially backed Saddam Hussein during the Gulf Crisis, thus linking the Gulf Crisis and the interethnic Intifada. However, between the dancing on the rooftops by Palestinians while Scud missiles fell in Tel-Aviv and the desperate situation of 400,000 Palestinian from Kuwait and Saudi Arabia the Intifada took a time-out. Very soon after the end of the Gulf War, diplomatic activity in the Arab–Israel arena resumed as did a low-scale version of the Intifada. The Intifada faded away with the opening of the Madrid conference on October 30, 1991, to be followed by the "Oslo" agreements in the latter part of 1993. In the ensuing years the withdrawal of the IDF from

Gaza and the major cities of the West Bank occurred. This cease-fire lasted until the outbreak of the second Intifada of October 2000. But before we turn to this major event we turn to the Jewish side in the conflict.

Religious and National Factors in the Jewish Attitude

Although there is no universally accepted map of the theological boundaries of the Land of Israel, there is no debate regarding the *core* of that region. Disagreements exist regarding the northern or the southern borders and to some extent regarding the East side of the Jordan River but there is no doubt that the area adjacent to the Jordan from the West constitutes, according to the Bible, the heart of the divinely promised Land of Israel. Similarly, from a historical perspective, the central mountains areas (Judea and Samaria) constituted the heart of the ancient Israelite and Judean kingdoms during both the first commonwealth (11 century B.C.E–586 B.C.E) and the second one (516 B.C.E–70 A.D.), even though the kingdoms' boundaries varied. The Judean kingdom started in the tribal capital Hebron (which according to the Old Testament is the burial place of the forefathers and foremothers of Israel and the Jewish nation) and then expanded and established the national capital in Jerusalem where the united kingdoms of David and Solomon resided. Shechem (Nablus) was the burial place of Joseph, the forefather of the competing dynasty from the tribe of Ephraim, and its surrounding mountains were witness to the entrance of the Israelites into the Land of Israel. The Tabernacle resided at Shilo, which according to the Bible was located in Samaria. (Samaria was the name of the capital of the Kingdom of Israel that emerged following the partition of the Davidic Kingdom.) Judea and Samaria were also the center of the Second Commonwealth and the Hasmonaean Kingdom. Yet, despite the religious sanctity of these regions, the Zionist movement on two occasions, in 1937 and 1947 as we shall see later, when faced with choice of a state or a religious-national dogmatic stand decided in favor of the first alternative.

No place in the Land of Israel has greater religious significance for the Jewish people than Jerusalem. Though the city has always combined religious, historical, and political elements, it was the religious element that overshadowed the others. Jerusalem—Zion, the Temple Mount—was where the Jewish Temple had twice been built and destroyed. This was the site to which Jews have prayed for millennia. The seat of government for Kings David and Solomon and the subsequent kings of Judea is identified with the glorious past of the Jews as well as with the future redemption and restoration of Jewish sovereignty. It is the only place in Palestine where a Jewish presence has never ceased to exist and where since the mid-nineteenth century the Jews have constituted the largest religious community in the city. The Zionist movement was named after one of the several names of Jerusalem. The city was the seat of the Zionist Executive (later the Executive of the Jewish Agency) and other important Jewish political, cultural, and religious organizations including Keren Hayesod, the JNF, the Va'ad Leumi, the Chief Rabbinate, and the Hebrew University. At the time of independence, 100,000 Jews, who constituted a sixth of the population of the Yishuv (as the Jewish community in Mandatory Palestine was called) resided in Jerusalem. And yet the Yishuv, like in the case of Judea and Samaria, was ready to accept the UN partition plan, which excluded Jerusalem from Israeli sovereignty, conferring on Jerusalem the status of corpus seperatum—or an international city (Sandler, 1984; Schueftan, 1986: 148–150). What does this imply regarding the role of religion in the Jewish behavior in the conflict?

Partition of the Land of Israel and Statehood

On two occasions the Zionist movement, following a very intensive debate, decided to accept proposals put down before it by the international community. The first event was the 1937 partition proposal of the Royal commission headed by Lord Peel, and the second was the UN partition Plan of November 29, 1947. In both cases, the Zionist movement acceded to surrender the heart of the Jewish historic land promised to them, according to their account, by the Balfour Declaration and later on by the League of Nations in favor of statehood. Even more significant was the Zionist compromise over Jerusalem. While not abdicating Jerusalem formally and demanding at least parts of the city, in effect on both occasions when faced with the opportunity to establish a state, the Zionist movement consented indirectly that Jerusalem would become part of a British (1937) or international (1947) enclave. In both cases the Zionist movement was ready to abdicate the religious locales of Jerusalem. Israeli decision makers asserted that when faced with the dilemma of no state or a state without Jerusalem they had no choice but to accept the state option (Brecher, 1972: 14–15). In contrast, the Revisionists (nationalists) and the religious parties (Mizrahi) objected to this decision in 1937, and so did many of the religious leaders in 1947 regardless of the threat to the state option. In both cases, David Ben-Gurion, the foremost Zionist leader and Israel's first prime minister, imposed his will on the Zionist national institutions to accept a compromise for the sake of a state.

How did Ben-Gurion, a secularist and the leader of a secularist party succeed in imposing his statist strategy on the religious parties for whom Judea and Samaria and especially Jerusalem symbolized sacred values? Moreover, how do we explain the minor role religion played in Israeli foreign affairs until 1967? Part of the answer lies in a political coalition he had established in the Zionist movement between the Labor and the religious Zionist movements even before the establishment of the state. In fact he picked up on an alliance that had started in 1902 when Theodor Herzel, the founder of political Zionism, reached a compromise with the leader of the religious Zionists Rabbi Jacob Reines (founder of the Mizrahi section in the Zionist Organization) on the question of secular-religious educational activity in the Zionist movement (Sandler, 1993: 30–31; Don Yehiya, 1983: 105–146). In this manner the founder of political Zionism also attracted the support of Rabbi Reines on the question of establishing a temporary Jewish colony in Eastern Africa. With the ascendance of Labor in the Zionist movement in the early 1930s, Ben-Gurion succeeded in turning the pivotal position of his party into hegemony by establishing a coalition with Mizrahi and its offshoot HaPoel haMizrahi parties. With time this relationship became the cornerstone of the political center during the pre-state (Yishuv) period and was carried on into the state era. It was this central array of parties that enabled Ben-Gurion to rule Israel without having to compromise with either the right-wing Herut party or the Moscow-oriented parties on his left on the main principles of Israeli foreign policy as he saw them.

The special relationship between MAPAI (The Israel Laborers Party) and the National Religious Party (NRP—previously Mizrahi/Hapoel Hamizrahi Parties) was termed in Israeli politics as the "historic alliance," while political scientists described it as a consociational relationship in accordance with the politics of accommodation model (Don Yehiya, 1975; Ljiphart, 1977). What this arrangement implied in the Israeli context was a trade-off between autonomy in areas like education for the NRP in exchange for Labor's control in foreign and security affairs. While the NRP identified with the civic symbols and the rituals of the Jewish state despite its secular nature the Ultraorthodox Agudat Israel, established in 1912, rejected the norm that redemption could come via secular Jews. While the NRP saw the establishment of the state as the beginning of redemption and hence approved of Labor government's foreign policy, Ultraorthodox Agudat Israel for the opposite reason also adopted a passive role in foreign policy.

Until 1967 foreign policy was the domain of MAPAI, as articulated by Israel's first Prime Minister David Ben-Gurion. The passive role of the NRP and Agudat Israel implied a lack of religious norms in foreign affairs. With the Arab states rejecting any compromise with Israel and Judea and Samaria beyond reach, a consensus on foreign policy emerged. Herut under the leadership of Irgun leader Menahem Begin was the only party that demanded the unification of the Land of Israel. But this was primarily an ethnonational-based claim that was based on historic rights rather than a religious one. The situation started to change following the Six Day War of 1967 in which Israel captured a significant amount of territory from its Arab neighbors including the Jewish holy sites in the Old City of Jerusalem. The traumatic experience that accompanied the May 1967 crisis and what seemed a miraculous victory in June brought out an outpour of religious feelings especially among the national-religious community. What seemed to the secularists as the demonstration of Israeli technology and modernity was interpreted as Divine intervention by others. Especially convincing was the fact that the ancient parts of the Land of Israel and most importantly Jerusalem were now under Israeli jurisdiction.

The National Religious Motif Ascendant

While playing a moderating role in the 1967 Crisis and its immediate aftermath the NRP could not stay indifferent for long to the regaining of the historic and religiously significant parts of the Land of Israel and the reunion of Jerusalem. The "young guard" in the NRP challenged the traditional leadership of the party that was in alliance with Labor and rejected its "land for peace" formula. Under the influence of many Rabbis, most of them coming from the "Mercaz Harav" Yeshiva (rabbinical college) the "Gush Emunim" (block of the faithful) movement emerged leading a settlement drive in the West Bank, renamed now according to its biblical term as Judea and Samaria. Many of the Gush leadership were followers of the redemption theology of Rabbi Abraham Yitzhak Kook, the founder of Mercaz Harav Yeshiva as interpreted by his son Rabbi Zvi Yehuda. In accordance with this approach the events of June 1967 constituted an advanced stage in the redemption of the Jewish people and the Land of Israel. Hence, no Jewish government had the right to turn over these genuine parts and holy places to non-Jewish control. In 1977 following the victory of the nationalist Likud headed by Herut leader Menahem Begin, the Labor–NRP alliance came to an end and instead an ethnonational-religious partnership commenced. Moreover, the NRP also brought in Ultraorthodox Agudat Israel into the coalition after over 25 years of nonparticipation in the Israeli government.

Power sharing between ethnonational and religious parties conceptually seems more natural. Indeed, the Likud and the hawkish new NRP were closer on foreign policy matters. Thus Prime Minister Begin encouraged the settlement drive of Gush Emunim in which the number of settlements grew from 27 in 1977 to 77 four years later (Sandler and Frisch, 1984: 139). Also in religious legislation and other matters of church and state Begin was more forthcoming to the NRP and Agudat Israel than Labor ever had been. The religious parties enjoyed automatic exemptions from the army for Rabbinical College students and larger budgets for their separate education systems. This exemption for Rabbinical students is particularly important since most Ultraorthodox males in Israel who can potentially be drafted define themselves as Rabbinical College students. But despite ideological proximity the Likud was now the government and Gush Emunim an extra-parliamentary organ. Hence, Begin and Defense Minister Sharon confronted the Gush in 1981 when the latter objected to the removal of settlements in the Sinai as a result of the Israeli–Egyptian peace agreement. More significant was the fact that the affinity between the two parties caused many to defect to the ruling party. Moreover, the radicalization of religious Zionists supporters encouraged the creation of more extreme national parties drawing electoral votes from the NRP. The result was that the NRP lost half of its parliamentary strength in the 1981 elections (Sandler, 1983). Significantly, the new parties that gained the votes from the NRP were nonclerical but ethnonational parties. In short, despite the emergence of the new religious-ethnonationalist alliance, it was ethnonationalism rather than religion that appeared forcefully on the Israeli political scene.

The act of signing the 1978 Camp David Accords has received full attention in the literature but primarily from an international political perspective. Most fascinating was the fact that the least expected leaders like devoted Muslim Anwar Sadat who was the most extreme foe of Israel in 1973 and nationalist Menahem Begin (himself a traditional person), always portrayed as a hawk, have succeeded where secular socialist leaders like Nasser and Golda Meir have failed. President Carter's religiosity was well known and the Camp David Accords were probably the greatest achievement of his otherwise failed presidency. The contribution of religiosity of all three leaders to the peace process is still to be studied.

The Radicalization of Religion

Religious radicalization of the religious Zionists found its expression in various nonelectoral arenas. While the main stream of Gush Emunim was leading the settlement drive in the late 1970s, a more dogmatic wing established the militant but legal "Movement to stop the withdrawal from Sinai." In parallel, a small covert group avowed to stop the peace process with Egypt via radical steps. Hence a Jewish underground composed of religious-Zionists emerged undertaking actions that challenged the state even though led by a right-wing coalition under the leadership of Begin. Within the underground the more "moderate" wing organized terror acts against Arab leaders in the West Bank. More extreme was the wing that aspired to remove the Dome of the Rock Mosque, an act that would have induced tumultuous reactions in the Arab and Muslim worlds and thus stopped the peace process.

It was at this juncture that the mark between a fundamentalist movement that essentially accepts the legitimacy of the regime and a radical one can be inferred. The leaders of the Jewish Underground that broke away from Gush Emunim had spiritual links with Mercaz Harav Rabbinical College (Shragai, 1995: 96–122). But in addition they were also influenced by *Kabala* (Jewish mystical) sources. According to one ideologue a Jewish state that was ruling without the rebuilding of the Temple, the renewal of the kingdom of Israel, and the restoration of the Sanhedrin (the Rabbinical Israelite Court) did not fulfill its Jewish mission. While for Gush Emunim Rabbis the creation of the state was a sign of the beginning of redemption, for some Underground leaders the fact that the Jewish state let the Dome of the Rock stand was proof that it was not progressing down the road to redemption (Don-Yehiya, 1994). For these leaders the state did not have any sanctity unless it proceeded in full to bring about redemption (Be'eri, 1996).

The reaction to the underground came from a variety of sources. The leading spiritual Rabbis of Mercaz Harav—Rabbis Y. Zukerman and

Z. Tau—denounced this approach because of anti-state ramifications. Since the state of Israel in itself is a sign of redemption delegitimizing the state was in itself a transgression. Most interesting was Rabbi Shlomo Aviner who asserted that the zealots' order of redemption was reverse; redemption must precede the restoration of the Temple (Shragai, 1995: 130–131). Gush Emunim leadership condemned it on the ground that it ruptured the relations between the state and the people on the one hand and the vanguard of the Israeli people namely Gush Emunim on the other hand. The most consequential reaction came from the nationalist government of Prime Minister Shamir who in 1984 apprehended the members of the underground. Secularist Shamir, though nationalist, grasped the dangers of such a group to the state. Shamir's reaction and the condemnations from the Right stopped the deterioration. In the ensuing years the extreme religious right wing abstained from radical actions and instead worked in tandem with the government even though most of the period Labor was a partner in the government.

In essence, Shamir tried to extend the tradition of power sharing between the secular and the religious parties to one between the national and the Labor camps. Following four years filled with recurrent political crises over foreign policy, in 1988, despite his victory and ability to establish a national religious coalition, Shamir established a national unity government with Labor (Elazar and Sandler, 1992: 280–286).

What brought down the Shamir government was a cross-cutting coalition, or, to use Keohane and Nye's language, a "trans-governmental" coalition that included Egypt, the Bush administration, and the Labor leadership (Keohane and Nye, 1973: 381–382). This coalition resulted from, the domestic split in the Israeli body politic between Labor, which supported a territorial compromise, and the national religious coalition that objected to any partition of the Land of Israel. Both the Mubarak proposal and an October 1989 more-limited five-points plan proposed by U.S. Secretary of State James Baker were accepted by the Labor ministers, including Rabin the hard-liner among them (Laqueur and Rubin, 1991: 556). In the following months intensive negotiations ensued among Israel, the United States, and Egypt. While the PLO was pressing via the Egyptians to enter the negotiations, Baker was pressuring Shamir to let the Palestinians in. Eventually, the disagreement between Israel and the United States narrowed down to two points: PLO participation in the negotiations and the participation of East Jerusalem Arabs in the elections (Arens, 1995: 110).

The religious factor played a role in the March 1990 collapse of the national unity government over Shamir's refusal to accede to Secretary Baker's proposals and the acceptance of the Baker Plan by Ministers Peres and Rabin. Peres who had convinced Shas to leave Shamir's national government ultimately failed to put together a majority in parliament, because of the refusal of the religious parties to join secular Labor. In contrast, in June Shamir succeeded in doing so. The new government was composed of the right-wing nationalist and religious members of the Knesset.

In 1992 after bringing down the Shamir government because of its readiness to enter the Madrid peace conference the national and religious Right was defeated and a Labor–Left coalition under Rabin formed the new government. In the new government not only all the nationalist parties were left out but Rabin abstained from inviting the NRP, which also traditionally represented the religious ticket to join the government. Instead he chose the ultraorthodox Shas Sephardi party to be a coalition member. The main reason for preferring Shas was that its spiritual leader Rabbi Ovadia Yosef ruled that territorial compromise was religiously acceptable if it was for the sake of peace and security. The NRP rabbis objected to such a ruling.

The Labor–Shas relationship was designed to enable the Rabin government to advance its agenda in foreign policy. Labor, despite the tradition of power sharing in religious affairs, did not intend to allow its religious partner to have a voice in foreign policy. Consequently, despite concessions in legislation by Rabin and the actual maintenance of the status quo in religious affairs, after two years Shas under the pressure of its voters formally left the government. Unwilling to compromise its position in foreign affairs, the Rabin government was kept in power with the help of the Israeli Arab parties, an unprecedented development in the political history of the Jewish state. The absence of religious parties from the government was also a precedent. To the majority of the Jewish public a foreign policy sustained by the religious parties was legitimate but not one supported by the Arab parties.

The lack of a religious party in government exacerbated an already tense situation in Israel in the wake of the Oslo agreements that paved the way for Yasser Arafat to enter the West Bank and Gaza. Against the background of mass unprecedented demonstrations by the Israeli national right-wing Dr. Baruch Goldstein, a supporter of Rabbi Meir Kahane, the most radical Jewish leader who supported the transfer of Arabs from the Land of Israel, gunned down 29 Palestinians in the Tomb of the Patriarchs in Hebron. In summer 1995 a group of rabbis from the national religious camp called upon the IDF soldiers to disobey possible government orders to evacuate settlements in Judea, Samaria, and the Gaza Strip. But the most extreme and unprecedented action came in November 4, 1995, when Yigal Amir a religious law student assassinated Prime Minister Yitzhak Rabin. Significantly, Rabin's successor, Shimon Peres invited Rabbi Yehuda Amital, the leader of Meimad—a centrist but very subdued religious Zionist movement to join his cabinet, thus trying to restore the remnants of power sharing with the religious camp. By doing so, Peres signaled what role he conceived for religion in foreign policy.

But Peres's takeover run was undermined by the eruption of Hamas and Islamic Jihad–inspired terrorist acts against Jews in the months that he followed Rabin and served as prime minister. To be sure terrorist attacks had started during the Rabin years and the most outstanding was the January 22, 1995 Hamas suicide bombing in Beit Leid in which 21 Israelis were assassinated. These acts had already reduced public support for Yitzhak Rabin. The reaction to the assassination was unprecedented support for his heir—Peres. However, the new round of terrorist suicide bombing that occurred during the months of Peres's reign slowly eroded his lead in the polls to the extent that he lost the elections in May 1996. The most obvious factor in this defeat were the suicide bombing executed by Muslim religious fanatics without the Palestinian Authority's PA's crackdown on them. When Arafat finally moved against the religious terror organizations, it was too late for Peres (Steinberg, 1998: 216–218). In short, the Palestinian religious extremism outbalanced the Jewish one and transformed the political regime in Israel.

Religion and Foreign Policy in the Al-Aqsa (Second) Intifada

Netanyahu, the winner of the May 1996 elections, who had objected to the Oslo agreements nonetheless continued to negotiate with the PA because of Israel's international obligations to do so. Israel even reached an agreement in January 1997 to evacuate almost all of Hebron, the second holiest city to Jews after Jerusalem. Unable to carry out a second pull back from 13 percent in the West Bank as agreed upon in the Wye agreement negotiated with Arafat in Wye Maryland because of the objection of his religious and national partners in parliament, Netanyahu called for new elections in which he was defeated in May 1999 by Ehud Barak, the leader of the Labor party. Understanding the potential power of religion Barak at the outset, assembled a broad coalition that included all the religious parties—Shas, Agudat Israel, and the NRP. At the same time he committed himself at Sharm al-Sheikh to reach a final framework peace accord within 15 months. The contradiction between the two commitments surfaced on the eve of the Camp David summit when both the NRP and Shas left the government in light of the forthcoming territorial concessions. Indeed in July 2000 at Camp David, under the auspices of President Clinton, Barak produced an unprecedented Israeli offer that reportedly included around 95 percent of the West Bank, all of the Gaza Strip, and even the Arab-populated parts of Jerusalem and shared rule over the Temple Mount. Barak continued with his offer even after the failure at Camp David while his government did not enjoy anymore a majority in the Knesset anymore. Presumably, the borders of the Palestinian state set forth by the PA were the pre-1967 lines and Eastern Jerusalem thus including over a hundred Israeli settlements with a combined population of 200,000 Jews living in the settlements. Two subjects however blocked an agreement. The first one was a religious one—Palestinian demand for control and full sovereignty over the Temple Mount. The second one was national—Palestinian right of return into Israel. Unable to reach an agreement regarding the final borders of the Palestinian state, ending Israeli occupation of the West Bank and Gaza Strip emerged as the official cause of the second Intifada.

A short review of the evolution of the second Intifada would unveil the relative strength of these issues.

The official trigger to the Intifada was the September 28 visit of opposition leader Ariel Sharon on the Temple Mount. In the ensuing violent demonstrations of the visit 20 Israeli policemen and 10 Palestinians were wounded. The next day following the Friday sermons at the Haram al-Sharif, as the Temple Mount is called by the Muslims, seven Palestinians were killed in violent clashes. The widening of the demonstrations brought more casualties. A significant expansion of the conflict occurred on October 1 when the Israeli Arabs joined the demonstrations and blocked strategic passes such as the Vadi Ara. In skirmishes with the Israeli police over the course of several days while trying to restore law and order, 13 Israeli Arabs were killed. While the religious bond between the two populations is deep the ethnonational axis seems as the more profound in attracting the Israeli Arabs into the Israeli–Palestinian conflict. The Palestinian toll reached 50 after a week of clashes. But another proximate nexus became evident right away and this was the one with the Hizballah, the Shiite militia, in Lebanon. The Hizballah's success in getting Israel out of Lebanon served as a model that the Palestinians could emulate to get the IDF out of the West Bank and Gaza and maybe beyond. Indeed, a series of side-road rigged explosions in the Gaza Strip in September preceded the Sharon visit. Following the Israeli pullback Arafat repeatedly proclaimed that he also demanded a total Israeli withdrawal in the West Bank and Gaza similar to that in Lebanon. The linkage with Lebanon was further strengthened on October 7 when Hizballah penetrated the international border between Israel and Lebanon and captured three Israeli soldiers. In late October, UN Secretary General Kofi Annan came to the Middle East to negotiate both the Palestinian and Hizballah confrontations with Israel without much success.

The operation of the Hizballah, mentioned earlier as associated with the sectarian civil war in Lebanon, in a way embodied the compound nature of conflict in the Middle East. Its support both military and financial, came from secular Syria and the theocratic Iran. For Syria it was a card to be played against Israel in its struggle to regain the Golan Heights. For Iran the role of Shiite militia a distance away from Iran was its participation in the struggle for the liberation of Jerusalem. At the same time, Assad has repeatedly signaled that a peace agreement with Damascus that would include Israeli withdrawal from the Golan Heights to the pre-1967 borders would eliminate the Hizballah (Ma'oz, 1995: 230–235). This option was never tested since Israel and Syria failed to reach a peace agreement in March 2000 in the Clinton–Assad meetings, and Barak decided on a unilateral withdrawal from Lebanon.

Apprehensive of a regional inflammation especially because of its religious tones, the Americans tried to take the Intifada asunder. President Clinton, striving to halt escalation intervened personally on October 16 rearranging a cease-fire between Israel and the PA in Sharm Al-Sheikh. On

November 8, Clinton appointed the Mitchell committee whose report was later accepted as a basis for negotiations. President Bush picked up on these attempts and the United States continued to send special envoys to the Middle East such as the head of the CIA George Tenet, General Ziny but to no avail. Ultimately, the president stated American support for an independent Palestinian state at the end of the road. A precondition for such a state to emerge was a reform of the PA. In other words the problem is political not religious.

Indeed, a comparison of the issues dominating the September 2000 Israeli–Palestinian crisis indicates that despite the weight of the religious dimension it was secondary to the national one. Comparing the saliency of the two issues that brought the 2000 Camp David negotiations to stalemate namely "Temple Mount" and the "right of return," it was the latter that caused the stalemate which ultimately induced the Intifada. The "right of return" issue is based on UN Resolution 194 from December 1948 and refers to the right of the Palestinians from all over the world to return to their homes within Israel. Of course for Israel, with almost 20 percent Arab minority, this implied demographic suicide. The addition of millions of refugees would have turned the Jews into a minority in their own state. Already at Camp David and in the Clinton proposals there seemed to be a potential dividing line in Jerusalem upon which the two sides appeared to agree. Moreover, the demand for Jerusalem was for it to be the Palestinian Capital not a holy city and this despite its name in Arabic Al-Quds (the Holy). The right of return, the main reason for the failure of Camp David 2000, in contrast, remained the hardest nut to crack. Significantly, Fatah and even the religious-oriented organizations — Hamas and Jihad — insisted on the right of return not because of religious reasons namely its holiness to Islam but rather due to international law and custom (Frisch and Sandler, 2003). Similarly, the PA conducted the battle over the Palestinian territories as a national liberation struggle not as a religious one. Significantly, the doctrine of Dar al Islam that sanctifies territories that were once held by Muslim peoples hardly played a role in the uprising against the Jews. In short, while the right of return was the motivating force of the Intifada it was the religious issue that was to mobilize the masses in the Arab and the Islamic worlds.

The strength of the religious component in the Intifada can also be tested in the external reaction to the outbreak of violence. Clearly, despite Arafat's attempt to pull in other Arab states, the main antagonists in the Intifada remained the Israelis and the Palestinians. The Intifada to be sure, evoked popular support in many Arab countries, with strong religious expressions in Muslim countries. In the ensuing weeks and despite ongoing violence moderate states like Egypt and Jordan warned against the use of violence. In the Arab summit all the Arab states supported the Palestinian Intifada, putting the full blame on Israel. The call to break relations was limited to the Arab states that did not sign an official peace treaty thus excluding Jordan and Egypt, which ultimately did call back their ambassadors but did not break relations. The more extreme bloc led by Syria, Yemen, and Iraq demanded more radical steps (*Yediot Ahronot* October 22, 2000: 2–3 and October 23: 11). Saddam Hussein moved some of his divisions to Western Iraq closer to Jordan's borders. In the ensuing years, Saddam forwarded funds in support of suicide bombers in Israel, a policy motivated more by his interest to divert attention from his actions and mobilize the Arab world behind him against the United States rather than by religious motives.

In retrospect, the Al-Aqsa Intifada has been the first unblended war between Jews and Palestinians. In all previous encounters even when the Palestinians were involved other actors participated in the hostilities either from outside of the region like Mandatory Britain in 1936–1939 or from within the region like Syria in 1982. The first Intifada, though unblended and despite casualties could not be defined as a war but rather as a civil uprising. Three and more years after September 2000 none of the either exterritorial or regional Arab countries dispatched worriers into the struggle. Political support on the international scene from both Arab and Muslim countries ran high, but so did support from many European states. Significantly, also religious international Islam did not consign expeditions of worriers into "Palestine." Cooperation between the two camps apparently did take place.

The ascension of the religious dimension of the Palestinian–Israeli conflict mirrored a similar rise of militant Islam in the global system. The first major concurrent action was an Islamist terrorist bombing on October 9 likely orchestrated by Osama Bin Laden, on the U.S.S. Cole refueling in a port in Yemen. Suicide bombings continued motivated by religious beliefs. On September 11, 2001, Al-Qaeda through suicide bombers that hijacked four planes and crashed them into predesignated targets destroyed the Twin Towers in New York and the West Wing in the Pentagon. President Bush's declaration of war against Islamist terror and especially against Bin Laden did not bring about cessation of religious terror neither in the Middle East nor on the global scene. Following its eradication from Afghanistan, Al-Qaeda tried to link its religious global war against the West to the Israeli–Palestinian conflict. In this sense it was comparable to Saddam Hussein's attempt to mobilize the Arab world behind him in his struggle against the United States. In short, the religious dimension was now not anymore a local Israeli–Palestinian, and this conflict was never only religious, but rather a global phenomenon that fed and was fed by intercommunal conflicts where one of the parties was Islam.

Summary and Conclusion

In summary, the origins of the Jewish–Palestinian conflict were set out at the beginning of the twentieth century as an intercommunal dispute that included both religious and ethnonational elements. In the middle of that century, coinciding with peak of the Cold War and aroused

Pan-Arabism, it shifted to an interstate secular confrontation. Socialist and statist ideologies that penetrated the region were secular. The new "embracement" interlocking the Palestinian and the Jewish communities since the June 1967 war ultimately revived the intercommunal elements of the conflict. At the outset it was the shocking victory that paradoxically induced ethnonational and religious longings among both Palestinians and Israelis. Aspirations of the return to Palestine and the whole of the Land of Israel ascended. The disengagement of Egypt and Jordan from the Gaza Strip and from West Bank had helped to crystalize an ethnonational Palestinian identity. The PLO that had demanded the total replacement of Israel by a Palestinian state, scored political victories both abroad and within the territory thus focusing its struggle on the West Bank and the Gaza Strip (Khalidi, 1991: 63–80). In like manner access to the historic sites of the West Bank (called Judea and Samaria according to their biblical Jewish names by Israeli religio-nationalists) activated an ethnonational momentum for Israel to keep the territory. The traumatic experience of the 1973 war, specifically disappointment with the failure of the international community to reward Israel's abstinence from preempting, which caused it heavy casualties, fanned the flames of Jewish ethnonationalism further. The reaction within the Israeli body politic was the emergence of the Gush Emunim settler movement in 1974, the victory of the nationalist Likud in 1977, and the big settlement drive of 1979.

But the ethnonational impulse in Israeli as well as the Palestinian societies fused with a religious motif. Smith in recent articles pointed to the linkage between religion and ethnonationalism (Smith, 1999, 2000). Indeed while many of the early forerunners of the Land of Israel movement were secular, most of the hard core settlements and settlers in Judea and Samaria were religious. Among the Palestinians the protagonists of both Intifadas and the hard core of opposition to the peace process were the Islamist organizations. Undoubtedly, it would be difficult to decouple the two sentiments. Nevertheless, what the aforementioned analysis demonstrated is that while both sentiments are linked in the Jewish–Palestinian context it was the national identity that predominated the conflict and it was the religious that exacerbated the intensity of the conflict.

One main reason to the dominancy of the national motif in the struggle is rooted in the norms of the international system. Even for the religious true believers and despite the strength of the religious sentiment in the Intifada as well as among the settlers, the international system has imposed its norms and procedures on the conflict. The relationship between the two sets of politics will be a major section in chapter 8.

This conflict also is clearly one that crosses borders. Many Arab states have been involved militarily at some point and many more politically. The presence of a non-Islamic state on holy Islamic territory and the treatment by Israel of the Palestinians has been a major issue for Islamic fundamentalists throughout the world. The conflict has attracted political

CHAPTER 8

TOWARD A THEORY OF INTERNATIONAL RELATIONS AND RELIGION

Throughout this book we focus upon and evaluate the extent that religion influences international relations. Our general argument is that religion has been ignored by international relations scholars for a variety of reasons even though it plays an important role. One of the most important of these reasons is that international relations tend to be Western-centric. That is, the major scholars of international relations theory have been Westerners who focused mostly on the West. The discipline has its origins in the Western experience of the Enlightenment and the belief that religion is becoming an epiphenon. The major theories of international relations and many of the methodologies for testing them also have not included religion.

We argue that this body of scholarship is partially flawed because it does not take religion into account. The role religion plays in international relations is not a simple monolithic one. Rather religion influences several aspects of international relations in a number of different ways. One such influence occurs because religion is a source of legitimacy that can be used by many actors in the world system including traditional policy makers and their opposition, both foreign and domestic. This is particularly important because many believe that normative values, including religious values, are playing an increasingly important role in international relations.

It is important to emphasize that this does not mean that the only relevant manifestation of religious legitimacy is its cynical use to legitimate policies that have purely nonreligious motivations, though this surely occurs. That is, religion is not merely a card to be played in the game of power politics. Often religious and secular motivations coincide. For instance, states often have realpolitik reasons for giving aid to those in need, but this in no way compromises the fact that most religions consider charity a virtue. Similarly, the policies of many states toward Israel are to a great extent motivated by their material interests in the Middle East and, at least in the case of the United States, its interest in supporting democracy and the free-market system throughout the world. Yet can policies toward Israel be fully separated from the disputes over the holy sites in Israel, whose value are mostly within the spiritual realm?

Thus, foreign policies can also be motivated by religious concerns. This can occur through the religious worldviews of the policy makers themselves, whether it is individual policy makers within a more secular government or a religious government such as that of Iran. Foreign policies can also be influenced through the religious worldviews of a population within a state that constrain the options of policy makers. For instance, returning to our example of Israel, both the Jews and Palestinians consider the Temple Mount to be a holy place that cannot be ceded to the other side of the conflict. An Israeli or Palestinian leader who gave up the Temple Mount in a peace settlement would likely be removed from office. Furthermore, since these constraints on the leaders are religious and absolutist in nature, there is little room for compromise on the issue. Constraints on leaders such as this one go a long way in explaining the difficulty in solving the conflict, despite considerable international attention to the issue.

Furthermore, if a policy is guided by religious beliefs, it should automatically have religious legitimacy for those who share similar beliefs. Thus, religious legitimacy and religious worldviews are inexorably intertwined.

Despite all this, religious legitimacy is not a unidirectional or universal tool. It can be used to promote peace as well as war (Appleby, 2000; Gopin, 2000). In fact, under the correct circumstances it can legitimize or delegitimize just about any policy or action. However, this ability to legitimize and motivate is limited. Not all people are religious and therefore receptive to religious arguments. Indeed, some may be automatically suspicious and hostile to any religious-based arguments for a variety of reasons. They themselves may not be religious and possibly have negative views of religion. Also, even religious people may be of the opinion that religion and state should be separate, giving religion no place in discourses over policy issues. Furthermore, religious legitimacy is not always transferable across religions. Invoking Christianity, for example, is less likely to influence members of other religions. Though, this limitation is not absolute because there are clearly some religious themes that do translate across religions. Finally, it is important to remember that religion is one among many competing sources of motivation and legitimacy. Often other such sources will trump religion. Also, policies can be so popular that religious opposition will not succeed in changing them.

A second way religion influences international relations is when domestic religious issues and conflicts cross borders and become international issues. We demonstrated in chapter 4 that this occurs with regard to international intervention in ethnic conflicts. Our analysis shows that intervention is more likely to occur in the religious conflicts, among these conflicts. It also shows that the vast majority of interveners intervene on behalf of minorities religiously similar to them. Thus, not only are ethnoreligious conflicts more likely to become international, the nature in which they become international is along religious lines. This finding is also indirect evidence that the motivations for international intervention include religious ones.

Religious conflicts, like most types of conflict, can cross borders in a number of other ways. Violent domestic conflicts can destabilize bordering states or even an entire region. Religious rebellions in one part of the world can inspire similar rebellions by similar groups living elsewhere. Religious conflicts often cause international refugee flows. Successful religious revolutions like those in Iran and Afghanistan often try to export their revolutions and provide training ground for militants from other states. Local religious conflicts can become internationalized with the two (or more) sides competing in international forums like the United Nations and through international NGOs. Local policies and conflicts over holy sites can quickly become international issues. Finally, all of these processes are exacerbated by the fact that the world is becoming a smaller place due to improvements in communications technology and the increasing economic interdependence of the international system. Nevertheless, this insight is based upon the traditional approach of state sovereignty that saw the borders of the territorial state as steadfast.

A third type of religious influence on the international system is through transnational religious phenomena. For instance, religious fundamentalist movements across the world have their origins in changes in the world system caused by the process of modernization. One of their goals is to resist the secular modern values of this system. Though, as discussed earlier, the values of the world system are influenced by religion, fundamentalists focus on the secular aspects of these values and consider the system not religious enough. While the near-term goals of most such movements are domestic, these motivations have international implications. If a fundamentalist movement succeeds in taking over a state government or influencing its policies, this will reverberate through the international system via that state's foreign policy. In the long term, however, the motivations of fundamentalists are international in that religious absolutes recognize no international borders. Thus, the eventual goal is often to convert the entire world to their ideology. Whether this is done through persuasion and missionaries or through force and terrorism, the effort has international implications.

Political Islam is, perhaps, the most visible of such movements but it is by no means the only one. It is also, perhaps, the most transnational of the various fundamentalist movements. Loosely associated Islamic fundamentalist movements exist in many, if not the majority, of states in the world. Their funding is often international. They also share many common policies and goals including spreading Islamic values and countering the influence of the West in their societies. Nevertheless, Islam is not monolithic and movements other than political Islam remain influential.

Religious terrorism is also becoming an increasingly important transnational issue. The majority of world terrorism since the 1980s has been by Islamic religious groups and the majority of new terrorist movements since then also fit into this category (Weinberg and Eubanks, 1998; Weinberg et al., 2002). The attacks of September 11, 2001 have increased both the awareness of international religious terrorism and its importance in foreign policy. Osama Bin Laden's Al-Qaeda network of terrorists is a truly international operation with a presence in as many as 60 states. More localized groups such as those in Algeria, Lebanon, and Israel have also caused violence that has had international implications. Clearly, this is related to the issue of fundamentalism as most such terrorists are fundamentalists. Yet, this manifestation of fundamentalism is of particular importance because of the direct and immediate impact of its violent acts. In the long term the more peaceful efforts by fundamentalists to change the nature of both domestic regimes and the international system may be of greater importance. But for the time being, states are more likely to rally around the cause of fighting terrorism's clear and present threat than the more existential threat posed by other fundamentalists.

The issue of human rights is among the international norms that is influenced by religion and is becoming an issue of increasing international importance. It is enshrined in international treaties and agreements and, increasingly, in international institutions. It is a justification for interfering with the sovereignty of a state, a value that was once considered absolute. Many of the international differences over this issue are precisely over religious values. For instance, views on the traditional role of women in Islam are often in conflict with views by others, especially the West, on the rights of women. Yet the basic values of equality and fairness, essential elements of the human rights regime, are also part of many religious doctrines.

Other issues of international importance such as population growth, contraception, and abortion also have religious aspects.

Despite all of these influences on various aspects of international relations, we do not claim that religion is the primary motivating force behind foreign policy. Rather, we claim it is an important aspect of the international system that has not been given nearly enough attention. It is also not a monolithic force that influences international relations in a simple and unidirectional manner. Rather its influence is an aggregate of multiple avenues of influence on different aspects of international relations. Each of these individual influences taken by themselves could seem to some to be trivial, though we do not believe that this is the case. But when taken as a whole these multiple avenues of influence create a cumulative effect that is undeniable. It influences and places constraints upon the decisions of many policy makers. Local religious issues and conflicts regularly spread across borders in a number of ways. It is also related to a number of transnational phenomena including religious fundamentalism, terrorism, and the human rights regime. Thus, while religion's influence on international relations is not a primary causal agency in international relations, it is among the most important, and perhaps the most important, of intervening variables.

Integrating Religion into General International Relations Theory

Since religion, while influential, is not the driving force behind international relations, the best way to account for its impact is to integrate it into existing international relations theory. Thus, we do not suggest that the dominant paradigms of international relations be scrapped, rather we argue that they need to be modified in order to account for religion.

Realist theory, the most influential theory in international relations scholarship, rests upon three assumptions that, in light of our findings on religion, need to be reassessed. First, that the goal of states' foreign policies is solely to accumulate power and material goods. Second, that the internal workings of a state can be placed in a "black box" and ignored, as all states have similar motivations and goals in the international system. Third, that the international system is a fully chaotic, self-help system.

Addressing the last of these assumptions first, it is clear that the international system is influenced by norms, including religious ones. For instance, the international laws on war are in part derived from religious concepts including those in St. Augustine's *City of God* and are mirrored by similar concepts in Islamic law.

There are actions that are simply considered unacceptable. Though imperfectly, these norms are enforced by international institutions and individual states. For instance, genocide and often lesser human rights abuses are considered sufficient justification for international organizations and individual states to intervene in the affairs of the states that perpetrate these crimes. Clearly, the application of such punishment is not consistent and the motivations for action or nonaction by states in enforcing international norms, either individually or through international institutions, is colored by other motivations including realist motivations. Nevertheless, while not a hierarchic structure the international system is bound by norms that remove a portion of the chaos from the international system and religion is one of the bases for these norms.

Also, it is important to note that there is some dispute over many of the norms that play a role in this regime. Interestingly, many of these disputes are along religious lines. For instance, the international human rights regime includes concepts like women's rights. This cause is championed by the Christian West. The greatest opposition to these norms comes from the Islamic world, where the Western concept of women's rights clashes with concepts of the traditional role of women. Similarly, the West, championed by the United States, has been trying with some success to spread the norm that democracy is the proper form of government. The success of this norm is apparent in the fact that even most dictatorships go through the motions of having elections even though the outcome is predetermined. However, as discussed in chapter 5, many Muslims have a very different concept of democracy than does the West, if they accept the concept at all. Many do not accept the concepts of separation of religion and state and equal treatment for religious minorities. These contradictions are recognized by many Muslims who, rather than address the tension between the two, prefer to question the validity of those elements of the concept of human rights that clash with their concept of Islam (Van der Vyver, 1996). Thus, religion is both one of the bases for a regime of international norms and one of the factors that has prevented the regime from becoming even stronger and more influential.

The second assumption of realists, placing all domestic factors within a "black box," also covers up the importance of religion. This is because religion's greatest influence on the international system is through its significant influence on domestic politics. It is a motivating force that guides many policy makers. It can also guide those who oppose specific policies. Thus, it is an important element of national debates over important issues. Its influence over foreign policy decisions can be seen in the fact that it influences the decision by states to intervene in domestic conflicts in other states. Its influence on public opinion can place constraints upon the decisions of policy makers. It can also provide justification for policies that decision makers support for other reasons. All of this reverberates into the international system through the foreign policies of individual states.

It is also important to remember that religion is not the only domestic factor that has been shown to influence international politics. The democratic peace literature has shown that democracies do not fight wars with each other, whether or not they may have realist reasons to do so. It also has been argued that states go to war in order to divert their populace's attention from domestic problems. In short, religion is another variable that influences international relations via the domestic system.

All of this brings into question the first assumption of realism that the prime and only motivations for foreign policies are the pursuit of power and material wealth. Clearly, foreign policies also include normative considerations, including religious ones. The domestic influences of religion on the decisions of foreign policy makers are sometimes difficult to place in the context of the pursuit of power. Furthermore, the international significance and attention given to holy sites also does not fit well with the pursuit of power. For example, the role of Jerusalem or the Temple Mount in Jerusalem's Old City cannot be measured by its territorial or strategic value.

Despite this, much of the influence of religion on international relations can be placed into a more realist context. Spreading a state's religious ideals to other states increases your influence on those states and the potential pool of allies, thus increasing that state's influence in the international system. Similarly, creating a system of international norms that effectively legislate a state's worldview, gives it an advantage over other states in the international system by providing justifications for that state's actions. For instance, the success of the United States and other Western states in spreading the norms of democracy and human rights help to justify their interference in the domestic politics of many nondemocratic states.

Another important power resource for states are diasporas. Populations of those who share ethnic, national, or religious bonds with a particular state or group of states living elsewhere can be a valuable resource for that state's foreign policy. Consider the influence of the Jewish lobby in the United States on U.S. policy toward Israel. Consider also the increasing organization by Muslim groups in the United States in support of the Palestinian cause. Both groups raise money that is sent abroad to help their cause and form lobby groups to directly influence U.S. policy toward the Palestinian–Israeli conflict.

Similarly, control over holy sites or other forms of religious symbols can be a power resource. The prestige of a holy site is transferable to secular leaders. This explains why Palestinian leader Yasser Arafat makes a point of attending Christmas celebrations at Christian holy sites in Bethlehem even though he is a Muslim. It explains why the White House, in addition to having a Christmas tree, also has a Hanukkah Menorah to celebrate the Jewish holiday. These symbols are important and being associated with them is important to leaders.

Religion is also a source of legitimacy that can be used to persuade others. The power to persuade is essential to policy makers both domestically and internationally. While a gun to one's head, a more classic realist source of power, is a powerful tool of persuasion, so is an appeal to one's religious morals. Even politicians who do not share these morals may not be willing to be seen by their constituents who do share these morals to be breaking them.

Nevertheless, to reduce religion to nothing more than one of many potential sources of power and influence is a mistake. This degrades the sincere beliefs held by a significant portion of the world's population. It is also ill-advised for more mundane reasons. Religion is one of the basic elements of many people's worldviews. It influences their decisions and how they view the world. While certainly this aspect of human nature can be manipulated by those who seek power, it is nonetheless an independent factor that can have a potent influence on people's behavior above and beyond its use as a power resource.

Religion similarly needs to be integrated into other theories of international relations. One such theory is liberalism, the body of theory that posits the need for building international institutions and norms in order to create a world civilization that will bring peace and prosperity to all. In this tradition, some like Appleby (2000) and Gopin (2000) have argued that religious norms can be used to bridge the gap between cultures and even resolve long-standing conflicts. Most religions have complex traditions that are open to multiple different interpretations. What is needed, according to this line of thought, is to find shared values that can be built upon as well as to emphasize those aspects of religions that promote peace, understanding, and cooperation.

Furthermore, as discussed in detail earlier and in chapter 3, existing international norms are, in part, based on religion. Thus, the concept of international regimes proposed by liberalism can accommodate the importance of religion in international politics. However, the theory also needs to account for the more divisive aspects of religion. Religion can be a powerful motivator for war. It has been associated with international intervention, ethnic conflict (Fox, 2002a), international conflict

(Henderson, 1997, 1998), terrorism (Rapoport, 1984, 1988, 1990; Hoffman, 1995), genocide (Fein, 1990: 49), and ethnic cleansing (Osiander, 2000: 785). Thus, while religion can potentially be a tool to legitimate and support a regime of international laws and institutions, it can also be one of the factors that prevents, damages, or destroys such a regime. As noted earlier, religious divisions are one of the factors that prevent such a regime, the human rights regime, from being more universally accepted.

Constructivism stresses process, as opposed to structure. This body of theory posits that the structure of international politics is dependent upon the norms and the construction of reality by the participants in the international forum. If states choose a power-oriented value system and behave anarchically, then the system resembles the system posited by realists and if states cooperate, it resembles the liberal perception. Constructivists tend to accept the dominant paradigm of the social sciences from the first eight or nine decades of the twentieth century and believe that religion is becoming irrelevant. However, other than this, there is no reason that religion cannot be included in a constructivist perception of international relations. Since religion can and does influence international institutions and hence the behavior of states it is part of the process and, thus, part of the international system.

Religion is, perhaps, most incompatible with Marxist theory and the body of international relations theory that derives from it. This is because this body of theory recognizes economics as the only motivating force in politics, including international relations. There is no way to adequately make this concept of international relations compatible with the notion that religion is an important influence, since in the end, Marxists consider it a false consciousness and the opiate of the masses. In doing so, even Marxists acknowledge its influence but predict that this influence will wane. Also, for that matter, it is difficult to reconcile Marxism with any of the other theories of international relations. Thus, the only approach is not to integrate religion into Marxist theory, as this would negate a basic assumption of that body of theory, but rather to integrate Marxism into the greater body of international relations theory. It is clear that economics influences international relations. Even realists acknowledge this. It is also clear that the world economic system benefits some countries more than others. Thus, if the insights of Marxism are taken in moderation and accepted as one of many influences in the international system, they can be used in combination with religion and other factors to better understand that system.

Another important element of the international system that has implications for integrating religion into international relations theory is nationalism. Nationalism and ethnicity are similar to religion in that they are sources of legitimacy, they influence the worldviews of leaders and their constituents, and form links of identity between populations across the globe. It is also a source of conflict that can cross borders and can be described as a transnational phenomenon. Until recently nationalism and ethnicity were, also like religion, ignored by international relations theory (Carment and James, 1997a,b). Yet, it has been recognized by international relations scholars that these factors do influence international politics. Articles on ethnicity and nationalism began to appear in international relations journals in the early 1990s and are now common. However, it is not clear that nationalism has yet been fully integrated into international relations theory, despite the obvious need for this to happen.

More interestingly, nationalism and religion are closely linked. Anthony Smith (1999, 2000), one of the pioneers in researching nationalism and international relations, has linked nationalism to religion. He argues that the two concepts have similar properties. Both include concepts of election—being the chosen people. Both include histories and myths with sacred or sacred-like qualities. Also, both include concepts of individual sacrifice for the group. Furthermore, these sacred-like qualities of nationalism are based on religious ideas. In addition to having qualities similar to religion, religious beliefs often shape and inspire specific modern national identities. Often there is a fusion between earlier religious myths and national ones. Thus in all, religion has influenced national myths and, even where there is no religious influence, national myths have "taken from these older traditions a vital component of its outlook" (Smith, 1999: 349). Thus, "modern concepts of national mission and national destiny are lineal descendants of the ancient beliefs in ethnic election, with their emphasis on the privileges and duties of the elect before God" (Smith, 1999: 350).

Implicit in this argument is that identity is an important element of modern politics, including international politics. Both nationalism and religion are important aspects of identity. People are more willing to help those with whom they share a common identity. States have a predisposition to ally with those who are similar to them. This includes those who look like them and share a common history, language, or religion.

Based on this, it is possible to conclude that Samuel Huntington's proposition that the clash of civilizations should be the new paradigm for international relations is correct. We argue that this is not the case. Identity, whether in Huntington's "civilizational" formulation or some other formulation based on ethnicity, nationalism, religion, or some other basis, is an important aspect of the world system, but it is certainly not the paradigmatic force that defines all international politics. Like religion it has its influence but this influence is only one among many. As discussed in chapter 6, conflict within identity groups is as common or perhaps even more common than conflict between them. For example, the increasing role of religious fundamentalism as a cause of conflict often pits fundamentalists and non-fundamentalists of the same religion and ethnicity against each other. This is especially true in the Islamic world where one of the most violent conflicts is the civil war in Algeria, which is between a more secular government run by Muslims against fundamentalist Muslim groups who wish to remake the state to fit with their concept of Islam. This conflict, and many like it, does not cross religious, ethnic, national, or civilizational identity lines.

In sum, realism's concept of the search for power in the international system is likely the dominant factor in international relations. It answers more questions better than does any other theory. But it does not answer all of them. For this we need to look elsewhere. International regimes, the process, economics, nationalism, ethnicity, and religion as well as a number of other factors also play a role. That the focus of this book is on religion is not to detract from any of these other significant and important influences on international relations. Rather it is intended to call attention to an important element of international relations that has been negligently overlooked.

Where to From Here?

This book is not intended to be the last word on religion and international relations. Rather it is meant to contribute to a debate on a topic that needs a considerable amount of further thought. While there is clearly a general need for international relations theorists, researchers, and practitioners to take religion into account, much needs to be done before the full influence of religion on international relations can be recognized.

Quantifying Religion

For instance, the quantitative branch of international relations scholarship needs to develop better variables to measure religion. The few purely international relations studies that include religion variables rely on simple measures like whether two states belong to a different religion[1] or the majority religion in a state.[2] Most studies of domestic politics use similarly simple measures including those mentioned earlier[3] or the extent to which a state is religiously homogeneous or heterogeneous.[4] However, some like Fox (1997, 1999a,b, 2000a,b,d, 2001c) have taken steps in the direction of more sophisticated measures. While some of the measures used in these studies are similar to those mentioned earlier, others are more sophisticated. These include complex variables measuring the extent of discrimination against an ethnic minority, the grievances expressed over this discrimination, and whether religious issues are more important than other issues in the conflict. While these specific variables may not be readily used in studies of international relations, similar ones could and should be developed to account for international conflict.

However, before we can do this, we need to develop more specific criteria describing how religion influences international relations. As implied earlier, the answers are not in international relations theory, as that body of theory has for too long neglected the topic of religion. Rather we need to explore the general social science literature on the topic of religion, searching for concepts that can be translated into international relations theory. As the lines between international relations and domestic politics are blurring, that the other social sciences focus on events that occur within a state should not hinder this process. While this book hopefully will have started this process, much still needs to be done.

For instance, we have established that religious legitimacy and world-views can significantly influence the behavior of leaders and such factors existing in a state's population can constrain that state's leaders' options. However, these concepts need to be refined further. When focusing on leaders we must ask do leaders who are religious behave differently than do leaders who are not religious? For instance, are they more likely to go to war? In order to answer this we need to develop a way to objectively measure the religiosity of world leaders. One way to do this would be to measure how often they refer to religious concepts like God or evil. However this avenue is somewhat problematic. How do we control for factors like whether a leader speaks in public more or less often? If we limit our study to U.S. presidents, for example, we could measure only State of the Union Addresses, which are given once a year by all U.S. presidents. If we were to limit our study to British prime ministers, we could use the times they are questioned in parliament. Yet how can we compare U.S. presidents and British prime ministers, as these two forums are so different that any comparison would be meaningless?

Furthermore, how can we be sure that any expression of religiosity by leaders is truly representative of their personal religiosity? Perhaps it is a cynically calculated campaign to gain the support of a religious con-stituency. For example, Sadam Hussein, known as a secular dictator, started using a religious vocabulary with the strengthening of Islam in the Arab world, especially when it suited his struggle against the United States. These problems of comparability also apply to our dependent variable of foreign policy. The influence of the U.S. president and the British prime minister on their states' foreign policies are not the same due to the very different structures of their governments. Also, leaders from different times and places generally deal with different types of issues in different contexts. Thus, while a quantitative study of the influence of leaders' reli-giosity is not impossible, it would be difficult and could only be applied in a limited context. For this reason, such studies are most likely to take the case study approach.

However, examining the influence of the religiosity of a population on that state's behavior is achievable. The dependent variable, state behavior in the international realm, already exists in a number of databases, espe-cially on the topic of war. Furthermore these databases include a number of control variables. Measures of the religiosity of the populations of many states are also available from sociologists. There are various sociological surveys that are done simultaneously in tens of states that include ques-tions intended to measure an individual's religiosity. These can be used to develop measures of the average religiosity of entire states. In fact, Barro and McCleary (2002) used this information to develop measures of reli-giosity for a study of the impact of religion on the economy. They used three different sets of surveys and have data on 59 different states.

However, the measures of religiosity from the different surveys are not exactly the same and not all of the surveys were taken at the same time. Thus, while this type of religiosity variable is useful, until there is a significant improvement in the current state of the available information it is seriously flawed.

A more promising avenue of research is to focus on state institutions and behavior as a surrogate variable for religiosity. That is factors like whether a state has an official religion, discriminates against religious minorities, or legislates the religion can be taken as indirect evidence of the religiosity of that state's population. It certainly reflects whether religion is an element of governing institutions. Some data has been collected on this. Chaves and Cann (1992) and Chaves et al. (1994) collected a variable that measures whether a state has an official church. They also collected 12 variables measuring the presence of various types of religious legislation.[5] Unfortunately this information was collected for only 18 states. Barret et al. (2001: 834–835) measures whether a state's "religion or philosophy" is religious. While this data is available for all world states, it is problematic in that there is little explanation as to how and based on what criteria this data was collected.

Variables measuring religious discrimination and religious freedom in a state are also available. For instance Freedom House provides a 12-point measure of religious freedom in 81 states.[6] Also Barret et al. (2001: 834–835) has measures for treatment of Christian minorities throughout the world. This data is limited in that it focuses only on Christian minorities and like his religious philosophy variable, there is little explanation as to how and based on what criteria this data was collected. As noted earlier Fox collected data on the treatment of ethnic minorities but, similar to Barret et al. (2001) this data looks only at the treatment of certain minorities and not others.

Thus, the existing cross-sectional data on the entanglement between religion and state is flawed. However, that this data has been collected demonstrates that better, more complete studies are possible. Thus it should be an important agenda for future research to develop and collect state-level variables on this topic, then use them to analyze state behavior in the international arena.

There is good reason to believe that such an endeavor will be fruitful. Specifically, existing quantitative studies on human behavior show a number of links between religion and behavior. A few of these studies deal with issues of international relations. The data in chapter 4 shows that international intervention is influenced by religion. Henderson (1997, 1998) shows that states belonging to different religions are more likely to go to war.

The majority of political science studies on religion deal with domestic issues. For instance, a series of studies by Fox (1997, 1999a,b, 2000a,b,d, 2001c, 2002a) show multiple links between religion and ethnic conflict. In an ethnic conflict involving separatism, the fact that religious issues are important can as much as double the level of violence. Religious institutions tend to deter ethnic conflict unless there are religious issues involved, in which case they exacerbate the conflict. When religious issues are not important religious legitimacy facilitates the formation of grievances over nonreligious issues. However, when religion is an important issue in a conflict, religious legitimacy inhibits the formation of nonreligious grievances and facilitates the formation of religious grievances. Both the presence of religious legitimacy and whether religion is an important issue in a conflict increase the extent of discrimination against ethnic minorities. Studies by Ellingsen (2000), Rummel (1997), and Reynal-Querol (2002) confirm these results showing that religious diversity in a state increases the extent of ethnic conflict.

Studies on other aspects of government structure and policy have also linked religion and politics. In a study of abortion policies Minkenberg (2002) found that low church attendance in a state is correlated with liberal abortion policies and the combination of high church attendance and the state being Catholic is associated with restrictive abortion policies. Chaves and Cann (1992) found that lower church attendance in a country is associated with higher government regulation of religion. As noted in chapter 5, there is also mixed evidence as to whether Islam is associated with autocratic governments.

There is also a considerable amount of sociological data that shows that religion influences behavior on the individual level. Many such studies show a link between religion and political opinions and attitudes toward other issues. Hayes (1995) demonstrates that religious identification, or the lack thereof, influences individual attitudes toward issues including abortion, working women, capital punishment, confidence in institutions, and support for religion in politics. Leak and Randall (1995) found that religiosity influences attitudes toward authoritarianism. Bruce (2000) found a correlation between religiosity and support for nationalist issues in Finland. Karpov (2002) found that Protestants in the United States and Poland are more likely to be illiberal than Catholics. Laythe et al. (2002a,b) and Kirkpatrick (1993) found that among college students, Christian beliefs are correlated with less racial prejudice and higher prejudice against homosexuals but religious fundamentalism is associated with prejudice against blacks, women, homosexuals, and Communists. Djupe (2000) links "religious brand loyalty" to partisanship and church attendance to voter turnout. Miller (1996) found that one's religious denomination influences one's attitude toward issues of morality, lifestyle, and tolerance of diversity. Similarly, Ebaugh and Haney (1978), Jelen (1984), Harris and Mills (1985), Scheepers and Van Der Silk (1998), and Woodrum (1988) all found that when controlling for education and income, religious denomination and involvement are the strongest predictors of moral attitudes.

There are also links between religion and individual violence. Cunradi et al. (2002) found that church attendance is associated with lower levels of violence by individuals. Nielson and Fultz (1995) found that someone who considers religion as an end in itself rather than a means to other ends is less likely to engage in conflict over social issues. While these are but a sampling of the existing sociological studies, they are enough to show that religion influences behavior and attitudes on the individual level. By implication, they provide further evidence of the likelihood that quantitative studies of international relations will also find a link between religion and the behavior of international actors.

Defining Religion

Another important issue is the question of what is religion and what is religious? From a philosophical perspective, and even from a social science perspective this question is difficult, if not impossible, to answer. Turner (1991: 242–246) in a brief discussion on "what is religion?" refers to over a dozen different and contradictory definitions and perspectives on this topic from the social sciences literature. Thus, a definitive definition is not realistic.

However, the question of what is religion can be limited in a way that makes it simpler to manage for the purposes of international relations theory and research. The key is to focus not on what religion is, but what it does. That is, rather than addressing the more philosophical issues involved in defining religion, it is easier to stress what role religion plays in society. This has the advantage of avoiding difficult philosophical and existential issues while focusing on the core issue of the social sciences, human behavior.

Four such roles have been discussed in this book. First, religion is one of the sources of people's worldviews. It influences people's behavior and those people influence the behavior of others. Whether we call this mechanism worldviews, beliefs, norms, or some other name, it is a powerful way in which religion intersects with individual and societal behavior. This aspect of religion explains the power of religion to guide and constrain foreign policy through the beliefs of the policy makers themselves and through the beliefs and expectations of their constituents.

Second, religion is a source of identity. In addition to influencing people's beliefs, it influences who they are. It gives them feelings of affinity to other members of their religion. This may cause them to feel responsible for their co-religionists, wherever they may live. This explains why states tend to intervene most often on behalf of groups religiously similar to them. It explains why states of similar religions are less likely to go to war with each other (Henderson, 1997, 1998). It explains why conflicts in one place can spread along religious lines to both neighboring states and places across the world. Though, clearly many nonreligious processes also contribute to this spread of conflict across borders.

Third, religion is a source of legitimacy. It can legitimize or delegitimize actions, including the foreign policies of states and the behavior of other international actors. Along with the first way religion intersects with international relations, this explains why many policy makers use religious terms and images to justify their actions.

Fourth, religion is associated with formal institutions. In some cases these institutions are themselves international actors, as is the case with the Catholic Church. In other cases these institutions play a role in domestic politics supporting regimes, opposing them, and lobbying them. These institutions also play a role in political mobilization. Sometimes, as is the case with Israel, as is described in chapter 7, religious institutions overlap with political parties that play a direct role in policy decisions.

The causes of transnational religious transnational phenomena tend to fit into more than one of these categories. For instance, religious fundamentalism is the result of threats to religious identities. Yet it also incorporates a desire or even an imperative to spread a belief system to others, often using religious institutions. Political Islam is a specific example of such a fundamentalist movement. Religious terrorism, which since the 1980s has mostly been perpetrated by Islamic groups (Weinberg and Eubanks, 1998; Weinberg et al., 2002) is a manifestation of fundamentalism where the threats to religious identity and the imperative to spread the belief system is so strong that violent acts are legitimized.

However, while helpful, this framework for understanding religion and others like it are still lacking in that they do not solve one central problem: where do we draw the line between what is religion and what is not? For instance, what is religion and what is culture? Western views on democracy and human rights can be described as part of the Enlightenments's rejection of religious ideals as the proper way to run governments and societies. If this is the case, these phenomena would be cultural developments. Yet many like Tocqueville make the argument that religion and religious values are essential elements of democracies. As the majority of Western democracies have established religions or give preference to certain religions (Stephan, 2000; Fox and Sandler, 2003c) there is considerable evidence for this argument.

On the Islamic side is it truly Islam that accounts for the fact that the Middle East is the most autocratic region of the world? (Jaggers and Gurr, 1995). If we include Muslims from outside of the Middle East, more than half of them live in democratic or near-democratic states (Stephan, 2000). This would imply that the link between Islam and autocracy is not religious, but something culturally specific to the Middle East. However, another study, while confirming that the Middle East is the most autocratic region of the world, also shows that even outside of the Middle East Islamic states are more autocratic than non-Islamic ones (Fox, 2001c). Thus, the evidence as to whether this difference between Western and Islamic states is religious or cultural is mixed.

Another difficult question of this nature is how do we determine if a person is religious? Sociologists use a number of different approaches in their survey studies. Some avoid the issue and compare different religions, like Protestants vs. Catholics without dealing with whether the respondents are religious. Others use church attendance. Others ask questions like: "Do you believe in God?" "Do you believe in Heaven and/or Hell?" or

"Do you believe in the supernatural?" All of these approaches will get different results. For instance, as Durkheim (1964) points out, Buddhists do not believe in a God so they would not be classified as religious. "Heaven" and "Hell", strictly speaking, are Christian concepts so Jews and Muslims may answer no even though these religions include concepts of an afterlife. Also, just because one believes in God or an afterlife does not mean one is religiously observant. On the other hand, not everyone who is religious regularly attends formal worship. Of course, there is the general problem of polls—that people do not always answer honestly.

This is not just a problem for poll-based studies and assessing trends within large populations. It is also a problem when trying to determine the motivations of policy makers. Assuming they profess to be religious, how do we determine if this is true or whether they do not truly believe but feel that saying they do will give them political advantage? Do they attend services for spiritual reasons or just to be seen there? To take an extreme example, videos of Saddam Hussein praying at Mosques can be seen on television but would a truly religious man use chemical weapons on entire Kurdish villages, especially considering these people are also Muslims? Yet there are clearly many politicians whose religious beliefs are sincere. How do we separate between the two?

There exists in the sociological literature an argument called the functionalist argument, which posits that any manifestation of religion in society is really some other secular force using religion. Thus, religion is seen as unimportant other than as a tool of other more relevant factors. The Marxist argument that "religion is the opiate of the masses" is a classic example of this body of thought, but by no means the only one. This theory, which dominated sociological thought on the issue for much of the twentieth century, is also a reflection of the basic question of what is religious and what is not.[7]

A basic argument of this book is that while religion is sometimes a tool used by other forces, it also has an independent influence. Also, even when used as a tool, this is also an important manifestation of religion in international politics. Nevertheless, the fact that it is sometimes a tool and sometimes an autonomous force further blurs the line between religion and other social and political forces.

Given this, even if we have an adequate definition of religion, we may not always be able to identify what is religious and what is not.

Some Final Thoughts

Will the discipline of international relations integrate religion into its framework? We think that it will be done in a similar manner to the way political science and international relations has adopted the study of nationalism, or to be more precise ethnonationalism. Though it is possible that international relation's adoption of religion will be done to a lesser degree. While originally ignoring nationalism and ethnonationalism, international relations nevertheless responded to the call of Walker Connor (1972) and Anthony Smith (1981) to supplant the notion of the integrated modern state with a more pluralistic approach. Thus, after years in which this dimension had been neglected in political science literature, the discipline has finally caught up with the reality that many of the conflicts taking place around the world are related to the politics of national or ethnic identity. T.R. Gurr (1993a), for instance, introduced the study of minorities and ethnic conflicts into the study of world politics while Pat James and David Carment (Carment and James, 1995, 1997b) have done it in the study of international crises. It is our expectation that following the international war against a source of terror so intertwined with religion, international relations as a discipline will have no choice but to pay attention to religion. Global terrorism will compel students of international politics to study the impact of religion at the international arena. As expected, once the phenomenon is recognized, the literature will grow extensively in both theoretical and empirical terms. In other words, the recognition of religion in comparative and international politics will follow ethnicity with a time lag.

While this book has begun the process of bringing religion into international relations, when all is said and done, it leaves us with as many questions as answers. We have succeeded in explaining why religion was ignored by international relations. We also succeeded in demonstrating a number of ways religion influences international relations and in providing a framework and agenda for dealing with religion's impact.

The questions that remain are not simple ones. One such question is how do we measure religion? While we discussed some ways to address this issue, the only way to get a more definitive answer is to actually use these methods or others to do so and see how they work. Another question that remains unresolved is how do we draw the line between what is religious and what is not? Both of these questions can be described as corollaries of a more central question—how do you make a concrete study of a topic that is often ambiguous and open to multiple interpretations? In more social science terms, how do you put together hard data on an inherently soft topic?

There may not be a perfect answer to these questions. The subtleties of human nature, the human psyche, and the soul where religion essentially resides may make these issues fundamentally unresolvable. Perhaps like the quest for perfection, a true answer to many of these questions is not achievable but the search itself may be rewarding. Thus, it is important to ask these questions and strive for answers. In doing so we will surely gain a better understanding of international relations, if not necessarily a perfect one.

Notes

Chapter 2   The Overlooked Dimension

1. For a survey of the literature on modernization, see, among others, Almond (1960), Apter (1965), Deutsch (1953), Foster-Carter (1985), Halpern (1964), Kautsky (1972), Randall and Theobald (1985), Rostow (1959), and Smith (1970, 1971, 1974).

2. While the focus of modernization theory is clearly on ethnicity, Appleby (1994: 7–8), Haynes (1994: 21–23), and Sahliyeh (1990: 3–4) make the argument that it is also meant to apply to religion. Also, most definitions of ethnicity include religion (e.g., see Gurr (1993a: 11)).

3. For a survey of the literature on secularization, see, among others, Beckford (1985), Bell (1971), Berger (1969), Glasner (1977), Martin (1978), Westhus (1976), and Wilson (1966, 1976, 1982).

4. For some criticisms of this theory, see Ellison (1995), Demerath (1995), and Williams (1994: 788–789).

5. *Sociology of Religion*, 6 (3), 1999.

6. These criticisms include: that Huntington has gotten the facts wrong or even misrepresented them; that his arguments are an oversimplification of reality; that his listing of civilizations is wrong; that he contradicts himself; that his evidence is wholly anecdotal; and that his analysis provides no systematic link between civilizations and conflict (Fox, 2001a: 182).

7. For a more comprehensive discussion of the debate over Huntington's theory see chapter 6 in this book and Fox (2001a,b).

8. See, e.g., Beyer (1994), Chaves (1994), Dobbelaere (1999), Lechner (1991), and Yamane (1997).

9. The new approach rebelled against the prevailing political science orthodoxy, emphasizing statist as opposed to pluralist politics. For a debate between the two approaches, see articles by Gabriel A. Almond, Eric A. Nordlinger, Theodor J. Lowi, and Sergio Fabrini in *American Political Science Review* 82 (3) (September 1988): 853–901.

10. For the neoliberal approach see Michael Doyle (1983, 1986). Mearsheimer defines institutions as "a set of rules that stipulate the ways in which states should cooperate and compete with each other. They prescribe acceptable forms of state behavior, and proscribe unacceptable kinds of behavior" (Mearsheimer, 1995: 8). Krasner, referred to it as an international regime and defined it as a setting in which international actors accept "sets of implicit or explicit principles, norms, rules and decision making procedures around which actors' expectations converge in a given area of international relations" (Krasner, 1983: 2). Jervis described security regimes, as "principles, rules, and norms that permit nations to be restrained in their behavior in the belief that others will reciprocate" (Jervis, 1982: 357).

11. See also Adler (1997: 319–363) and Hopf (1998: 171–200). Such an argument would be difficult for realists to accept in light of the practice of international politics. But, they accept, as Mearsheimer in the "The False Promise of Institutionalism," asserted that clearly realism was the hegemonic discourse or theory in world politics at least since the emergence of the Westphelian inter-state system (Mearsheimer, 1995: 42–44).

12. For a comprehensive discussion of the schemes used by these studies to measure the influence of religion on ethnic conflict, the reasoning behind it, and a summary of the results, see Fox (1999c, 2000c).

Chapter 3   Religion and Legitimacy

1. See, e.g., Baldwin (1993) and Waltz (1979).

2. Seth Maydens "In Indonesia, Political Leaders Seek a Mystical Mandate to Govern" *International Herald Tribune*, 8/22/01, 2.

3. U.S. Department of State Annual Report on International Religious Freedom for 1999: Iran. Minorities at Risk report on the Bahai Minority in Iran, available at www.cidcm.umd.edu/inscr/mar.

4. For a more detailed discussion of instrumentalism in the national and ethnic contexts see Comoroff and Stern (1995), Connor (1972).

5. A more complete discussion of the concept of *jihad* is provided later in this chapter.

6. See chapter 7 for more details on the role of religion in the Palestinian–Israeli conflict.

7. See, among others, Gurr (1994: 356–358), Russett et al. (2000), Fox (2001a,b, 2002b), Henderson (1998), Henderson and Tucker (2001), and Henderson and Singer (2000).

8. See, among others, Gungwu (1997a,b), Harris (1996), Murphey (1998), Naff (1998), Seamon (1998), and Walid (1997).

9. For a discussion of St. Augustine's views on war see Deane (1963: 154–171).

10. For a more general discussion of the Western concept of just war see Walzer (1977).

11. For a discussion of the Jewish tradition on the laws of war see Cohen (2003) and Inbar (1987).

12. For a more detailed discussion of Durkheim's views on religion see Pickering (1975, 1984).

13. For a more detailed discussion of the views of Marx and Weber, among others, on religion and society see Turner (1991).

14. For a more detailed discussion of the views of Weber on religion and society see Turner (1991) and Latin (1978).

15. While Fox (2000a) and Fisch (2002) both use only one measure of democracy, finding Islam linked with autocracy, Midlarsky (1998) used three and found Islam to be correlated with autocracy as measured by two of them. It is important to note that this view is not uncontested. Price (1999, 2002) found that Islam neither undermines or supports democracy and/or human rights.

16. Huntington (1996a: 47) admits, his definitions are, to a great extent, based on religion. The civilizations he describes tend to be religiously homogeneous. He defines the Sinic/Confucian civilization as the Confucian Chinese, Chinese minorities outside of China and "the related cultures of Vietnam and Korea." The Japanese civilization appears to include the Japanese and only the

Japanese. The Hindu and Islamic civilizations appear to be wholly defined by religion, even if Huntington claims otherwise. The Slavic-Orthodox civilization seems to be a combination of the Orthodox Christian religion combined with a common historical experience. The Western civilization is basically the United States, Western Europe, Australia, and New Zealand, which are mostly Protestant Christians but include some Catholics. The Latin American is distinguished by being Catholic and "incorporates indigenous cultures." Finally, the "possible" African civilization is based on a developing common identity. Many others argue that Huntington's concept of civilizations is highly correlated with religion. These include: Eisenstadt (2000a: 591), Esposito and (2000: 616), Laustsen and Waever (2000: 705), Smith (2000: 791), and Tibi (2000: 844).

17. See, e.g., Kirkpatrick et al. (1993), Halliday (2000: 20), Hunter (1998), Kader (1998), and Rosecrance (1998).

18. See, e.g., Anwar (1998), Ikenberry (1997), and Tipson (1997).

19. For a more comprehensive discussion of this debate see Fox (2001a,f, 2002b).

Chapter 4   Local Religious Conflicts are International Issues

1. This information is taken from the Minorities at Risk dataset, which is described in more detail later.

2. Minorities were included in the dataset if they meet one or both of two criteria: if the group is currently politically active in pursuit of group interests and if the group suffers from persistent discrimination or differential treatment (Gurr, 2000: 7–8). It is important to note that some, including Fearon and Latin (1997) have criticized the MAR data on grounds of selection bias. Gurr (2000: 10–13) addresses these criticisms, arguing that the project has systematically collected a list of groups that are treated differentially and/or politically active. Thus, the project represents a reasonably complete record of all serious conflicts between ethnic groups and governments.

   The dataset is designed to assess the relationship between specific minorities and specific states because each such relationship is posited to be unique. Accordingly many minorities appear several times, once for each state in which they live. For example, the Kurds are coded three times, once each for Turkey, Iraq, and Iran. Similarly, many states have several minorities living in them, each of which are coded separately.

3. Unless otherwise noted, the variables used in this study are taken from the MAR dataset that is available, along with a codebook, at the MAR website at www.cidcm.umd.edu/inscr/mar.

4. This variable is available in "dataset2" of the "Jonathan Fox—Project Operationalizing Huntington's Civilizations" section of the MAR links webpage.

5. While the identities of the foreign governments who intervened in the conflict are not available in the MAR dataset, the project did collect the information. We, therefore, obtained copies of the relevant portions of the original codesheets in order to code this variable.

6. This variable is available in "dataset2" of the "Jonathan Fox—Project Operationalizing Huntington's Civilizations" section of the MAR links webpage.

7. The United States did not intervene militarily or politically on behalf of any minorities of the same denomination as the U.S. majority (Protestant Christian) from 1990 to 1995. It intervened politically on behalf of 17 Christian minorities (same religion, different denomination) and 13 minorities of non-Christian faiths. It militarily intervened on behalf of 5 Christian minorities and 3 minorities of non-Christian faiths.

8. This variable is a modified form of the ethnic differences variable used in the MAR dataset. The original variable (ethdifxx) is a composite variable that includes differences in religion, language, race, and customs. The modified variable removes the religious element because this is accounted for by the religion variable from this study. This is accomplished by subtracting the MAR religion variable (belief) from the ethnic differences variable (ethdifxx). For details on this, as well as all other variables from the MAR dataset, see the MAR website at www.cidcm.umd.edu/inscr/mar.

9. This variable was constructed by adding five variables from the MAR dataset that measure cultural differences. These variables measure the following: different ethnicity or nationality (culdifx1); different language (culdifx2); different historical origins (culdifx3); different social customs (culdifx5); and different residence (culdifx6).

10. Both the protest and rebellion variables are coded yearly in the MAR dataset. The two variables used here total the individual scores for protest and rebellion for the six-year period of 1990–1995 covered in this study.

11. This variable was created by taking the MAR variables for political discrimination, economic discrimination, and cultural discrimination, scaling them to 10 and adding the result.

12. The MAR dataset includes a democracy variable taken from the POLITY dataset that measures the extent of a state's institutional democracy. See Jaggers and Gurr (1995) for details.

13. These variables measure the mean level of protest (iconpro) and rebellion (iconreb) in the region during the 1980s and 1990s.

14. A third variable for whether the minority is neither Christian or Muslim would be redundant because only one of the three variables would be coded as positive for any given case.

15. Youssef M. Ibrahim "Arabs Raise a Nervous Cry over Iranian Militancy" *New York Times*, December 12, 1992.

16. U.S. State Department Report: "Patterns of Global Terrorism, 2000" released April 2001.

17. Judith Miller "Killing for the Glory of God, In a Land Far From Home" *New York Times*, January 16, 2001.

18. Stephen Engelberg "One Man and a Global Web of Violence" *New York Times*, January 14, 2001.

19. John F. Burns "Little Sympathy in Yemen for Condemned Militant" *New York Times*, September 17, 1999.

20. Carlotta Gall "Dagestan Skirmish is Big Russian Risk" *New York Times*, August 13, 1999.

21. Youssef M. Ibrahim "Arabs Raise a Nervous Cry over Iranian Militancy" *New York Times*, December 21, 1992.

22. Stephen Engelberg "One Man and a Global Web of Violence" *New York Times*, January 14, 2001.

23. Philip Shenon "Holy War is Home to Haunt the Saudis" *New York Times*, July 14, 1996.

24. John F. Burns "Little Sympathy in Yemen for Condemned Militant" *New York Times*, September 17, 1999; Raymond Bonner, "After the Attack: the Guerillas" *New York Times*, August 27, 1998; Tim Weiner "Blowback From Afghan Battlefield" *New York Times*, March 13, 1994.

25. While newspapers cite 55–60 as the number of states in which Al-Qaeda has a presence, our research has only identified 54. These include Afghanistan, Algeria, Australia, Azerbaijan, Bangladesh, Belgium, Bosnia, Bulgaria, Burma, Cambodia, Canada, China, the Czech Republic, Dubai, Egypt, Eritrea, France, Germany, Hungary, India, Indonesia, Iran, Iraq, Israel, Italy, Jordan, Kenya, Kosovo, Kuwait, Kyrgyzistan, Lebanon, Libya, Malaysia, Morocco, Nairobi, Netherlands, Pakistan, Philippines, Russia, Saudi Arabia, Singapore, Spain, Somalia, Sudan, Syria, Tajikistan, Tanzania, Turkey, Turkmenistan, United Arab Emirates, United Kingdom, United States, Uzbekistan, and Yemen. However if we include Chechnya, Hong Kong, Kashmir, and the Palestinian-controlled territories, all of which are either semi-independent territories or territories seeking independence, the number is increased to 58. For the sources for this list, see the following footnote.

26. "Who is Osama bin Laden" *International Herald Tribune*, September 14, 2001; Laura Mansnerus "Man Is Guilty In Bomb Plot At Millennium" *New York Times*, July 14, 2001; Emma Daly "Spain Arrests Terror Suspect Said to Be Linked to bin Laden" *New York Times*, June 23, 2001; Alan Feuer and Benjamin Weiser "Translation: 'The How-To Book of Terrorism'" *New York Times*, April 5, 2001; Benjamin Weiser "Ex-Aide to bin Laden Describes Terror Campaign Aimed at U.S." *New York Times*, February 7, 2001; Judith Miller " Killing for the Glory of God, In a Land Far From Home," *New York Times*, January 16, 2001; Judith Miller "On Jordan's Death Row, Convicted Terrorist Says He Has No Regrets" *New York Times*, January 15, 2001; Stephen Engelberg "One Man and a Global Web of Violence" *New York Times*, January 14, 2001; Celia W. Dugger "India Accuses 4 of Plotting To Bomb U.S. Consulates" *New York Times*, January 21, 1999; Benjamin Weiser "Bin Laden Linked to Embassy Blasy by an Ex-Soldier" *New York Times*, October 21, 2000; Tim Weiner "US Fury on 2 Continents" *New York Times*, August 21, 1998; Raymond Bonner and Steve LeVine "After the Attack" *New York Times*, August 27, 1998; Douglas Frantz and Raymond Bonner "A Far-Flung Terrorist Network" *International Herald Tribune*, September 24, 2001; "Former Aide of Bin Laden Bared Plots in Mideast" *International Herald Tribune*, October 1, 2001; Keith B. Richburg "Suspect Describes Plot Against Paris Embassy" *International Herald Tribune*, October 23, 2001; Peter Finn "Hijacker Reportedly Met Iraqi Official" *International Herald Tribune*, September 7, 2001; Tim Weiner "U.S. is Likely to Target Groups in East Asia Linked to Bin Laden" *International Herald Tribune*, October 31, 2001; Bob Woodward "With Case, Bin Laden 'Owns and Operates' Taliban, CIA Believes" *International Herald Tribune*, October 12, 2001; Jane Perlez "Saudis Uncooperative, White House Aides Say" *International Herald Tribune*, October 12, 2001; Susan Sachs "Qaida at Work: Islamic Jihad Trial Papers Detail Ruthless Tactics" *International Herald Tribune*, November 22, 2001; Michael Richardson "U.S. Seeks Indonesia's Anti-Terror Help" *International Herald Tribune*, November 22, 2001; Keith B. Richburg "Papers Discarded by Taliban Show Extent of Their Foreign Network" *International Herald Tribune*, November 23, 2001; "Australian Who Trained with Bin Laden Forces is Captured" *International Herald Tribune*, December 13, 2001; Elizabeth Rosenthall "Beijing Wants Chinese Qaida

Fighters for Trial" *International Herald Tribune*, December 13, 2001; Seth Mydans "15 Muslims are Acc-used of Plot to Blow Up Targets in Singapore" *International Herald Tribune*, January 7, 2002; Howard, Schneider "Car Bomb Misses Joedan Anti-Terror Investigator" *International Herald Tribune*, March 1, 2002; David Rhode and C.J. Chivers "The Jihad Files: Qaeda Lifr in Afghanistan" *International Herald Tribune*, March 18, 2002; Barry James "17 Suspects pf Qaeda Links Arrested Across Europe" *International Herald Tribune*, April 25, 2002; Marlise Simons "Militants Recruit in Netherlands" *International Herald Tribune*, June 1, 2002; "Saudis Arrested in Gibraltar Terror Plot" *International Herald Tribune*, June 12, 2002; Dexter Filkins "Qaeda Suspects are U.S. Citizens, Pakistanis Believe" *International Herald Tribune*, June 13, 2002; "France Holds 5 Suspects Linked to U.K. Shoe Bomber" *International Herald Tribune*, June 13, 2002; Howard Schneider "Saudis Hold 13 Tied to Terror Plots in Kingdom" *International Herald Tribune*, June 19, 2002; "3 Held in Hong Kong on Alleged Qaeda Deal" *International Herald Tribune*, November 6, 2002; Emily Wax "Israelis Targeted in Kenya Attacks" *International Herald Tribune*, November 29, 2002; Robert M. Frank "Qaeda at Work in Canada, Intelligence Experts Allege" *International Herald Tribune*, December 18, 2002; "U.K. Police Arrest 7 in Terror Raids" *International Herald Tribune*, December 19, 2002; Seth Mydans "Outsiders are Nourishing Islam Among Cambodians" *International Herald Tribune*, December 23, 2002.

27. Brian Knowlton "U.S. Seeks Other Plotters" *International Herald Tribune*, June 12, 2002; Michael Grunwald and Amy Goldstein "A Catholic Latino Turned Muslim Terrorism Suspect" *International Herald Tribune*, June 12, 2002; Dexter Filkins "Qaeda Suspects are US Citizens, Pakistanis Believe" *International Herald Tribune*, June 13, 2002.

28. This description of the events surrounding the Durban conference is based on: Elizabeth Becker "Annan Says Race Conference Must Chart Way for Future" *New York Times*, July 31, 2001; Neil A. Lewis "U.S. Pushes to Refocus Racism Conference" *New York Times*, August 1, 2001; "U.N. Racism Panel is Deadlocked on Israel" *New York Times*, August 9, 2001; Elizabeth Olson "Racism Talks Are Stumbling On Language About Israel" *New York Times*, August 12, 2001; Rachel L. Swarns "Rancor and Powell's Absence Cloud Racism Parley" *New York Times*, August 31, 2001; Rachel L. Swarns "Palestinians Give U.N. Racism Conference a Mixed Message" *New York Times*, September 1, 2001; Rachel L. Swarns "U.S. and Israel Threaten Boycott of U.N. Conference on Race" *New York Times*, September 3, 2001; John H. Cushman Jr. "The Racism Walkout: The Washington View" *New York Times*, September 4, 2001; Rachel L. Swarns "Conferees Fail To Resolve Their Disputes At Race Talks" *New York Times*, September 7, 2001; Rachel L. Swarns "Racism Talks Still Seek to End Impasses on Israel and Slavery" *New York Times*, September 8, 2001; Rachel L. Swarns "Race Talks Finally Reach Accord On Slavery and Palestinian Plight" *New York Times*, September 9, 2001; "UN Rights Chief Dismayed Iran Blocked Jews, Bahais from Racism Conference" *Jerusalem Post*, February 23, 2001.

29. For more details on the conflict over Jerusalem's holy sites see chapter 7.

30. Paul Watson "War on Art: Taliban Took Ax to Culture" *International Herald Tribune*, November 24–25, 2001.

31. "Pre-Islam Idols Being Broken Under Decree By Afghans" *New York Times*, March 2, 2001; "U.N. Pleads With Taliban Not to Destroy Buddha Statues" *New York Times*, March 3, 2001; Charles A. Radin "Scholars Lament Afghan Relic Purge Buddhist Sites Under Siege" *Boston Globe*, March 2, 2001; "Afghans Reject Appeals to Spare Statues" *New York Times*, March 6, 2001; "Taliban Chief Defies World Criticism" *Newsday*, March 6, 2001; Destruction of Ancient Works is Almost Complete, Taliban Says" *St. Louis Post Dispatch*, March 11, 2001; Berry Berrak "Afghan Says Destruction Of Buddhas is Complete" *New York Times*, March 12, 2001.

32. See the MAR report on Muslims in France for more details. The report is available at www.cidcm.umd.edu/inscr/mar.

33. See the MAR report on Turks in Germany for more details. The report is available at www.cidcm.umd.edu/inscr/mar.

Chapter 5　Transnational Religious Phenomena

1. Many others make similar arguments. These include, among others: Eisenstadt (2000a), Esposito (1998), Lawrence (1989: 229), Lechner (1993), Laustsen and Waever (2000: 705), Mendelsohn (1993), and Tehranian (1993).

2. Amos Harel "The PA Steals from Me, Hamas Takes Care of Me" *Ha'aretz English Edition*, 6/27/02.

3. For similar arguments see Haynes (1994: 64), Juergensmeyer (1993), Monshpouri (1998: 26), Tibi (2000: 846), Zubadia (2000: 60).

4. This information is also taken from The U.S. Office of the Secretary of State, *2000 Annual Report on International Religious Freedom* (Washington, DC: U.S. Secretary of State, Bureau of Democracy, Human Rights, and Labor, 2001).

5. The U.S. Office of the Secretary of State, *2000 Annual Report on International Religious Freedom* (Washington, DC: U.S. Secretary of State, Bureau of Democracy, Human Rights, and Labor, 2000).

6. The U.S. Office of the Secretary of State, *2001 Annual Report on International Religious Freedom* (Washington, DC: U.S. Secretary of State, Bureau of Democracy, Human Rights, and Labor, 2002). Andrea Morigi, Vittorio Emanuele, Vernole Chiara Verna, "Report 2000 on Religious Freedom in the World" *Aid to the Church in Need*, 2000.

7. The U.S. Office of the Secretary of State, *2000 Annual Report on International Religious Freedom* (Washington, DC: U.S. Secretary of State, Bureau of Democracy, Human Rights, and Labor, 2001).

8. International Coalition for Religious Freedom, *Religious Freedom Report: Iraq*, www.religiousfreedom.com.

9. It must be noted that the Kuwaiti government only officially recognizes three Churches: The Catholic Church, the Anglican Church, and the National Evangelical Church of Kuwait (Protestant). These Churches enjoy "full recognition" and are permitted to build temples and worship publicly. The other, unrecognized, churches are permitted private worship in private homes, Office of the Secretary of State, *1999 Annual Report on International Religious Freedom* (Washington, DC: U.S. Secretary of State, Bureau of Democracy, Human Rights, and Labor, 2000).

10. The U.S. Office of the Secretary of State, *Report on Human Rights Practices, 1999* (Washington, DC: U.S. Secretary of State, Bureau of Democracy, Human

Rights, and Labor, 2000), "Lebanon: Thinking the Holy Unthinkable" *The Economist*, March 28, 1998, 45.

11. Office of the Secretary of State, *2001 Annual Report on International Religious Freedom* (Washington, DC: U.S. Secretary of State, Bureau of Democracy, Human Rights, and Labor, 2002).

12. The U.S. Office of the Secretary of State, *2001 Annual Report on International Religious Freedom* (Washington, DC: U.S. Secretary of State, Bureau of Democracy, Human Rights, and Labor, 2002).

13. Office of the Secretary of State, *2001 Annual Report on International Religious Freedom* (Washington, DC: U.S. Secretary of State, Bureau of Democracy, Human Rights, and Labor, 2001); Andrea Morigi, Vittorio Emanuele, Vernole Chiara Verna, "Report 2000 on Religious Freedom in the World" *Aid to the Church in Need, 2000*; "Qatar," *Religious Freedom World Report*, www.religious-freedom.com.

14. Office of the Secretary of State, *2001 Annual Report on International Religious Freedom* (Washington, DC: U.S. Secretary of State, Bureau of Democracy, Human Rights, and Labor, 2001).

15. The U.S. Office of the Secretary of State, *1999 Annual Report on International Religious Freedom* (Washington, DC: U.S. Secretary of State, Bureau of Democracy, Human Rights, and Labor, 2000); Andrea Morigi, Vittorio Emanuele, Vernole Chiara Verna, "Report 2000 on Religious Freedom in the World" *Aid to the Church in Need*, 2000.

16. U.S. Office of the Secretary of State, *2001 Annual Report on International Religious Freedom* (Washington, DC: U.S. Secretary of State, Bureau of Democracy, Human Rights, and Labor, 2002); U.S. Office of the Secretary of State, *Report on Human Rights Practices, 2001* (Washington, DC: U.S. Secretary of State, Bureau of Democracy, Human Rights, and Labor, 2002); Andrea Morigi, Vittorio Emanuele, Vernole Chiara Verna, "Report 2000 on Religious Freedom in the World" *Aid to the Church in Need, 2000*; "UAE," *Religious Freedom World Report*, www.religiousfreedom.com.

17. The U.S. Office of the Secretary of State, *2001 Annual Report on International Religious Freedom* (Washington, DC: U.S. Secretary of State, Bureau of Democracy, Human Rights, and Labor, 2002).

18. The U.S. Office of the Secretary of State, *2000 Annual Report on International Religious Freedom* (Washington, DC: U.S. Secretary of State, Bureau of Democracy, Human Rights, and Labor, 2001).

19. The U.S. Office of the Secretary of State, *2001 Annual Report on International Religious Freedom* (Washington, DC: U.S. Secretary of State, Bureau of Democracy, Human Rights, and Labor, 2002).

20. "Annual Report, 1999" *International Helsinki Foundation for Human Rights*, www.ihf-hr.org/reports/ar99/ar99tur.htm.

21. U.S. Office of the Secretary of State, *Report on Human Rights Practices, 1992* (Washington, DC: U.S. Secretary of State, Bureau of Democracy, Human Rights, and Labor, 1993).

22. The U.S. Office of the Secretary of State, *2001 Annual Report on International Religious Freedom* (Washington, DC: U.S. Secretary of State, Bureau of Democracy, Human Rights, and Labor, 2002).

23. The U.S. Office of the Secretary of State, *2001 Annual Report on International Religious Freedom* (Washington, DC: U.S. Secretary of State, Bureau of Democracy, Human Rights, and Labor, 2002).

24. The U.S. Office of the Secretary of State, *2001 Annual Report on International Religious Freedom* (Washington, DC: U.S. Secretary of State, Bureau of Democracy, Human Rights, and Labor, 2002).

25. See, e.g., Gregg (1997), Gungwu (1997a,b), Hardjono (1997), Harris (1996), Lewis (1993), Murphey (1998), Naff (1998), Seamon (1998), and Walid (1997).

26. U.S. Office of the Secretary of State, *2000 Annual Report on International Religious Freedom: France.*

27. U.S. Office of the Secretary of State, *2000 Annual Report on International Religious Freedom: Greece.*

Chapter 6   The Clash of Civilizations Debate

1. Italics added by the authors.

2. See, e.g., Nussbaum (1997), Smith (1997), and Tipson (1997).

3. It is unclear whether Buddhism is included in the Confucian/Sinic civilization. This is discussed in more detail later in this chapter.

4. Italics added by the authors.

5. For a reply to this study see Huntington (2000).

6. A similar argument is made by many scholars with regard to ethnic conflict. See, e.g., Horowitz (1985).

7. See, e.g., Appleby (2000) and Gopin (2000).

8. For a more detailed discussion of the MAR dataset see chapter 6.

9. The scale for protest is as follows: 0—none reported; 1—verbal opposition (public letters, petitions, posters, publications, agitation, etc.); 2—scattered acts of symbolic resistance (e.g., sit-ins, blockage of traffic), sabotage, symbolic destruction of property; 3—political organizing activity on a substantial scale. (includes mobilization for autonomy and/or secession by a minority-controlled regional government.); 4—a few demonstrations, rallies, strikes, and/or riots, total participation less than 10,000; 5—demonstrations, rallies, strikes, and/or riots, total participation estimated between 10,000 and 100,000; 6—demonstrations, rallies, strikes, and/or riots, total participation over 100,000 .

10. The scale for rebellion is as follows: 0—none; 1—political banditry, sporadic terrorism; 2—campaigns of terrorism; 3—local rebellions (armed attempts to seize power in a locale, includes declarations of independence by a minority-controlled regional government); 4—small-scale guerrilla activity; 5—intermediate-scale guerrilla activity; 6—large-scale guerrilla activity; 7—protracted civil war, fought by rebel military with base areas.

11. This variable is based on the SEPX variable in the MAR dataset. A group is considered separatist in this study if SEPX is coded as 1 or higher.

12. The scores for religious and civilizational conflict in this figure are taken from figure 8.1. The average score is the average for all groups.

13. It is important to note that his finding diverges from that of another study of the MAR data by Fox (1997), which found no real difference in the levels of violence between Islamic and other groups. These different results can be explained by several factors. First, the Fox (1997) study focused on religious and not civilizational differences. Second, conflicts involving Islamic majority groups and Islamic minority groups were considered separately by Fox (1997) as opposed to this study that only examines whether one or both groups involved are Islamic without regard to which group is the minority or majority

group. Third, the Fox (1997) study looks only at 105 religious conflicts within the MAR dataset and not all 275 as does this one.

Chapter 8   Toward a Theory of International Relations and Religion

1. See, e.g., Henderson (1997, 1998).
2. See, e.g., Midlarsky (1998).
3. See, e.g., Rummel (1997) and Reynal-Querol (2002).
4. See, e.g., Reynal-Querol (2002).
5. These variables are as follows: state authority to rule on internal church matters; state sovereign officially related to church; state department of religious affairs; state positions reserved for religious leaders; state approves or appoints church leaders; state directly pays church personnel salaries; ecclesiastical taxes; state legally recognizes or gives preference to specific churches; state directly subsidizes church expenses; state funds or grants money to churches for specific social services; state subsidies for religious educational institutions; and tax exemptions for church property or income.
6. For more information on the Freedom House Data see www.freedomcouse. org/religion.
7. For more discussion of the functionalist argument see Fox (2002a: 65–75).

BIBLIOGRAPHY

Adler, Emanuel "Seizing the Middle Ground: Constructivism in World Politics" *European Journal of International Relations*, 3 (3), 1997, 319–363.

Ahari, M.E. "The Clash of Civilizations: An Old Story or New Truth" *New Perspectives Quarterly*, 14 (2), 1997, 56–61.

Ajami, Faoud "The Summoning" *Foreign Affairs*, 72 (4), 1993, 2–9.

Akbar, Ahmed S. "Media Mongols at the Gates of Baghdad" *New Perspectives Quarterly*, 19 (1), 2002, 46–61.

Akiner, Shirin "Religion's Gap" *Harvard International Review*, 22 (1), 2000, 62–65.

Albrecht-Carrie, Rene. *Europe After 1815*, New Jersey: Littlefield, 1972.

Almond, Gabriel "Introduction: A Functional Approach to Comparative Politics" in Almond and James C. Coleman eds. *The Politics of the Developing Areas*, Princeton: Princeton University Press, 1960.

Al-Sabbah, Sheikh Saud Nassr "Political Islamists Have Hijacked Arab World" *New Perspectives Quarterly*, 19 (1), 2002, 12–15.

Ammerman, Nancy T. "Accounting for Christian Fundamentalisms: Social Dynamics and Rhetorical Strategies" in Martin E. Marty and R. Scott Appleby eds. *Accounting for Fundamentalisms: The Dynamic Character of Movements*, Chicago: University of Chicago Press, 1994b, 149–170.

An-Na'im, Abdullahi Ahmed "The Islamic Counter-Reformation" *New Perspectives Quarterly*, 19 (1), 2002, 29–35.

Antonius, George, *The Arab Awakening*, New York: Capricorn Books, 1965.

Anwar, Said Tariq "Civilizations Versus Civilizations in a New Multipolar World" *Journal of Marketing*, 62 (2), 1998, 125–128.

Appleby, R. Scott *Religious Fundamentalisms and Global Conflict*, New York: Foreign Policy Association Headline Series #301, 1994.

Appleby, R. Scott *The Ambivalence of the Sacred: Religion, Violence, and Reconciliation*, New York: Rowman and Littlefield, 2000.

Apter, David *The Politics of Modernization*, Chicago: University of Chicago Press, 1965.

Arens, Moshe *Broken Covenant*, Tel Aviv: Yediot Ahronot, 1995 (in Hebrew).

Aroian L. and Mitchell R. *The Modern Middle East and North Africa*, New York: Macmillan Publishing, 1984.

Avigur, Shaul, et al. *A Short History of the Hagana*, Tel Aviv: Am Oved, 1978 (in Hebrew).

Aysha, Emad El Din "Samuel Huntington and the Geopolitics of American Identity: The Function of Foreign Policy in America's Domestic Clash of Civilizations" *International Studies Perspectives*, 4 (2), 2003, 113–132.

Bachi, Roberto *The Population of Israel*, Jerusalem: The Hebrew University of Jerusalem, 1974.

Baldwin, David A. ed. *Neorealism and Neoliberalism: The Contemporary Debate*, New York: Columbia University Press, 1993.

Barber, Benjamin R. "Fantasy of Fear" *Harvard International Review*, 20 (1), Winter 1997/1998, 66–71.

Barfield, Thomas "Idol Threats" *Religion in the News*, 4 (2), 2001, 4–7.

Barret, D.B., G.T. Kurian, and T.M. Johnson *World Christian Encyclopedia*, 2nd ed., Oxford: Oxford University Press, 2001.

Barro, Robert J. and Rachel McCleary "Religion and Political Economy in an International Panel" www.wcfia.harvard.edu/programs/prpes/, 2002.

Bartley, Robert L. "The Case for Optimism" (a reply to Hunnington's "The Clash of Civilizations?"), *Foreign Affairs*, 72 (4), 1993, 15–18.

Beckford, James A. "The Insulation and Isolation of the Sociology of Religion" *Sociological Analysis*, 46 (4), 1985, 347–354.

Beedham, Brian "The New Geopolitics: A Fading Hell" *The Economist*, July 31, 1999, s10.

Be'eri, D. "The Routes have Parted" *Nekuda*, 193, March 1996, 38–42 (in Hebrew).

Be'eri, Eli'ezer *The Palestinians Under Jordanian Rule—Three Issues*, Jerusalem: The Magness Press, 1978.

Bell, D. "Religion in the Sixties" *Social Research*, 38, 1971, 447–497.

Bell, Bowyer J. "Contemporary Revolutionary Organizations" in Keohane, Robert O. and Joseph S. Nye, Jr. eds. *Transnational Relations and World Politics*, Cambridge: Harvard University Press, 1970.

Bellah, Robert N. "Christianity and Symbolic Realism" *Journal for the Scientific Study of Religion*, 9, 1970, 89–96.

Ben-Yehuda, H.A. and Shmuel Sandler *The Arab-Israeli Conflict Transformed*, New York, NY: State University of New York Press, 2002.

Berger, Peter L. *The Sacred Canopy*, Garden City: Doubleday, 1969.

Berryman, Phillip *Liberation Theology*, Philadelphia: Temple University 1987.

Beyer, Peter *Religion and Globalization*, London: Sage, 1994.

Bolce, Louis and Gerald De Maio "The Anti-Christian Fundamentalist Factor in Contemporary Politics" *Public Opinion Quarterly* 63, 1999, 508–542.

Boyle, Kevin and Juliet Sheet eds. *Freedom of Religion and Belief: A World Report*, London: Routledge, 1997.

Brand, Laurie A. "The Intifada and the Arab World: Old Players, New Roles" *International Journal*, 45 (3), 1990, 501–527.

Brecher, Michael *The Foreign Policy System of Israel*, London: Oxford University Press, 1972.

Bruce, Steve "The Supply Side Model of Religion: The Nordic and Baltic States" *Journal for the Scientific Study of Religion*, 39 (1), 2000, 32–46.

Bryan, Hehir H. "Expanding Military Intervention: Promise or Peril?" *Social Research*, 62 (1), 1995, 41–50.

Carment, David and Patrick James "Internal Constraints and Interstate Ethnic Conflict: Toward a Crisis-Based Assessment of Irridentism" *Journal of Conflict Resolution*, 39, 1995, 137–150.

Carment, David and Patrick James "The International Politics of Ethnic Conflict: New Perspectives on Theory and Policy" *Global Society*, 11 (2), 1997a, 205–232.

Carment, David and Patrick James eds. *Wars in the Midst of Peace*, Pittsburgh: University of Pittsburgh Press, 1997b.

Carment, David and Patrick James "Escalation of Ethnic Conflict" *International Politics*, 35, 1998, 65–82.

Chaves, Mark "Secularization as Declining Religious Authority" *Social Forces*, 72 (3), March 1994, 749–774.

Chaves, Mark and David E. Cann "Religion, Pluralism and Religious Market Structure" *Rationality and Society*, 4 (3), 1992, 272–290.

Chaves, Mark, Peter J. Schraeder, and Mario Sprindys "State Regulation of Religion and Muslim Religious Vitality in the Industrialized West" *Journal of Politics*, 56 (4), 1994, 1087–1097.

Clark, Anne M. and Elisabeth J. Friedman "Sovereignty in the Balance: Claims and Bargains at the UN Conferences on the Environment, Human Rights, and Women" *International Studies Quarterly*, 44 (4), 2000, 591–614.

Cobban, Helena *The Palestine Liberation Organization: People, Power and Politics*, Cambridge: Cambridge University Press, 1984.

Cohen, Amnon *Political Parties in the West Bank Under the Hashemite Regime*, Jerusalem: The Magness Press, 1980 (in Hebrew).

Cohen, Stuart "The Changing Jewish Halakic Discourse on Armed Conflict" delivered at the May 2003 conference on The Religious Dimension of World Politics at Bar Ilan University, Ramat Gan, Israel.

Comaroff, John L. and Paul C. Stern eds. *Perspectives on Nationalism and War*, Luxembourg: Gordon & Breach, 1995.

Connolly, William E. *Political Theory and Modernity*, Oxford: Basil Blackwell, 1988.

Connor, Walker "Nation Building or Nation Destroying?" *World Politics*, 24 (3), 1972, 319–355.

Cortell, Andrew P. and James W. Davis "Understanding the Impact of International Norms: A Research Agenda" *International Studies Review*, 1 (2), 2000, 65–87.

Crouch, Colin "The Quiet Continent: Religion and Politics in Europe" *The Political Quarterly*, 71 (Supplement 1), 2000, 90–103.

Cunradi, Carol B., Raul Caetano, and John Schafer "Religious Affiliation, Denominational Homogamy, and Intimate Partner Violence Among US Couples" *Journal for the Scientific Study of Religion*, 41 (1), 2002, 139–151.

Dalacoura, Katrina "Unexceptional Politics? The Impact of Islam on International Relations" *Millennium*, 29 (3), 2000, 879–887.

David, Steven R. "Internal War: Causes and Cures" *World Politics*, 49, 1997, 552–576.

Davis, David R. and Will H. Moore "Ethnicity Matters: Transnational Ethnic Alliances and Foreign Policy Behavior" *International Studies Quarterly*, 41 (1), March 1997, 171–184.

Davis, David R., Keith Jaggers and Will H. Moore "Ethnicity, Minorities, and International Conflict" in David Carment and Patrick James eds. *Wars in the Midst of Peace*, Pittsburgh: University of Pittsburgh Press, 1997, 148–163.

Deane, Herbert A. *The Political and Social Ideas of St. Augustine*, New York: Columbia University Press, 1963.

Demerath, N.J. III "Rational Paradigms, A-Rational Religion, and the Debate over Secularization" *Journal for the Scientific Study of Religion*, 34 (1), 1995, 105–112.

Deutsch, Karl *Nationalism and Social Communication*, Cambridge: MIT Press, 1953.

Deutsch, Karl W. "On Nationalism, World Regions, and the Nature of the West" Per Torsvik ed. *Mobilization, Center-Periphery Structures, and Nation Building*, Oslo: Universitesforlaget, 1981, 51–93.

Djupe, Paul A. "Religious Brand Loyalty and Political Loyalties" *Journal for the Scientific Study of Religion*, 39 (1), 2000, 78–89.

Dobbelaere, Karel "Towards an Integrated Perspective of the Processes Related to the Descriptive Concept of Secularization" *Sociology of Religion*, 60 (3), 1999, 229–247.

Don Yehiya, Eliezer "Religion and Coalition" in Asher Arian ed., *Elections in Israel, 1973*, Jerusalem: Israel Academic Press, 1975.

Don-Yehiya, Eliezer "The Book and the Sword: The Nationalist Yeshivot and Political Radicalism in Israel" in Martin E. Marty and R. Scott Appleby eds. *Accounting for Fundamentalisms: The Dynamic Character of Movements*, Chicago: University of Chicago Press, 1994, 264–302.

Don-Yehiya, Eliezer "Conflict Management of Religious Issues: The Israeli Case in Comparative Perspective" in Reuven Y. Hazan and Moshe Maor, *Parties, Elections and Cleavages: Israel in Comparative and Theoretical Perspective*, London: Frank Kass, 2000, 86–108.

Dothan, Shmuel *Partition of Eretz-Israel in the Mandatory Period, The Jewish Controversy*, Jerusalem: Yad Yitzhak Ben-Zvi, 1979.

Douglass, William "A Critique of Recent Trends in the Analysis of Ethnonationalism" *Ethnic and Racial Studies*, 2 (2), 1988, 192–206.

Dowty, Alan *Middle East Crisis: US Decision-Making in 1958, 1970 and 1973*, Berkeley and Los Angeles: University of California Press, 1984.

Doyle Michael "Kant Liberal Legacies, and Foreign Affairs" *Philosophy and Public Affairs*, 12, 1983, 205–35.

Doyle Michael "Liberalism and World Politics" *American Political Science Review*, 80 (4), 1986, 1151–69.

Drake, C.J.M. "The Role of Ideology in Terrorists' Target Selection" *Terrorism and Political Violence*, 10 (2), 1998, 53–85.

Durkheim, Emile *The Elementary Forms of Religious Life*, trans. Joseph Ward Swain, London: George Allen & Unwin Ltd., 1964.

Ebaugh, Helen R.F. and Allen Haney "Church Attendance and Attitudes Toward Abortion: Differentials in Liberal and Conservative Churches" *Journal for the Scientific Study of Religion*, 17, 1978, 107–143.

Eckstein, Harry "Theoretical Approaches to Explaining Collective Political Violence" in T.R. Gurr, ed. *Handbook of Political Conflict: Theories and Research*, New York: The Free Press, 1980.

Eisenberg, Laura and Neil Caplan *Negotiating Arab-Israeli Peace*, Bloomington: Indiana University Press, 1998.

Eisenstadt, S.N. "The Reconstruction of Religious Arenas in the Framework of 'Multiple Modernities' " *Millennium*, 29 (3), 2000a, 591–611.

Eisenstadt, S.N. "The Resurgence of Religious Movements in Processes of Globalisation—Beyond End of History or Clash of Civilisations" *MOST, Journal on Multicultural Societies*, 2 (1), 2000b, www.unesco.org./most/vl1n1ris.htm.

Elazar, Daniel and Shmuel Sandler, eds. *Who is the Boss in Israel, Israel at the Polls 1988–89*, Detroit: Wayne Sate University Press, 1992.

El Fadal, Khalid A. "The Rules of Killing at War: An Inquiry into Classical Sources" *The Muslim World*, 89 (2), 1999, 144–157.

Ellingsen, Tanja "Colorful Community or Ethnic Witches' Brew? Multiethnicity and Domestic Conflict During and After the Cold War" *Journal of Conflict Resolution*, 44 (2), 2000, 228–249.

Ellison, Christopher G. "Rational Choice Explanations of Individual Religious Behavior: Notes on the Problem of Social Embeddedness" *Journal for the Scientific Study of Religion*, 34 (1), 1995, 89–97.

Ellison, Christopher G., John P. Bartkowski, and Kristin L. Anderson "Are There Religious Variations in Domestic Violence" *Journal of Family Issues*, 20 (1), 1999, 87–113.

Emmett, Chad F. "The Capital Cities of Jerusalem" *Geographical Review*, 86 (2), 1996, 233–258.

Enders Walter and Todd Sandler "Transnational Terrorism in the Post-Cold War Era" *International Studies Quarterly*, 43 (1), 1999, 145–167.

Esposito, John L. *The Islamic Threat: Myth or Reality?*, 2nd ed., Oxford: Oxford University Press, 1995.

Esposito, John L. "Religion and Global Affairs: Political Challenges" *SAIS Review*, Summer–Fall, 1998, 19–24.

Esposito, John L. and John O. Voll *Islam and Democracy*. New York: Oxford University Press, 1996.

Esposito, John L. and John O. Voll "Islam and the West: Muslim Voices of Dialogue" *Millennium*, 29 (3), 2000, 613–639.

Evans, Peter, Dietrich Rueschemeyer, and Theda Skocpol, eds. *Bringing the State Back in*, Cambridge: Cambridge University Press, 1985.

Fairbanks, Stephen C. "Iran: No Easy Answers" *Journal of International Affairs*, 54 (2), 2001, 447–464.

Falconer, Alan D. "The Role of Religion in Situations of Armed Conflict: The Case of Northern Ireland" *Bulletin of Peace Proposals*, 21 (3), 1990, 273–280.

Fawcett, Liz *Religion, Ethnicity, and Social Change*, New York: St. Martin's, 2000.

Fearon, James D. and David D. Latin "A Cross-Sectional Study of Large-Scale Ethnic Violence in the Postwar Period" Unpublished paper, Department of Political Science, University of Chicago, September 30, 1997.

Fearon, James and David D. Laitin. "Ethnicity, Insurgency, and Civil War" *American Political Science Review*, 97 (1), February 2003, 75–90.

Fein, Helen "Genocide: A Sociological Perspective" *Current Sociology*, 38 (1), Spring 1990, 1–126.

Fein, Helen "Accounting for Genocide After 1945: Theories and Findings" *International Journal of Group Rights*, 1 (1), 1993, 79–106.

Fenton, Steve *Ethnicity: Racism, Class, and Culture*, London: McMillan, 1999.

Fisch, M. Steven "Islam and Authoritarianism" *World Politics*, 55 (1), 2002, 4–37.

Fischer, Michael, M.J. "Islam: The Odd Civilization Out" *New Perspectives Quarterly*, 19 (1), 2002, 62–71.

Foster-Carter, A. "The Sociology of Development" in M. Haralambos ed., *Sociology: New Directions*, Ormskirk: Causeway, 1985.

Fox, Jonathan "The Salience of Religious Issues in Ethnic Conflicts: A Large-N Study" *Nationalism and Ethnic Politics*, 3 (3), Autumn 1997, 1–19.

Fox, Jonathan "Do Religious Institutions Support Violence or the Status Quo?" *Studies in Conflict and Terrorism*, 22 (2), 1999a, 119–139.

Fox, Jonathan "The Influence of Religious Legitimacy on Grievance Formation by Ethnoreligious Minorities" *Journal of Peace Research*, 36 (3), 1999b, 289–307.

Fox, Jonathan "Towards a Dynamic Theory of Ethno-religious Conflict" *Nations and Nationalism*, 5 (4), October 1999c, 431–463.

Fox, Jonathan "Is Islam More Conflict Prone than Other Religions? A Cross-Sectional Study of Ethnoreligious Conflict" *Nationalism and Ethnic Politics*, 6 (2), Summer 2000a, 1–23.

Fox, Jonathan "Religious Causes of Ethnic Discrimination" *International Studies Quarterly*, 44 (3), September 2000b, 423–450.

Fox, Jonathan "The Ethnic-Religious Nexus: The Impact of Religion on Ethnic Conflict" *Civil Wars*, 3 (3), Autumn 2000c, 1–22.

Fox, Jonathan "The Effects of Religious Discrimination on Ethnic Protest and Rebellion" *Journal of Conflict Studies*, 20 (2), Fall 2000d, 16–43.

Fox, Jonathan "The Copts in Egypt: A Christian Minority in an Islamic Society" in Ted Robert Gurr, *Peoples versus States: Minorities at Risk in the New Century*, Washington, DC: United States Institute of Peace Press, 2000e, 138–142.

Fox, Jonathan "Civilizational, Religious, and National Explanations for Ethnic Rebellion in the Post-Cold War Middle East" *Jewish Political Studies Review*, 13 (1–2), Spring, 2001a, 177–204.

Fox, Jonathan "Islam and the West: The Influence of Two Civilizations on Ethnic Conflict" *Journal of Peace Research*, 38 (4), July 2001b, 459–472.

Fox, Jonathan "Are Middle East Conflicts More Religious?" *Middle East Quarterly*, 8 (4), Fall 2001c, 31–40.

Fox, Jonathan "Religion: An Oft Overlooked Element of International Studies" *International Studies Review*, 3 (3), Fall 2001d, 53–73.

Fox, Jonathan "Religious Causes of International Intervention in Ethnic Conflicts" *International Politics*, 38 (4), December 2001e, 515–531.

Fox, Jonathan "Clash of Civilizations or Clash of Religions, Which is a More Important Determinant of Ethnic Conflict?" *Ethnicities*, 1 (3), December 2001f, 295–320.

Fox, Jonathan *Ethnoreligious Conflict in the Late 20th Century: A General Theory*, Lanham, MD: Lexington Books, 2002a.

Fox, Jonathan "Ethnic Minorities and the Clash of Civilizations: A Quantitative Analysis of Huntington's Thesis" *British Journal of Political Science*, 32 (3), 2002b, 415–434.

Fox, Jonathan "In the Name of God and Nation: The Overlapping Influence of Separatism and Religion on Ethnic Conflict" *Social Identities*, 8 (3), 2002c.

Fox, Jonathan "Are Ethno-Religious Minorities more Militant than Other Ethnic Minorities?" *Alternatives*, 28 (1), 2003a, 91–114.

Fox, Jonathan "State Failure and the Clash of Civilisations: An Examination of the Magnitude and Extent of Domestic Civilisational Conflict from 1950 to 1996" *Australian Journal of Political Science*, 38 (2), 2003b, 195–213.

Fox, Jonathan and Shmuel Sandler "Quantifying Religion: Toward Building More Effective Ways of Measuring Religious Influence on State-Level Behavior" *Journal of Church and State*, 45 (3), 2003c.

Frisch, Hillel "The Evolution of Palestinian Nationalist Islamic Doctrine: Territorializing: A Universal Religion" *Canadian Review in Nationalism*, 21 (1–2), 1994, 45–55.

Frisch, Hillel and Shmuel Sandler "Religion, State and the International System in the Israeli-Palestinian Conflict" *International Political Science Review* (2003).

Fuller, Graham E. and Ian O. Lesser *A Sense of Seige: The Geopolitics of Islam and the West*, Boulder: Westview, 1995.

Gal-Nor, Yitzhak "The Territorial Partition of Palestine: The Decision of 1937" in *Studies in Israel's Independence*, Sde Boker: Ben-Gurion University, 1991 (in Hebrew).

Gaus, Gregory F. III. "The Kingdom in the Middle: Saudi Arabia's Double Game" in James H. Hoge Jr. and Gideon Rose eds. *How Did This Happen? Terrorism and the New War*, Oxford: Public Affairs, 109–122.

Geertz, Clifford *The Interpretation of Culture*, New York: Basic Books, 1973.

Geertz, Clifford "Centers, Kings and Charisma: Reflections on the Symbolics of Power" in J. Ben-David and C. Nichols Clark eds., *Culture and Its Creators*, Chicago: Chicago University Press, 1977.

Gellner, Ernest *Postmodernism, Reason and Religion*, London, Routledge, 1992.

Gill, Anthony *Rendering Unto Caesar: The Catholic Church and the State in Latin America*, Chicago: University of Chicago Press, 1998.

Gill, Anthony and Arang Keshavarzian "State Building and Religious Resources: An Institutional Theory of Church-State Relations in Iran and Mexico" *Politics and Society*, 27 (3), 1999, 431–465.

Girard, Rene *Violence and the Sacred*, trans. Patrick Gregory, Baltimore: The Johns Hopkins University Press, 1977.

Glasner, Peter E. *The Sociology of Secularization: A Critique of a Concept*, London: Routledge & Kegan Paul, 1977.

Glynn, Patrick "Racial Reconciliation: Can Religion Work Where Politics has Failed?" *American Behavioral Scientist*, 41 (6), 1998, 834–841.

Gold, Dore. *Hatereds Kingdom How Saudi Arabia Supports the New Global Terrorism* Washington, DC: Regnery, 2003.

Gopin, Marc *Between Eden and Armageddon: The Future of World Religions, Violence, and Peacemaking*, Oxford: Oxford University Press, 2000.

Gray, John "Global Utopias and Clashing Civilizations: Misunderstanding the Prosperity" *International Affairs*, 74 (1), 1998, 149–164.

Greely, Andrew M. *Religion: A Secular Theory*, New York: Free Press, 1982.

Gregg, Donald P. "A Case for Continued US Engagement" *Orbis*, 41 (3), 1997, 375–384.

Gungwu, Wang "A Machiavelli for Our Times" *The National Interest* (46), 1997a, 69–73.

Gungwu, Wang "Learn from the Past" *Far Eastern Economic Review*, 160 (18), May 1, 1997b, 37–38.

Gurr, Ted R. *Minorities At Risk*, United States Institute of Peace, 1993a.

Gurr, Ted R. "Why Minorities Rebel" *International Political Science Review*, 14 (2), 1993b, 161–201.

Gurr, Ted R. "Peoples Against the State: Ethnopolitical Conflict and the Changing World System" *International Studies Quarterly*, 38 (3), 1994, 347–377.

Gurr, Ted R. *Peoples Versus States: Minorities at Risk in the New Century*, Washington, DC: United States Institute of Peace Press, 2000.

Gurr, Ted R. and Barbara Harff *Ethnic Conflict in World Politics*, Boulder: Westview, 1994.

Haas, Ernst "What Is Nationalism and Why Should We Study It?" *International Organization*, 40 (3), 1986, 707–744.

Hadden, Jeffrey K. "Toward Desacralizing Secularization Theory" *Social Forces*, 65 (3), 1987b, 587–611.

Hall, Rodney B. "Moral Authority as a Power Resource" *International Organization*, 51 (4), 1997, 591–622.

Halliday, Fred *Islam and the Myth of Confrontation: Religion and Politics in the Middle East*, New York: St. Martin's Press, 1996.

Halliday, Fred "A New World Myth" *New Statesman*, 10 (447), 1997, 42–43.

Halliday, Fred *Nation and Religion in the Middle East*, Boulder, CO: Lynne Rienner, 2000.

Halpern "Toward Further Modernization of the Study of New Nations" *World Politics*, 17, October 1964, 157–181.

Hamid, Rashid "What is the PLO?" *Journal of Palestine Studies*, 4 (4), 1975, 90–109.

Hardjono, Ratih "The Clash of Civilizations and the Remaking of World Order" *Nieman Reports*, 51 (1), 1997, 87–88.

Harkabi, Yehoshafat *Arab Strategies and Israel's Response*, New York: The Free Press, 1977.

Harkabi, Yehoshafat *The Palestinian Covenant and Its Meaning*, London: Valentine, Mitchell, 1979.

Harris, Fredrick C. "Something Within: Religion as a Mobilizer of African-American Political Activism" *Journal of Politics*, 56 (1), 1994, 42–68.

Harris, Richard and Edgar W. Mills "Religion, Values, and Attitudes Toward Abortion" *Journal for the Scientific Study of Religion*, 24, 1985, 137–154.

Harris, Robin "War of the World Views" *National Review*, 48 (20), 1996, 69.

Hasenclever, Andreas and Volker Rittberger "Does Religion Make a Difference? Theoretical Approaches to the Impact of Faith on Political Conflict" *Millennium*, 29 (3), 2000, 641–674.

Hassner, Pierre "Morally Objectionable, Politically Dangerous" *The National Interest* (46), Winter 1997a, 63–69.

Hassner, Pierre "Clashing On" *The National Interest* (48), Summer 1997b, 105–111.

Hashimi, Sohail H. "Saving and Taking Life in War: Three Modern Views" *The Muslim World*, 89 (2), 1999, 158–180.

Hayes, Bernadette C. "The Impact of Religious Identification on Political Attitudes: An International Comparison" *Sociology of Religion*, 56 (2), 1995, 177–194.

Haynes, Jeff *Religion in Third World Politics*, Boulder: Lynne Rienner Publishers, 1994.

Haynes, Jeff *Religion in Global Politics*, New York: Longman, 1998.

Heilbrunn, Jacob "The Clash of Samuel Huntingtons" *The American Prospect* (39), 1998, 22–28.

Henderson, Errol A. "Culture or Contiguity: Ethnic Conflict, the Similarity of States, and the Onset of War, 1820–1989" *Journal of Conflict Resolution*, 41 (5), October 1997, 649–668.

Henderson, Errol A. "The Democratic Peace Through the Lens of Culture, 1820–1989" *International Studies Quarterly*, 42 (3), September 1998, 461–484.

Henderson, Errol A. "Testing the Clash of Civilizations Thesis in Light of Democratic Peace Claims" Paper presented at the International Studies Association 43rd annual conference in New Orleans, March 2002.

Henderson, Errol A. and J. David Singer "Civil War in the Post-Colonial World, 1946–92" *Journal of Peace Research*, 37 (3), 2000, 275–299.

Henderson, Errol A and Richard Tucker "Clear and Present Strangers: The Clash of Civilizations and International Conflict" *International Studies Quarterly*, 45 (2), 2001, 317–338.

Herz, John "Rise and Demise of the Territorial State" *World Politics*, 9 (2), 1957, 473–493.

Hickey, John *Religion and the Northern Ireland Problem*, New Jersey: Barnes & Noble, 1984.

Hoffman, Bruce *The Failure of British Military Strategy Within Palestine 1939–1947*, Ramat-Gan: Bar-Ilan University Press, 1983.

Hoffman, Bruce " 'Holy Terror': The Implications of Terrorism Motivated by a Religious Imperative" *Studies in Conflict and Terrorism*, 18, 1995, 271–284.

Holsti, K.J. *International Politics*, Englewood Cliffs, NJ: Prentice-Hall, 1983.

Holsti, K.J. *The Dividing Discipline*, Boston: Allen and Unwin, 1987.

Hopf, Ted "The Promise of Constructivism in International Relations Theory" *International Security*, 23 (1), 1998, 171–200.

Horowitz, Donald L. *Ethnic Groups in Conflict*, Berkeley: University of California Press, 1985.

Horowitz, J.C. *The Struggle for Palestine*, New York: Greenwood Press, 1968.

Howell, David "East Comes West" *Foreign Affairs*, 76 (2), 1997, 164.

Hunter, Shirleen T. *The Future of Islam and the West: Clash of Civilizations or Peaceful Coexistence?* Westport, CT: Praeger; with the Center for Strategic and International Studies, Washington, DC, 1998.

Huntington, Samuel P. *Political Order in Changing Societies*, New Haven: Yale University Press, 1968.

Huntington, Samuel P. "The Clash of Civilizations?" *Foreign Affairs*, 72 (3), 1993a, 22–49.

Huntington, Samuel P. "If Not Civilizations, What? Paradigms of the Post-Cold War" *Foreign Affairs*, 72 (5), 1993b, 186–194.

Huntington, Samuel P. *The Clash of Civilizations and the Remaking of the World Order*, New York: Simon and Schuster, 1996a.

Huntington, Samuel P. "The West: Unique, Not Universal" *Foreign Affairs*, 75 (6), 1996b, 28–46.

Huntington, Samuel P. "Try Again: A Reply to Russett, Oneal, and Cox" *Journal of Peace Research*, 37 (5), 2000, 609–610.

Huntington, Samuel P. "Osama bin Laden has Given Common Identity Back to the West" *New Perspectives Quarterly*, 19 (1), 2002, 5–8.

Hurd, Ian "Legitimacy and Authority in International Politics" *International Organizations*, 53 (2), 1999, 379–408.

Iannaccone, Laurence R. "Voodoo Economics? Reviewing the Rational Choice Approach to Religion" *Journal for the Scientific Study of Religion*, 34 (1), 1995a, 76–89.

Iannaccone, Lawrence R. "Second Thoughts: A Response to Chaves, Demerath, and Ellison" *Journal for the Scientific Study of Religion*, 34 (1), 1995b, 113–120.

Ibrahim, Anwar "Terror Attacks Set Back Cause of Democracy in Islam" *New Perspectives Quarterly*, 19 (1), 2002, 9–11.

Ikenberry, John G. "Just Like The Rest" *Foreign Affairs*, 76 (2), 1997, 162–163.

Inbar, Efraim "War in the Jewish Tradition" Jerusalem Journal of International Relations, 9 (2), 1987.

Indyk, Martin "The Clinton Administration's Approach to the Middle East" in Kenneth Katzman ed., *US Iranian Relations: An Analytic Compendium of US Policies, Laws and Regulations*, Washington, DC: The Atlantic Council of the United States, 1999.

Jaggers, Keith and Ted R. Gurr "Tracking Democracy's Third Wave with the Polity III Data" *Journal of Peace Research*, 32 (4), 1995, 469–482.

Jelen, Ted G. "Respect for Life, Sexual Morality, and Opposition to Abortion" *Review of Religious Research*, 25, 1984, 220–231.

Jervis, Robert "Security Regimes" *International Organizations*, 38 (2), 1982, 357–378.

Johnson, James T. *The Holy War Idea in Western and Islamic Traditions*, University Park: Pennsylvania State University Press, 1997.

Johnson, James T. "Maintaining the Protection of Non-Combatants" *Journal of Peace Research*, 37 (4), 2000, 481–488.

Johnston, Hank and Jozef Figa "The Church and Political Opposition: Comparative Perspectives on Mobilization Against Authoritarian Regimes" *Journal for the Scientific Study of Religion*, 27 (1), 1988, 32–47.

Juergensmeyer, Mark "Sacrifice and Cosmic War" *Terrorism and Political Violence*, 3 (3), 1991, 101–117.

Juergensmeyer, Mark *The New Cold War?* Berkeley: University of California, 1993.

Juergensmeyer, Mark *Terror in the Mind of God: The Global Rise of Religious Violence*, Berkeley: University of California Press, 2000.

Kabalkova, Vendulka "Towards and International Political Theology" *Millennium*, 29 (3), 2000, 675–704.

Kader, Zerougui A. "The Clash of Civilizations and the Remaking of World Order" *Arab Studies Quarterly*, 20 (1), 1998, 89–92.

Kalberg, Stephen "The Rationalization of Action in Max Weber's Sociology of Religion" *Sociological Theory*, 8 (1), Spring 1990, 58–84.

Kantori, Louis, J. "Religion and Politics in Egypt" in Michael Curtis ed. *Religion and Politics in the Middle East*, Boulder, CO: Westview Press, 1981, 77–90.

Kaplan, Jeffrey "Introduction" *Terrorism and Political Violence*, 14 (1), 2002, 1–24.

Karpov, Vycheslav "Religiosity and Tolerance in the United States and Poland" *Journal for the Scientific Study of Religion*, 41 (2), 2002, 267–288.

Katz, Yossi "The Formation of the Jewish Agency's Partition Proposal of Borders, 1937–1938" *Zion*, 56 (4), 1992, 401–439.

Kaufmann, Chaim D. "Possible and Impossible Solutions to Ethnic Civil Wars" *International Security*, 20 (4), 1996a, 136–175.

Kautsky, J. *The Political Consequences of Modernization*, New York: John Wiley, 1972.

Keane, John "Secularism?" *The Political Quarterly*, 71 (Supplement 1), 2000, 5–19.

Kennedy, Robert "Is One Person's Terrorist Another's Freedom Fighter? Western and Islamic Approaches to 'Just War' Compared" *Terrorism and Political Violence*, 11 (1), 1999, 1–21.

Keohane, Robert O. and Joseph S. Nye, Jr. eds., *Transnational Relations and World Politics*, Cambridge: Harvard University Press, 1970.

Keohane, Robert and Joseph S. Nye Jr. *Power and Interdependence: World Power in Transition*, Boston: Little Brown, 1977.

Kerr, Malcolm *The Arab Cold War: Gamal Abd Al-Nasir and His Rivals*, London: Oxford University Press, 1971.

Khalidi, Rashid "Policymaking within the Palestinian Polity" in Judith Kipper and Harold H.Saunders eds., *The Middle East in Global Perspective*, Washington DC: American Enterprise Institute, 1991.

Khosla, Deepa "Third World States as Intervenors in Ethnic Conflicts: Implications for Regional and International Security" *Third World Quarterly*, 20 (6), 1999, 1143–1156.

Khouri, Fred *The Arab–Israeli Dilemma*, Syracuse, NY: Syracuse University Press, 1966.

Kirkpatrick, Jeane J. and others "The Modernizing Imperative" *Foreign Affairs*, 72 (4), 1993, 22–26.

Kirkpatrick, Lee A. "Fundamentalism, Christian Orthodoxy, and Intrinsic Religious Orientation as Predictors of Discriminatory Attitudes" *Journal for the Scientific Study of Religion*, 32 (3), 1993, 256–268.

Kirth, James "The Real Clash" *The National Interest* (37), Fall 1994, 3–14.

Kissinger, Henry *A World Restored*, Boston: Houghton Mifflin, 1957.

Kokosalakis, Nikos "Legitimation, Power and Religion in Modern Society" *Sociological Analysis*, 46 (4), 1985, 367–376.

Kowalewski, David and Arthur L. Greil "Religion as Opiate: Religion as Opiate in Comparative Perspective" *Journal of Church and State*, 1990, 511–526.

Krasner, Stephen *Defending the National Interest: Raw Materials Investments and US Foreign Policy*, Princeton: Princeton University Press, 1978.

Krasner, Stephen *International Regimes*, Ithaca, NY: Cornell University Press, 1983.

Krasner, Stephen "Approaches to the State, Conceptions and Historical Dynamics" *Comparative Politics* 16 (1), 1984, 223–246.

Kuhn, Thomas S. *The Structure of Scientific Revolutions*, 2nd ed., Chicago: University of Chicago Press, 1970.

Kuran, Timur "Fundamentalism and the Economy" in Martin E. Marty and R. Scott Appleby eds. *Fundamentalisms and the State: Remaking Politics, Economies and Militance*, Chicago: University of Chicago Press, 1991, 289–301.

Laqueur, Walter and Barry Rubin, eds., *The Israel Arab Reader*, New York: Penguin, 1991.

Latin, David "Religion, Political Culture, and the Webarian Tradition" *World Politics*, 30 (4), 1978, 563–593.

Laustsen, Carsten B. and Ole Waever "In Defense of Religion: Sacred Referent Objects for Securitization" *Millennium*, 29 (3), 2000, 705–739.

Lawrence, Bruce B. *Defenders of God: The Fundamentalist Revolt Against the Modern Age*, San Francisco: Harper & Row, 1989.

Laythe, Brian, Deborah Finkel, and Lee A. Kirkpatrick "Predicting Prejudice from Religious Fundamentalism and Right Wing Authoritarianism: A Multiple Regression Approach" *Journal for the Scientific Study of Religion*, 40 (1), 2002a, 1–10.

Laythe, Brian, Deborah G. Finkel, Robert G. Bringle, and Lee A. Kirkpatrick "Religious Fundamentalism as a Predictor of Prejudice: A Two Component Model" *Journal for the Scientific Study of Religion*, 41 (4), 2002b, 623–635.

Leak, Gary K. and Brandy A. Randall "Clarification of the Link Between Right-Wing Authoritarianism and Religiousness: The Role of Religious Maturity" *Journal for the Scientific Study of Religion*, 34 (2), 1995, 245–252.

Lechner, Frank A. "The Case Against Secularization: A Rebuttal" *Social Forces*, 69 (4), June 1991, 1103–1119.

Lewis, Bernard, "The Return of Islam" in Michael Curtis ed. *Religion and Politics in the Middle East*, Boulder, CO: Westview Press, 1981, 9–30.

Lewis, Bernard "Introduction" in *Islam, From the Prophet Muhammad to the Capture of Constantinople, Vol. 1: Politics and War*, edited and translated by Bernard Lewis, New York: Oxford University Press, 1987.

Lewis, Bernard *Islam and the West*, Oxford: Oxford University Press, 1993.

Lewis, Bernard "License to Kill: Usama bin Ladin's Declaration of Jihad" *Foreign Affairs*, 77 (6), 1998, 14–19.

Lewy, Gunther *Religion and Revolution*, New York: Oxford, 1974.

Lichbach, Mark I. "An Evaluation of 'Does Economic Inequality Breed Political Conflict?' Studies" *World Politics*, 1989, 431–70.

Ljiphart, Arend *Democracy in Plural Societies*, New Haven: Yale University Press, 1977.

Lincoln, Bruce ed. *Religion, Rebellion and Revolution*, London: Macmillan, 1985.

Little, David *Ukraine: The Legacy of Intolerance*, Washington, DC: United States Institute of Peace Press, 1991.

Little, David "Religious Militancy" in Chester A. Crocker and Fen O. Hampson eds., *Managing Global Chaos: Sources of and Responses to International Conflict*, Washington, DC: United States Institute of Peace Press, 1996a, 79–91.

Little, David "Studying 'Religious Human Right': Methodological Foundations" in John D. van der Vyver and John Witte Jr. *Religious Human Rights in Global Perspective: Legal Perspectives*, Boston: Martinus Njhoff, 1996b, 45–77.

Litwak, Meir "The Islamization of the Palestinian-Israeli Conflict: The Case of Hamas" *Middle Eastern Studies*, 34 (10), 1998, 148–163.

Mahbubani, Kishore "The Dangers of Decadence" *Foreign Affairs*, 72 (4), 1993, 10–14.

Ma'oz, Moshe *Syria and Israel, From War to Peace-making*, Oxford: Oxford University Press, 1995.

Marquand, D and R.L. Nettler "Forward" *The Political Quarterly*, 71 (Supplement 1), 2000, 1–4.

Marshall, Paul "Religion and Global Affairs: Disregarding Religion" *SAIS Review*, Summer-Fall, 1998, 13–18.

Martin, David A. *A General Theory of Secularization*, Oxford: Blackwell, 1978.

Marty, Martin E. and R. Scott Appleby eds., *Fundamentalisms and the State: Remaking Politics, Economies and Militance*, Chicago: University of Chicago Press, 1991.

Marty, Martin E. and R. Scott Appleby eds., *Fundamentalisms and Society: Reclaiming the Sciences, the Family, and Education*, Chicago: University of Chicago Press, 1993.

Marty, Martin E. and R. Scott Appleby eds., *Accounting for Fundamentalisms: The Dynamic Character of Movements*, Chicago: University of Chicago Press, 1994.

Mearsheimer, John J. "The False Promise of International Institutions" *International Security*, 19 (3), 1995, 5–79.

Mendelsohn, Everett "Religious Fundamentalism and the Sciences" in Martin E. Marty and R. Scott Appleby eds., *Fundamentalisms and Society: Reclaiming the Sciences, the Family, and Education*, Chicago: University of Chicago Press, 1993, 23–41.

Midlarsky, Manus I. "Democracy and Islam: Implications for Civilizational Conflict and the Democratic Peace" *International Studies Quarterly*, 42 (3), 1998, 458–511.

Miller, Alan S. "The Influence of Religious Affiliation on the Clustering of Social Attitudes" *Review of Religious Research*, 37 (3), March 1996, 123–136.

Minkenberg, Michael "Religion and Public Policy: Institutional, Cultural, and Political Impact on the Shaping of Abortion Policies in Western Democracies" *Comparative Political Studies*, 35 (2), 2002, 221–247.

Misztal, Bronislaw and Anson Shupe eds. *Religion and Politics in Comparative Perspective: Revival of Religious Fundamentalism in East and West*, Westport: Praeger, 1992.

Molov, Ben *Power and Transcendence: Hans J. Morgenthau and the Jewish Experience*, Lanham: Lexington Books, 2002.

Monshipouri, Mahmood "The West's Modern Encounter with Islam: From Discourse to Reality" *Journal of Church and State*, 40 (1), 1998, 25–56.

Morgenthau, Hans *Politics Among Nations*, New York: Alfred Knopf, 1956.

Morgenthau, Hans *A New Foreign Policy for the United States*, New York: Praeger, 1969.

Morris, Benny *The Birth of the Palestinian Refugee Problem, 1947–1949*, Cambridge: Cambridge University Press, 1987.

Moshiri, Farrokh "Iran: Islamic Revolution Against Westernization" in Jack A. Goldstone, Ted Robert Gurr, and Farrokh Moshiri eds., *Revolutions of the Late Twentieth Century*, Boulder: Westview, 1991, 116–135.

Murphey, Dwight C. "The Clash of Civilizations" *The Journal of Social, Political, and Economic Studies*, 23 (2), 1998, 215–216.

Naff, William E. "The Clash of Civilizations and the Remaking of World Order" *Annals of the American Academy of Political and Social Science*, 556, 1998, 198–199.

Neckermann, Peter "The Promise of Globalization or the Clash of Civilizations" *The World and I*, 13 (12), 1998.

Nettl, J.B. "The State as a Conceptual Variable," *World Politics* 20 (3), 1968, 559, 592.

Nettler, Ronald L. "Islam, Politics, and Democracy: Mohamed Talbi and Islamic Modernism" *The Political Quarterly*, 71 (Supplement 1), 2000, 50–59.

Nielson, Michael E. and Jim Fultz "Further Examination of the Relationships of Religious Orientation to Religious Conflict" *Review of Religious Research*, 36 (4), June 1995, 369–381.

Nussbaum, Bruce "Capital, Not Culture" *Foreign Affairs*, 76 (2), 1997, 165.

Olson, Mancur, Jr. *The Logic of Collective Action*, Cambridge: Harvard University Press, 1971.

Olzak, Susan *The Dynamics of Ethnic Competition and Conflict*, Stanford: Stanford University Press, 1992.

Olzak, Susan and Joane Nagel eds., *Competitive Ethnic Relations*, New York: Academic Press, 1986.

Organski, A.F.K. *The Stages of Political Development*, New York: Alfred Knopf, 1965.

Osiander, Andreas "Religion and Politics in Western Civilization: The Ancient World as Matrix and Mirror of the Modern" *Millennium*, 29 (3), 2000, 761–790.

Partner, Peter *God of Battles: Holy Wars of Christianity and Islam*, Princeton: Princeton University Press, 1998.

Perkin, Harold "American Fundamentalism and the Selling of God" *Political Quarterly*, 71 (Supplement 1), 2000, 79–89.

Perry, Glenn E. *The Middle East , Fourteen Islamic Centuries*, Englewood, NJ: Prentice Hall, 1983.

Pfaff, William "The Reality of Human Affairs" *World Policy Journal*, 14 (2), 1997, 89–96.

Philpott, Daniel "The Religious Roots of Modern International Relations" *World Politics*, 52, 2000, 206–245.

Pickering, W.S.F. *Durkheim on Religion: A Selection of Readings with Bibliographies*, London: Routledge & Kegan Paul, 1975.

Pickering, W.S.F. *Durkheim's Sociology of Religion: Themes and Theories*, London: Routledge & Kegan Paul, 1984.

Pipes, Daniel "A New Round of Anger and Humiliation: Islam after 9/11" in Wladyslaw Pleszczynski ed., *Our Brave New World: Essays on the Impact of September 11*, Stanford: Hoover Institution Press, 2002, 41–61.

Pipes, Daniel "God and Mammon: Does Poverty Cause Militant Islam?" *The National Interest*, Winter 2001–2002.

Pollis, Adamantia "Greece: A Problematic Secular State" in William Safran, ed., *The Secular and the Sacred: Nation, Religion, and Politics*, London: Frank Cass, 2002, 143–156.

Porath, Yehoshua *The Emergence of the Palestinian-Arab National Movement, 1918–1929*, Tel-Aviv: Am Oved, 1976 (in Hebrew).

Porath, Yehoshua *The Emergence of the Palestinian-Arab National Movement, From Riots to Rebellion*, Jerusalem: Tel-Aviv: Am Oved, 1978 (In Hebrew).

Pottenger, John R. "Liberation Theology: Its Methodological Foundation for Violence" in David C. Rapoport and Yonah Alexander eds., *The Morality of Terrorism: Religious and Secular Justifications*, 2nd ed., New York: Columbia University Press, 1989, 99–123.

Price, Daniel E. *Islamic Political Culture, Democracy, and Human Rights*, Westport, CT: Praeger, 1999.

Price, Daniel E. "Islam and Human Rights: A Case of Deceptive First Appearances" *Journal for the Scientific Study of Religion*, 41 (2), 2002, 213–225.

Puchala, Donald *International Politics Today*, New York: Harper and Row, 1971.

Randall, V. and R. Theobald *Political Change and Underdevelopment: A Critical Introduction to Third World Politics*, London: Macmillan, 1985.

Rapoport, David C. "Fear and Trembling: Terrorism in Three Religious Traditions" *American Political Science Review*, 78, 1984, 658–677.

Rapoport, David C. "Messianic Sanctions for Terror" *Comparative Politics*, 20 (2), January 1988, 195–213.

Rapoport, David C. "Sacred Terror: A Contemporary Example from Islam" in Walter Reich ed., *Origins of Terrorism: Psychologies, Ideologies, Theologies, States of Mind*, Cambridge: Cambridge University Press, 1990, 103–130.

Rapoport, David "Some General Observations on Religion and Violence" *Journal of Terrorism and Political Violence*, 3 (3), 1991a, 118–139.

Regan, Patrick M. "Choosing to Intervene: Outside Interventions in Internal Conflicts" *The Journal of Politics*, 60 (3), 1998, 754–779.

Reynal-Querol, Marta "Ethnicity, Political Systems, and Civil Wars" *Journal of Conflict Resolution*, 46 (1), 2002, 29–54.

Ritcheson, Philip L. "Iranian Military Resurgence: Scope, Motivations, and Implications for Regional Security" *Armed Forces and Society*, 21 (4), 1995, 573–592.

Roelofs, H. Mark "Liberation Theology: The Recovery of Biblical Radicalism" *American Political Science Review*, 88 (2), 1988, 549–566.

Romanucci-Ross, Lola and George DeVos, eds. *Ethnic Identity: Creation, Conflict, and Accommodation*, 3rd ed., London: Alta Mira, 1995.

Rosecrance, Richard "The Clash of Civilizations and the Remaking of World Order" *American Political Science Review*, 92 (4), 1998, 978–980.

Rosenau, James *Linkage Politics*, New York: The Free Press, 1969.

Rostow, W. *The Stages of Economic Growth: A Non-Communist Manifesto*, Cambridge: Cambridge University Press, 1959.

Rubin, Barry *Islamic Fundamentalism in Egyptian Politics*, London: Macmillan, 1990.

Rubin, Barry "Religion and International Affairs" in Douglas Johnston and Cynthia Sampson eds. *Religion, the Missing Dimension of Statecraft*, Oxford: Oxford University Press, 1994, 20–34.

Rummel, Rudolph J. "Is Collective Violence Correlated with Social Pluralism?" *Journal of Peace Research*, 34 (2), 1997, 163–175.

Russett, Bruce, John R. Oneal, and Michalene Cox "Clash of Civilizations, or Realism and Liberalism Deja Vu? Some Evidence" *Journal of Peace Research*, 37 (5), 2000, 583–608.

Sadri, Houman A. "Trends in the Foreign Policy of Revolutionary Iran" *Journal of Third World Studies*, Spring, 1998, 13–37.

Sahliyeh, Emile *In Search of Leadership: West Bank Politics Since 1967*, Washington, DC: Brookings Institution, 1968.

Sahliyeh, Emile ed., *Religious Resurgence and Politics in the Contemporary World*, New York: State University of New York Press, 1990.

Sandler, Shmuel "The Religious Parties," in Howard R. Penniman and Daniel J. Elazar eds., *Israel at the Polls , 1981*, Bloomington: Indian University Press, 1983.

Sandler, Shmuel and Hillel Frisch, *Israel, Jordan and the West Bank*, Lexington: Lexington Books, 1984.

Sandler, Shmuel "The Protracted Arab-Israeli Conflict: A Temporal Spatial Analysis" *The Jerusalem Journal of International Relations*, 10 (4), 1988, 54–78.

Sandler, Shmuel *The State of Israel, The Land of Israel: The Statist and Ethnonational Dimensions of Foreign Policy*, Westport: Greenwood, 1993.

Sandler, Shmuel "Religious Zionism and the State: Political Accomodation and Religious Radicalism in Israel" *Terrorism and Political Violence*, 8 (2), Summer 1996, 133–154.

Sarkees, Meredith Reid, Frank Whelon Wayman, and J. David Singer "Inter-State, Intra-State, and Extra State Wars: A Comprehensive Look At Their Distribution over Time" *International Studies Quarterly*, 47 (1), March, 49–70.

Sayigh, Yezid *Armed Struggle and the Search for a State: The Palestine National Movement 1949–1993*, Oxford: Clarendon Press, 1997.

Scheepers, Peer and Frans Van Der Silk "Religion and Attitudes on Moral Issues: Effects of Individual, Spouse and Parental Characteristics" *Journal for the Scientific Study of Religion*, 37 (4), 1998, 678–691.

Schueftan, Dan *A Jordanian Option*, Ramat Efal: Yad Tabenkin, 1986 (in Hebrew).

Seamon, Richard "The Clash of Civilizations: And the Remaking of World Order" *United States Naval Institute. Proceedings*, 124 (3), 1998, 116–118.

Senghass, Dieter "A Clash of Civilizations—An Idea Fixe?" *Journal of Peace Research*, 35 (1), 1998, 127–132.

Seul, Jefferey R. " 'Ours is the Way of God': Religion, Identity and Intergroup Conflict" *Journal of Peace Research*, 36 (3), 1999, 553–569.

Shalev, Arie *The Intifada, Causes and Effects*, Tel Aviv: The Jaffe Center for Strategic Studies, 1990.

Sherkat Daren E. and Christopher G. Ellison "Recent Development and Controversies in the Sociology of Religion" *Annual Review of Sociology*, 25, 1999, 363–394.

Schiff, Zeev and Ehud Yaari, *Intifada*, Jerusalem: Shocken, 1990.

Shils, Edward, *Center and Periphery: Essays in Macrosociology*, Chicago: Chicago University Press, 1978.

Shragai, Nadav *The Temple Mount Conflict*, Jerusalem, Keter, 1995.

Shupe, Anson "The Stubborn Persistence of Religion in the Global Arena" in Emile Sahliyeh ed. *Religious Resurgence and Politics in the Contemporary World*, New York: State University of New York Press, 1990, 17–26.

Singhua, Liu "History as Antagonism" *Far Eastern Economic Review*, 160 (18), May 1, 1997, 37.

Skreslet, Stanley H. "God of Battles: Holy Wars of Christianity and Islam/The Holy War Idea in Western and Islamic Traditions" *Interpretation*, 53 (4), 1999, 416–418.

Smith, A. D. "States and Homelands: The Social and Geopolitical Implications of National Territory," *Journal of International Studies*, 10 (3), Autumn, 1981, 187–202.

Smith, Anthony D. "Ethnic Election and National Destiny: Some Religious Origins of Nationalist Ideals" *Nations and Nationalism*, 5 (3), 1999, 331–355.

Smith, Anthony D. "The Sacred Dimension of Nationalism" *Millennium*, 29 (3), 2000, 791–814.

Smith, Donald E. *Religion and Political Development*, Boston: Little Brown, 1970.

Smith, Donald E. ed. *Religion, Politics and Social Change in the Third World*, New York: Free Press, 1971.

Smith, Donald E. ed. *Religion and Political Modernization*, New Haven: Yale University Press, 1974.

Smith, Tony "Dangerous Conjecture" *Foreign Affairs*, 76 (2), 1997, 163–164.

Spanier, John *American Foreign Policy Since World War II*, New York: Praeger, 1965.

Spiro, Melford E. "Religion: Problems of Definition and Explanation" in Banton, Michael ed. *Anthropological Approaches to the Study of Religion*, London: Tavistock Publications, 1966, 85–126.

Stark, Rodney and William Bainbridge "Of Churches, Sect, and Cults: Preliminary Concepts for a Theory of Religious Movements" *Journal for the Scientific Study of Religion*, 18, 1979, 117–133.

Stark, Rodney and William Bainbridge *The Future of Religion: Secularization, Revival and Cult Formation*, Berkeley: University of California Press, 1985.

Steinberg, Gerald "Peace, Security and Terror the 1996 Elections" in Daniel J. Elazar and Shmuel Sandler eds., *Israel at the Polls 1996*, London: Frank Cass, 1998, 209–236.

Stephan, Alfred "Religion, Democracy, and the 'Twin Tolerations'" *Journal of Democracy*, 11 (4), 2000, 37–56.

Sullivan, Michael P. *International Relations: Theories and Evidence*, Englewood, NJ: Prentice-Hall, 1976.

Sykes, Christopher *Cross Roads to Israel*, London: Nel Mentor, 1967.

Takeyh, Ray "Pragmatic Theocracy: A Contradiction in Terms?" *The National Interest*, 59, Spring, 2000, 94–100.

Talhami, Ghada Hashem "The Modern History of Islamic Jerusalem: Academic Myths and Propaganda" *Middle East Policy*, 7 (2), 2000, 113–129.

Taylor, Alan *The Arab Balance of Power*, Syracuse, NY: Syracuse University Press, 1982.

Taylor, Maxwell *The Fanatics*, London: Brassey's, 1991.

Tehranian, Majid "Fundamentalist Impact on Education and the Media: An Overview" in Martin E. Marty and R. Scott Appleby eds., *Fundamentalisms and Society: Reclaiming the Sciences, the Family, and Education*, Chicago: University of Chicago Press, 1993, 313–340.

Thomas, Scott M. "Taking Religious and Cultural Pluralism Seriously: The Global Resurgence of Religion and the Transformation of International Society" *Millennium*, 29 (3), 2000, 815–841.

Tibi, Bassam "Post-Bipolar Disorder in Crisis: The Challenge of Politicized Islam" *Millennium*, 29 (4), 2000, 843–859.

Tilly, Charles *The Formation of National States in Western Europe*, Princeton: Princeton University Press, 1975.

Tilly, Charles *From Mobilization to Revolution*, Reading: Addison-Wesley, 1978.

Tipson, Frederick S. "Culture Clash-ification: A Verse to Huntington's Curse" *Foreign Affairs*, 76 (2), 1997, 166–169.

Turner, Brian S. *Religion and Social Theory*, 2nd ed., London: Sage, 1991.

Vallier, Ivan "The Roman Catholic Church: A Transnational Actor" in Robert O. Keohane and Joseph S. Nye eds., *Transnational Relations and World Politics*, Cambridge: Harvard University Press, 1970, 129–152.

Van der Vyver, Johan D. "Religious Fundamentalism and Human Rights" *Journal of International Affairs*, 50 (1), 1996, 21–40.

Vasquez, John "The Realist Paradigm and Degenerative versus Progressive Research Programs: An Appraisal of Neotraditional Research on Waltz's Balancing Proposition" *American Political Science Review*, 91 (4), 1997, 899–911.

Vasquez, John A. *The Power of Power Politics: From Classical Realism to Neotraditionalism* , Cambridge: Cambridge University Press, 1998.

Verba, Sidney, Kay L. Scholzman, Henry Bradey, and Norman H. Nie "Race, Ethnicity, and Political Resources: Participation in the United States" *British Journal of Political Science*, 23 (4), 1993, 453–497.

Viorst, Milton "The Coming Instability" *The Washington Quarterly*, 20 (4), 1997, 153–167.

Voye, Liliane "Secularization in a Context of Advanced Modernity" *Sociology of Religion*, 60 (3), 1999, 275–288.

Walid, Abdurrahman "Future Shock" *Far Eastern Economic Review*, 160 (18), May 1, 1997, 38–39.

Walsh, Andrew "The Pope Among the Orthodox" *Religion in the News*, 4 (2), 2001, 11–13.

Walt, Stephen N. "Building Up New Bogeymen" *Foreign Policy*, 106, 1997, 177–189.

Waltz, Kenneth *Theory of International Politics*, New York: Random House, 1979.

Waltz, Kenneth N. "Evaluating Theories," *American Political Science Review*, 91 (4), 1997: 913–917.

Walzer, Michael *Just and Unjust Wars*, United States: HarperCollins, 1977.

Warner, R. Stephen "Work in Progress Toward a New Paradigm for the Sociological Study of Religion in the United States" *American Journal of Sociology*, 98 (5), March 1993, 1044–1093.

Warr, Kevin "The Normative Promise of Religious Organizations in Global Civil Society" *Journal of Church and State*, 41 (3), 1999, 499–523.

Weigel, George "Religion and Peace: An Argument Complexified" in Sheryl J. Brown and Kimber M. Schraub eds., *Resolving Third World Conflict: Challenges for a New Era*, Washington DC: United States Institute for Peace, 1992, 172–192.

Weinberg, Leonard B. and William L. Eubank "Terrorism and Democracy: What Recent Events Disclose" *Terrorism and Political Violence*, 10 (1), 1998, 108–118.

Weinberg, Leonard, William Eubank, and Ami Pedahzur "Characteristics of Terrorist Organizations 1910–2000" Presented at the 25th Annual Meeting of the International Society of Political Psychology in Berlin, Germany, July 2002.

Wendt, Alexander "Anarchy is what States Make of it" *International Organization*, 20 (1), Spring 1992, 391–425.

Wentz, Richard *Why People Do Bad Things in the Name of Religion*, Macon, GA: Mercer, 1987.

Westhus, Kenneth "The Church in Opposition" *Sociological Analysis*, 37 (4), 1976, 299–314.

Williams, Rhys H. "Movement Dynamics and Social Change: Transforming Fundamentalist Ideologies and Organizations" in Martin E. Marty and R. Scott Appleby eds., *Accounting for Fundamentalisms: The Dynamic Character of Movements*, Chicago: University of Chicago Press, 1994, 785–833.

Wilmer, Franke *The Indigenous Voice in World Politics*, Newbury Park: Sage, 1993.

Wilson, Bryan R. *Religion in Secular Society*, Baltimore: Penguin, 1966.

Wilson, Bryan R. "Aspects of Secularization in the West" *Japanese Journal of Religious Studies*, 3 (4), 1976, 259–276.

Wilson, Bryan R. *Religion in Sociological Perspective*, Oxford: Oxford University Press, 1982.

Woodrum, Eric "Determinants of Moral Attitudes" *Journal for the Scientific Study of Religion*, 27, 1988, 553–573.

Yamane, David "Secularization on Trial: In Defense of a Neosecularization Paradigm" *Journal for the Scientific Study of Religion*, 36 (1), 1997, 109–122.

Yamazaki, Masakazu "Asia, A Civilization in the Making" *Foreign Affairs*, 75 (4), 1996, 106–128.

Yaniv, Avner *PLO—A Profile*, Haifa: Israel Universities Study Group for Middle Eastern Affairs, 1974.

Zitrin, Steve "Milleniarianism and Violence" *Journal of Conflict Studies*, 12 (2), 1998, 110–115.

Zubadia, Sami "Trajectories of Political Islam: Egypt, Iran and Turkey" *Political Quarterly*, 71 (Supplement 1), 2000, 60–78.

Zionism, A Collection of Political Documents, Jerusalem: Ahiassaf, 1943 (in Hebrew).

INDEX

DATE DUE

iLL (FAU) 53252301 5/17/09		

DEMCO 138298

Printed in the United States
106860LV00001B/83/A

9 781403 976031